American Philosophy
and the Romantic Tradition

Cambridge Studies in American Literature and Culture

Editor
Albert Gelpi, Stanford University

Advisory Board
Nina Baym, University of Illinois, Champaign–Urbana
Sacvan Bercovitch, Harvard University
David Levin, University of Virginia
Joel Porte, Cornell University
Eric Sundquist, University of California, Berkeley
Tony Tanner, Cambridge University
Mike Weaver, Oxford University

Selected books in the series
Charles Altieri, *Painterly Abstraction in Modernist American Poetry*
Douglas Anderson, *A House Undivided*
Sacvan Bercovitch and Myra Jehlen (eds.), *Ideology and Classic American Literature*★
Ronald Bush (ed.), *T. S. Eliot*
Michael Davidson, *The San Francisco Renaissance*
George Dekker, *The American Historical Romance*★
Stephen Fredman, *Poets' Prose,* 2nd Edition
Susan Friedman, *Penelope's Web*
Albert Gelpi (ed.), *Wallace Stevens*★
Richard Godden, *Fictions of Capital*
Richard Gray, *Writing the South*★
Ezra Greenspan, *Walt Whitman and the American Reader*
Alfred Habegger, *Henry James and the "Woman Business"*
David Halliburton, *The Color of the Sky*
Susan K. Harris, *19th Century American Women's Novels*
Robert Lawson-Peebles, *Landscape and Written Expression in Revolutionary America*
Robert S. Levine, *Conspiracy and Romance*
John Limon, *The Place of Fiction in the Time of Science*
John McWilliams, *The American Epic*
Susan Manning, *The Puritan-Provincial Vision*
David Miller, *Dark Eden*
Michael Oriard, *Sporting with the Gods*
Tim Redman, *Ezra Pound and Italian Fascism*
Eric Sigg, *The American T. S. Eliot*
Brook Thomas, *Cross Examinations of Law and Literature*★
David Wyatt, *The Fall into Eden*★

★Published in hardcover and paperback

For a complete listing of books in the series, see the pages following the Index.

AMERICAN PHILOSOPHY
AND THE
ROMANTIC TRADITION

RUSSELL B. GOODMAN
Department of Philosophy
University of New Mexico

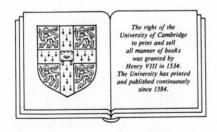

The right of the
University of Cambridge
to print and sell
all manner of books
was granted by
Henry VIII in 1534.
The University has printed
and published continuously
since 1584.

CAMBRIDGE UNIVERSITY PRESS

CAMBRIDGE

NEW YORK   PORT CHESTER   MELBOURNE   SYDNEY

Published by the Press Syndicate of the University of Cambridge
The Pitt Building, Trumpington Street, Cambridge CB2 1RP
40 West 20th Street, New York, NY 10011, USA
10 Stamford Road, Oakleigh, Melbourne 3166, Australia

© Cambridge University Press 1990

First published 1990

Printed in the United States of America

Library of Congress Cataloging-in-Publication Data
Goodman, Russell B.
American philosophy and the romantic tradition / Russell B.
Goodman.
p.   cm. – (Cambridge studies in American literature and
culture)
Includes bibliographical references and index.
ISBN 0-521-39443-0
1. Philosophy, American.   2. Romanticism – United States.
3. Emerson, Ralph Waldo, 1803–1882.   4. James, William, 1842–1910.
5. Dewey, John, 1859–1952.   I. Title.   II. Series.
B893.G66   1990
191 – dc20   90-36093
                                                       CIP

British Library Cataloguing in Publication Data
Goodman, Russell B.
American philosophy and the romantic tradition.
1. American philosophy
I. Title
   191

ISBN 0-521-39443-0 hardback

CONTENTS

v

*In memory of Harry, Sadie, and Regina,
who came to America*

PREFACE

Although I didn't know it at the time, this book started many years ago with my reading Stanley Cavell's *The Senses of Walden*. Even before making much sense of Cavell's book (something I began to do years later, camped for a week on a mountain ridge in New Mexico's Gila Wilderness), I found the following passage provocative:

> Study of *Walden* would perhaps not have become such an obsession with me had it not presented itself as a response to questions with which I was already obsessed: Why has America never expressed itself philosophically? Or has it – in the metaphysical riot of its greatest literature? Has the impulse to philosophical speculation been absorbed, or exhausted, by speculation in territory, as in such thoughts as Manifest Destiny? Or are such questions not really intelligible?[1]

It was not clear to me that such questions were intelligible or even worthwhile, and so it was easy enough to ask back: "Why should America express itself philosophically? Must every country do so? Is a figure like Aristotle or Descartes not an international figure, not an expression of Greek or French culture?" I could have said too that there was an American philosophy, enunciated by such figures as C. I. Lewis and W. V. O. Quine, and before them, perhaps (for I was thinking as someone trained in postwar "Anglo-American" departments of philosophy, where they have traditionally not been viewed as serious contributors to the philosophical dialogue), Dewey and James. Nevertheless Cavell's question stuck, so that the lack of a distinctive and weighty American tradition became part of the philosophical landscape for me, much as – to use an example from William James's *Psychology* – one feels a missing tooth.

Cavell's speculation, or complaint, occurs in a book in which he attempts to discern ("inherit," he later termed it) just such an American philosophy, one he finds hidden in accepted masterpieces of literature to which professional philosophers – including those writing about "American philosophy" – pay no serious attention. (Emerson and Thoreau are accorded minor and tangential places in many histories and overviews of American philosophy,[2] and it is only recently – for example, in the work of Richard Poirier and Cornel West – that Emerson's contributions to the development of later American philosophy have begun to be adequately assessed.)[3] Cavell convincingly makes out Emerson's and Thoreau's scrupulous and philosophical attention to issues of language, knowledge, and being.

One reason Cavell's question stuck with me, I confess, is that I found appealing the idea of there being an American philosophical tradition rooted in transcendentalism: In some sense I wanted it to be true. (In *The Will to Believe*, James argues that such desires play a major role in the development of all philosophical positions.) I found much, if by no means all, of what passed as philosophy in the "profession" to be unexciting, trivial, and insular. I wanted a philosophy that was not embarrassed by literature or by the idea of searching "for the best human life."[4] Wouldn't it be wonderful, I thought, if such a philosophy could be found already established – if considerably "repressed"[5] – in American soil?

Cavell's thought about the transcendentalists has become increasingly bound up with an interest in European Romanticism, particularly in the writings of Wordsworth and Coleridge. In his paper "In Quest of the Ordinary" (which I heard at the University of New Mexico in 1983) Cavell examines Wordsworth's concern for the revitalization and expansion of experience.[6] In an imaginative discussion of Coleridge's "Rime of the Ancient Mariner," Cavell aligns "the frozen world" through which the mariner journeys with the position of philosophical skeptics like Descartes and even Kant. The Romantic interest in the recovery or revitalization of everyday experience, Cavell argues, is both historically (as in Coleridge) and conceptually or "mythically" a response to Kant's *Critique of Pure Reason:* "Romanticism is understandable in part as an effort to overcome both skepticism and philosophy's responses to skepticism."[7]

What precipitated this book, however, was not Emerson, Thoreau, or Cavell, but John Dewey. I had taught Dewey's *The Quest for Certainty* and *Experience and Nature* for years in epistemology courses and had thought of him as a somewhat plodding and unenthusiastic writer, albeit with far-reaching criticisms of traditional epistemological enterprises such as the Cartesian quest for certainty. Finding *The Quest for Certainty* out of print and looking for a more complete view of Dewey's philosophy, I chose John McDermott's anthology *The Philosophy of John Dewey* and there encountered some key portions of *Art as Experience*. I was surprised by the passion with which Dewey speaks in this book of reforming our experience of the world and by his extensive use of Romantic poetry in thinking about this goal. In *Art as Experience,* Dewey joins epistemological and poetic issues in a way completely unlike "standard" treatments of our knowledge of and position in the world, such as those offered by Hume or Russell. But Dewey's concern for the poetry of the ordinary resembles nothing so much as the Romantic philosophy that Cavell, at work on the English Romantic poets and American transcendentalists, has been uncovering and developing. The more I looked at Dewey's writing, early and late, and then at James's, the more convinced I became that the tradition for which Cavell searches does exist here and that the pragmatists Dewey and James – whom Cavell does not discuss – are important figures in it.

In 1910, a quarter of a century before he published *Art as Experience,* Dewey produced a memorial for William James, in which he wrote: "When our country comes to itself in consciousness, when it transmutes into articulate ideas what are still obscure and blind strivings, two men, Emerson and William James, will, I think, stand out as the prophetic forerunners of the attained creed of values."[8] "Romanticism" (of which I certainly owe my readers an account, to be given in Chapter 1) is the key to the new cut that I make through the layers of American philosophical writing. Emerson and James do stand out in the strata this cut exposes, but Dewey himself and Cavell emerge, too.

There are some significant historical connections between America and the English Romantics. Coleridge planned to found a new society in America, going as far as to make plans with Robert Southey for a ship and provisions. Soon after he left his Unitarian ministry, the young Waldo Emerson made a pilgrimage to England, meeting Wordsworth, Coleridge (in an encounter he described as "rather a spectacle than a conversation"),[9] and, to better effect, Carlyle. There are links among the Americans: James's father, Henry James, Sr., was Emerson's friend and fellow admirer of Swedenborg; Emerson was a frequent guest in the James home when William was a child;[10] and William gave a major talk at the Emerson centenary celebration in 1903. But Dewey, who was James's contemporary and follower and never met Emerson, was more appreciative of Emerson's philosophical importance than was James himself.

In the following pages, I consider the Americans' European Romantic predecessors, following Cavell in concentrating on Wordsworth, Coleridge, and Kant (who, as Cavell puts it, "heralds Romanticism").[11] But my focus is on the Americans. Romanticism is not a simple movement, and although I use it to expose connections among the American writers, I do not wish to obscure the writers' individuality and vivacity by reducing them to commentators on a limited set of themes. James wrote that "the books of all the great philosophers are like so many men. Our sense of an essential personal flavor in each one of them, typical but indescribable, is the finest fruit of our philosophic education."[12] I seek to convey the "essential personal flavor" of Emerson, James, and Dewey in the context of their development of an American Romantic philosophical tradition.

I do not claim that this is the only way to look at American philosophy. Nor do I claim that the writers I treat are the only American Romantic philosophers (one could make a case for Bushnell, Royce, or Whitehead and could clearly give more attention to Thoreau than I have chosen to). My interpretations are, to use a word of Emerson's, "initial." Nevertheless, in working on them I have felt my position to be that described in Emerson's great essay "Experience," in which he writes of being

> apprised of my vicinity to a new and excellent region of life. By persisting to read or to think, this region gives further sign of itself, as it were in flashes of light, in sudden discoveries of its profound beauty and repose, as if the clouds that covered it parted at intervals, and showed the approaching traveller the inland mountains, with the tranquil eternal meadows spread at their base, whereon flocks graze and shepherds pipe and dance. But every insight from this realm of thought is felt as initial, and promises a sequel.[13]

Such a region, what Emerson calls "a new . . . America," is so vast and so various – mythological, philosophical, literary, and historical – that I could not hope to survey it all here, even if I should have such an all-encompassing wish. I want only to walk in, to chart some routes through the new terrain, and to open certain prospects to general view.

ACKNOWLEDGMENTS

Many friends and colleagues helped me make this a better book than it would otherwise have been. During the early stages the encouragement of Stanley Cavell and John McDermott were especially important to me. Throughout the course of the writing and rewriting, my wife, Anne Doughty Goodman, provided criticism, editorial skills, and sustaining companionship. William C. Dowling made masterly suggestions about structure and style.

I also wish to thank Thomas Alexander, Brom Anderson, Stephen Barker, Gus Blaisdell, Richard Bernstein, John Bussanich, Sharon Cameron, Linda Dowling, David Dunaway, Albert Gelpi, George L. Kline, Bruce Kuklick, Henry Samuel Levinson, Hilary Putnam, Paul Schmidt, George Frederick Schueler, R. W. Sleeper, Howard Tuttle, Hugh Witemeyer, Margaret B. Yamashita, and an anonymous reader for Cambridge University Press. I am grateful to the members of the Society for the Advancement of American Philosophy for providing a friendly forum for the airing and criticism of my ideas.

I began work on the book with the aid of a sabbatical leave granted me by the Department of Philosophy and the College of Arts and Sciences of the University of New Mexico and was aided by several teaching reductions allowed me by the department. A computer provided by the College of Arts and Sciences of the University of New Mexico enabled me to bring the book to completion more easily. Sandy Robbins and Glenda Baxter helped with proofreading.

Finally, I wish to acknowledge the constant support of my parents and to thank my dear children, Elizabeth and Jacob, for their patience during the arduous days of work on "daddy's book."

Corrales, New Mexico
July 26, 1990

1

THE MARRIAGE OF SELF
AND WORLD

I. WITTGENSTEIN, CAVELL, AND SKEPTICISM

This book is about a tradition in American philosophy, running through the writings of Ralph Waldo Emerson, William James, and John Dewey, that has its origins in Romanticism as a movement in European thought. The oddity of these origins having gone unremarked even by students of American philosophy will be part of my subject in the following pages, but I want to begin with the work of the one contemporary philosopher who has not only been conscious of the Romantic strain in American philosophy but who, increasingly and especially in his most recent work, has been led to identify himself with its tradition. This is Stanley Cavell, speaking in a recent paper on Emerson, for instance, of his work as a "philosophical journey" toward locating "an inheritance of Wittgenstein and Heidegger, and before them of Emerson and Thoreau, for all of whom there seems to be some question whether the individual or the community as yet, or any longer, exist."[1]

As such a remark may suggest, the origins of Cavell's own involvement with the Romantic tradition lie most clearly in his own early work on Wittgenstein and, in particular, on the problem of skepticism as it is isolated and attacked in Wittgenstein's writings. This is the significance of Cavell's insistence, heterodox enough at the time, on Wittgenstein as a confessional and therapeutic writer, like Augustine or Freud. His early (1962) essay "The Availability of Wittgenstein's Later Philosophy"[2] contains a devastating attack on the then-reigning interpretation of Wittgenstein presented by David Pole and shows how inaccessible Wittgenstein's philosophy can become if one ignores his method – interprets him, for example, as producing "theses" for which he offers "arguments." Wittgenstein's philosophy employs a unique method and requires a special kind of reading. As with the linguistic phenomena to which Wittgenstein tries to bring us back, we are "unable to notice" Wittgenstein's philosophy, Cavell argues, even though it is right before our eyes.[3] Cavell's analysis of Wittgenstein points to problems within us, that is, within the human subjects engaged in philosophy, as part of our difficulty with the phenomena we seek to understand.

Cavell contends that Wittgenstein's voices in the conversations in *Philosophical Investigations* do not so much express Wittgenstein's own lack of clarity as they record and encourage a confrontation with various forms of philosophical temptation, particularly the temptations to certainty and completeness from which skepticism arises. Pointing to Wittgenstein's claim that philosophical methods are "like different therapies,"[4] Cavell ends his essay with remarks about the style of the *Investigations,* which clearly apply to his own style as well: "Why does he write that way? Why doesn't he just say what he means, and draw instead of insinuate conclusions?" In characterizing Wittgenstein's writing as confessional, Cavell sees it not as explaining or justifying but, rather, as describing "how it is with you." He asks what the point of such writing is, where "there is virtually nothing . . . which we should ordinarily call reasoning," where there are "questions, jokes, parables, and propositions so striking (the way lines are in poetry) that they stun mere belief." Wittgenstein's project is to overcome some of the blinders, dogmas, and established ways of thinking that seem so obvious and comfortable that we would not think even of questioning them, let alone doing away with them. Wittgenstein wishes, according to Cavell, to end our "subjection to modes of thought and sensibility whose origins are unseen or unremembered." He agrees with Freud in opposing "understanding which is unaccompanied by inner change."[5]

From his earliest work to the present, then, Cavell is trying to discover or uncover problems – such as that of "other minds" (which includes the problem of one's own, including his own, mind) – which even he does not clearly see. His writing is meant to work on its readers, as well as on its writer, so that – as he says of *Walden* – not only are we to read the book, but also the book is to read us. This means that the process of reading is crucial. We can't just ask what Cavell's results are, as we may do in a scientific treatise or in much of the professional philosophy to which he stands opposed. If we are to get anything out of it, we must go through it, and Cavell's writing is in this sense like music. It would be pointless to ask what the results of the *Eroica* are, as if we could just skip the development of the symphony. The development is the symphony. In the same way, the development of Cavell's thought – the voices, examples, themes and variations, counterthemes and associations – is Cavell's philosophy.[6] Similarly, Wittgenstein saw philosophy as a directed process, with original positions (philosophers' problems), development, and resolutions. He characterized philosophy as the search for a clear view of things, for a way out of a state of confusion to a state of "peace," and wrote that "a philosophical problem has the form: 'I don't know my way about'." "The aspects of things that are most important for us," Wittgenstein wrote, "are hidden because of their simplicity and familiarity . . . we fail to be struck by what, once seen, is most striking and most powerful."[7] Like Wittgenstein's, Cavell's writing expresses the sense of something hidden from us, but hidden as much because of our nature as because of the nature of what we seek. "I am trying," he explains, "to discover the problem of others."[8]

The tendency of Cavell's work, even at this early stage, is to isolate skepticism as a problem to which Romanticism, as both an intellectual and a literary movement, may be seen as an attempted solution. This view of skepticism emerges perhaps most clearly in "The Avoidance of Love," an essay on *King Lear* published in 1969 and included by Cavell in his book of essays, *Must We Mean What We Say?* Cavell's interest in Shakespeare is an interest in the bard's depiction of ways in which we live our skepticism concerning other minds, that is, ways in which radical doubts about our knowledge of others turn out not to be just a philosopher's thought experiment but indeed the fabric of our lives. Cavell holds that our lack of knowledge (or our avoidance) of others has its roots in ourselves, in our own motives and passions. Lear, for example, fails to acknowledge both Gloucester's and Cordelia's love for him, and this failure of recognition is "explained by . . . [his] attempt to avoid recognition."[9] Afraid of his own imperfection, ashamed of letting others see him, Lear avoids the direct offers of love and friendship that those who love him make. To Gloucester's "O! Let me kiss that hand," Lear replies, "Let me wipe it first, it smells of mortality." To Cordelia's loving silence, he replies, "Nothing will come of nothing." Cavell's thesis is that "recognizing a person depends upon allowing oneself to be recognized by him" and that the skepticism that we live, our failures to recognize others, are failures to let others recognize us, "a fear of what is revealed to them."[10]

We are responsible, then, for our failures to acknowledge others, for our living skepticism concerning other minds. But if our skepticism receives the correct therapy, we may be able to alter it by ending the unwillingnesses on which it depends. This message, implicit throughout Cavell's enterprise, is one he generalizes as early as "The Avoidance of Love" to skepticism concerning the "external world": "We think skepticism must mean that we cannot know the world exists, and hence that perhaps there isn't one (a conclusion some profess to admire and others to fear). Whereas what skepticism suggests is that since we cannot know the world exists, its presentness to us cannot be a function of knowing. The world is to be *accepted;* as the presentness of other minds is not to be known, but acknowledged."[11]

Cavell's increasingly elaborate interpretation of Wittgenstein tends toward an isolation of skepticism, about both the world and other minds, as the central issue of his own philosophical enterprise. That issue dominates "Between Acknowledgment and Avoidance," a book-length work contained in *The Claim of Reason,* published in 1979. It is headed by a quotation from Wordsworth ("to be mistaught is worse than to be untaught") but begins with Wittgenstein, though with a characteristically interpretative and introspective question: "In what spirit does Wittgenstein 'deny' the 'possibility' of private language?" The discussion moves to Wittgenstein's questioning of his linguistic and other obsessions, so that his relations to those other self-inquirers, "Thoreau or Kierkegaard or Nietzsche, for example,"[12] become relevant. Literary examples and explorations abound, even in the essay's first thirty pages. Sometimes they are used as examples, as is Dickens's Captain Cuttle, with his vocal doodle (in connection with defining the meaning of an arbitrary symbol), but at other times – for example, in Cavell's use of Othello and Lear, the *Chanson du Roland* or *For Whom the Bell Tolls* – they operate on their own as avenues of inquiry. Although he begins with Wittgenstein, Cavell's discussion of the problems of other minds (including his own) soon becomes a hall of voices, including those of Kant, Nietzsche, Freud, Thoreau, Shakespeare, and Heidegger.[13] Cavell also confronts Christianity, horror movies, the Social Contract, insanity, confession, and his own previous writings.[14]

In *The Claim of Reason* Cavell presents his investigations as logical ones. His notion of logic (which he also calls "grammar," following Wittgenstein, or "myth," perhaps following Frye) is a broadly Kantian one, and he affirms its subjective origin as well as its objective status.[15] Cavell attacks some myths – the myth of privacy, of the body as a veil, for example. Other myths, such as that depicting the body as giving expression to the soul, require understanding, not rejection.[16] Cavell takes from Wittgenstein (who wrote, famously, that "*essence* is expressed by grammar")[17] the idea that the way we speak and the language games we play reveal the logical structure of the world.

The variety of material in "Between Acknowledgment and Avoidance" and the claim to uncover the logic of the phenomena treated have something in common with Hegel's encyclopedic approach to philosophy, but the form and tone of Cavell's text are entirely different from the self-confident certainties of Hegelian dialectic, much more closely resembling those of Hegel's great antagonist Kierkegaard. This is the context in which to appreciate the suggestion that what Cavell's critics call his self-involvement is really a mode of self-inquiry, one stemming from the view – which he shares with Kierkegaard and also with philosophers as diverse as Socrates and Wittgenstein – that working on philosophy is working on oneself.[18] Wordsworth's remark that "no errors are so difficult to root out as those which the understanding has pledged its credit to uphold" begins this section of *The Claim of Reason*. Rooting out such errors requires a critical examination of the very understanding that seeks to find them.[19] Reading Cavell means taking one's time, letting the language work on and with oneself. Cavell might have said what Wittgenstein once said of himself: "I really want my copious punctuation marks to slow down the speed of reading. Because I should like to be read slowly. (As I myself read.)"[20]

Although the style and much of the content of "Between Acknowledgment and Avoidance" are thus far from those of most current professional philosophical writing, the piece displays logical and epistemological structures as precise as those prized by "analytic" philosophers, and it examines epistemological problems central to modern philosophy as it is understood in the Anglo-American philosophical establishment in which Cavell was trained. ("I am not exactly single or unified myself," Cavell confesses in a recent paper. "I am also other to the Anglo-American profession of philosophy, to which at the same time I belong.")[21]

The major turn toward Romanticism in Cavell's work occurs, however, only when his long exploration of such problems as acknowledgment also begins to suggest a certain solution to the problem of skepticism concerning the external world. For this is skepticism in its "classical" (i.e., post-Cartesian) form, skepticism concerning other minds being most often thought of as an adjunct to or an extension of skepticism about "objects" or the "external world" they compose. Standard external world skepticism asks whether the world is there, whether, for example, there is a world of objects "behind" my ideas of them. Skepticism concerning other minds is thought to ask the same sort of question with respect to one set of objects in the world, that is, people, that skeptics such as Descartes ask of the world generally; namely, is there another "level" of existence "behind" the bodily behavior that we observe, a level of consciousness? Skepticism concerning other people is thus thought of as parallel to external world skepticism in that the other's body, like my "veil" of ideas, may be thought to hide a domain of psychic reality that I either have to learn to peer into, to arrive at by some sort of inference, or just to accept, as I accept the world of objects when I am not doing philosophy.

Although he eventually moves toward an alignment of external world with other minds skepticism – toward the idea of a romance with the world as well as with other people – Cavell begins by challenging the view that these forms of skepticism are symmetrical. He argues, for example, that the real problem in my relations with others is not their barrier to me, not their body that fails to let me "in," but my barriers to them. This is a point to which Cavell finds *Lear* and *Othello* relevant. Lear avoids recognizing the love of his daughter Cordelia, who refuses the public display of love demanded by her father; rather, he participates in the deception of his feelings practiced by his other daughters, Goneril and Regan. Like the philosopher in need of Wittgensteinian therapy, Lear fails to notice what is before his eyes. Similarly, the paradigmatic slave owners that Cavell discusses avoid recognizing the humanity of their "property," the other human beings "whom they know, or all but know to be human beings."[22] In the cases of both Lear and the slave owners, the barrier to knowledge of the other lies in the knower.

There thus seems an asymmetry between external world and other minds skepticism stemming from the role the self plays in the latter but not in the former. If there is a Cartesian evil genius deceiving me in a drastic way, then the responsibility is not mine. It is not that I have failed but that I have been deceived by another being more powerful than myself; the criteria that I (and we all) use will have turned out not to work. But if I fail to know (and here Cavell frequently employs the word "acknowledge") another, then the problem is mine, just as Lear's problem with Cordelia or the slave owner's with a slave is his own. My knowledge of other minds "seems more deeply up to me, to my attitudes and sensibility," as Cavell puts it, than does my knowledge or acceptance of external objects. If material objects do not exist, "I suffer a generalized *trompe l'oeil*," but if no other human beings exist I suffer a "massive *trompe l'âme*."[23]

Cavell's use of the word *l'âme*, "soul," derives from Wittgenstein, who wrote in the *Investigations* that "my attitude towards him is an attitude towards a soul. I am not of the *opinion* that he has a soul."[24] Cavell develops an account of our "attitude" toward souls (which we presumably learn as we learn language), employing the term "empathic projection" to describe it. He conceives of empathic projection as the basis for our knowledge of others. By naming this projection as the basis, Cavell registers the sense of separateness we have from one another, for we project onto something distinct from us. By calling it empathic, he records the sense that "my identification of you as a human being is not merely an identification *of* you but *with* you."[25]

Empathic projection is then an attitude found throughout a series of actions and is not just an act of will present on a single occasion. In his early essay "Knowing and Acknowledging," Cavell wrote that "the concept of acknowledgment . . . is not a description of a given response but a category in terms of which a given response is evaluated."[26] As such a category, acknowledgment resembles what Kierkegaard calls the ethical sphere of existence, which both requires a choice or act of will (a "response" in Cavell's terms) and, when chosen, "changes everything."

When one chooses rather than drifts through one's life, according to Kierkegaard, one comes to live it in terms of the unmediated polarity expressed by his famous formula "either/or." One has then reached the ethical sphere. "My either/or," Kierkegaard states, "does not in the first instance denote the choice between good and evil, it denotes the choice whereby one chooses good *and* evil/or excludes them. Here the question is under what determinants one would contemplate the whole of existence and would himself live."[27] Cavell's terms "acknowledgment," "avoidance," and "empathic projection" describe such determinants.

One case Cavell considers in making the point that the will is "not a phenomenon but an attitude toward phenomena" is that of Mark Tapley in Dickens's *Martin Chuzzlewit*. Seasick, as are most of the ship's passengers on a stormy ocean voyage, Tapley has "just that sea of experiences possessed by everyone around him, but without inflecting himself toward it as the others do, e.g., without their seamoans and their wild languors of misery; instead, he moves about the ship as it were in the valleys between swells of nausea, attending to the others." Calling this an "exercise of a will," Cavell regards the will not "as a kind of strength, which I may have more or less of, but as a perspective which I may or may not be able to take upon myself."[28] Tapley is, as Wittgenstein put it, "happy in spite of the misery of the world."[29] In his discussions of slavery, Lear and Cordelia, and Wittgenstein and Kierkegaard in "Between Acknowledgment and Avoidance," Cavell provides what one might call a phenomenology of the will, a treatment of "what it is like" to have a will.[30]

This is the point at which there begins to emerge from Cavell's voluntaristic idea of empathic projection a further important asymmetry between material object and other minds skepticism. In traditional accounts of our knowledge of objects, the basis for such knowledge is held to be sensing (as in the expression "sensing sense-data" that applies whether we are really perceiving objects or merely having an hallucination). Sensing is something less than seeing – seeing is sensing sense-data plus the proper relation (causal or otherwise) between these sense-data and the objects they reveal. Now if empathic projection is the basis for our knowledge of others, then that knowledge is based on something more than seeing. Another asymmetry follows from this one. If the doubt raised by the material object skeptic turns out to be justified – in the sense that the world I take myself to be seeing is only a creation in my mind produced by an evil genius – that would make no difference in my experience. That is, the world would be "sensuously indistinguishable" from the way it now is. (For this reason, the positivists held that radical skepticism was cognitively meaningless – its truth would make no difference in experience.) But if the possibility represented by the other minds

skeptic were realized, I would have "lost the feat" of projecting, and the
world would then not be indistinguishable from the one I now inhabit.
"If I stopped projecting, I would no longer take anything to be human,
or rather I would see no radical difference between humans and other
things."[31] Cavell eventually finds in Romanticism – in the "celestial
light" of the "Immortality Ode" and the "frozen world" of "The Rime
of the Ancient Mariner" – a notion of external world skepticism according to which skepticism does make a difference in our experience.

What Cavell terms "best cases" bring to light yet another asymmetry
between material object and other minds skepticism. Best cases are those
objects or situations – Descartes by the fire in his bathrobe, for example –
about which if we know anything, we know these things. They are precisely not cases in which, say, the light is bad or the perceiver is sleepy
or drugged. The force of the skeptic's position is that it sows the seeds
of doubt in such fields. There also are best cases of knowing others.
Fathers' (say Lear's) knowledge of their daughters are such cases (who
could know Cordelia better than Lear?); spouses' (say Othello's and
Desdemona's) relation to each other are such cases as well. But there is
the following asymmetry between these cases: We (like Lear or Othello)
avoid the best cases of knowing other people or avoid recognizing that
they are best cases or, alternatively, find these everyday life cases disap-
pointing, whereas in the case of the external world "it makes no sense to
try to avoid the best; the best is my milieu, my life with objects."[32] Lear,
for example, avoids the best cases of his knowledge of Cordelia – his daily
life with her – and demands a public and inherently duplicitous testimony
of love from her at the opening of the play. About Cordelia's situation in
the face of that demand, Cavell writes that "to pretend publicly to love,
where you do not love, is easy; to pretend to love, where you really do
love, is not obviously possible."[33] Othello similarly avoids recognizing
that he knows Desdemona as well as a man can know a woman. Consumed by jealousy, he demands a proof of fidelity that is impossible to ob-
tain except through her death. Might it not be, Cavell muses,

> that just this haphazard, unsponsored state of the world, just this radia-
> tion of relationships, of my cares and commitments, provides the milieu
> in which my knowledge of others can best be expressed? Just *this* – say
> expecting someone to tea; or returning a favor; waving goodbye; reluc-
> tantly or happily laying in groceries for a friend with a cold; feeling re-
> buked, and feeling it would be humiliating to admit the feeling; pretend-
> ing not to understand that the other has taken my expression, with a
> certain justice, as meaning more than I sincerely wished it to mean; hid-
> ing inside a marriage; hiding outside a marriage – just such things are
> perhaps the most that knowing others comes to, or has come to for me.[34]

Yet we feel a disappointment with such best cases, a disappointment that
we do not feel with best cases of knowledge of objects.

One may say that we do feel such disappointment with objects, that this is what a skeptic like Descartes or Hume registers (and so the asymmetry turns out to be a symmetry, after all).[35] But here – and this is the final asymmetry we shall discuss – there is the crucial difference that such disappointment with objects requires philosophy in order for it to be felt, whereas our disappointment with the best cases of our knowledge of other minds haunts our everyday lives. Cavell puts this by saying that we live our skepticism concerning other minds.[36]

That we don't live our skepticism concerning the external world was Hume's point in contrasting his philosophical thinking in his "chamber" with the easy and unskeptical life in the streets or the billiard hall, from whose perspective his philosophical musings seemed "cold, strained, and ridiculous."[37] It is a point also made by Wittgenstein in *On Certainty*, regarding the difficulty of taking seriously external world skepticism in daily life:

> Why is it not possible for me to doubt that I have never been on the moon? And how could I try to doubt it?
> First and foremost, the supposition that perhaps I have been there would strike me as idle. Nothing would follow from it, nothing would be explained by it. It would not tie in with anything in my life.[38]
>
> My life shows that I know or am certain that there is a chair over there, or a door, and so on.[39]

Cavell's point – which he often illustrates through examples of drama or literature – is that our life shows that we do not know and are not certain about our knowledge of others. Take the case of Nora, in Ibsen's *Doll's House*. Surely, one might think, she at least knows herself, even if her pompous and condescending husband does not. Yet at the end of the play she says to him, "I used to think I was; but I haven't ever been happy."[40] And *Othello* shows in excruciating detail how doubts about the foundations of our human relationships work their way into our daily life. Our doubts about our knowledge of human beings are, tragically, not idle. Cavell writes that

> there is no everyday *alternative* to skepticism concerning other minds. There is no competing common sense of the matter; there is nothing about other minds that satisfies me for *all* (practical) purposes; I already know everything skepticism concludes, that my ignorance of the existence of others is not the fate of my natural condition as a human knower, but my way of inhabiting that condition; that I cannot close my eyes to my doubts of others and to their doubts and denials of me, that my relations with others are restricted, that I cannot trust them blindly.[41]

When he asserts that other minds skepticism is the way I inhabit the human condition, he is playing on the theme that my knowledge of others is "up to me" in a way that external world skepticism is not. When he states that "there is no competing common sense of the matter," he is alluding to the "moment" in standard skeptical recitals when the skeptic maintains that such doubts are only hyperbolical or ridiculous and that one would have to be insane to live according to them. For the traditional skeptic there is a "common sense of the matter" that competes (rather successfully) with the skeptical sense of the matter. This moment is not found in other minds skepticism: "I cannot close my eyes to my doubts of others." But this is the point at which Cavell begins to grasp skepticism in a way that draws him increasingly toward Romanticism as an intellectual and literary movement and toward the tradition in American philosophy that I myself will be describing as Romantic.

II. ROMANTICISM AND SKEPTICISM

The turn toward Romanticism in Cavell's work occurs most dramatically at the moment he begins to scrutinize, from the viewpoint of his earlier philosophy, our relations primarily not with people but with the world. In the 1970s and 1980s Cavell followed a line of thought running through the American writers Emerson and Thoreau, who are even more "outside" the traditions of "Anglo-American philosophy" than is Kierkegaard or Freud or the "therapeutic" Wittgenstein that Cavell finds at work in *Philosophical Investigations*. Cavell comes increasingly to understand both their work and his own as "Romantic."

In a parenthetical remark in *The Claim of Reason*, Cavell anticipates some of the themes of his recent writing: "It would not hurt my intuitions, to anticipate further than this book actually goes, were someone to be able to show that my discoveries in the regions of the skeptical problem of the other are, rightly understood, further characterizations of (material object) skepticism, of skepticism as such."[42] Could our relation with the world be as murderous as Othello's is with Desdemona? Is something like jealousy operative in Descartes's (and modern philosophy's) attempt to identify irrefutable knowledge of the world? Does external world skepticism express an underlying but unnecessary disappointment with our knowledge of the world? These are questions Cavell finds explored in Romanticism, a topic usually thought of as the province of literary critics and intellectual historians but that has become the new context within which he places his enterprise. Cavell writes of "a Romanticism represented for me by William Wordsworth, Samuel Taylor Coleridge, Ralph Waldo Emerson, and Henry David Thoreau, whose defining mission I have sketched as the redemption of philosophy and poetry by one another. I am coming to think of what I do as seeking my relation to some such mission."[43]

We see the reason for Cavell's interest in Romanticism when we see the ways in which this movement, with such profound consequences for the development of modern thought, is an encounter with the problem of skepticism. Or, rather, when we see that Romanticism is an encounter with what loomed as a monumental and finally unsatisfactory attempt to deal with the problem of skepticism (in its Cartesian or Humean form) once and for all: Kant's epistemology. Romanticism, in Cavell's characterization, holds that what the world needs "redeeming from is . . . at once skepticism and the answer to skepticism provided in the *Critique of Pure Reason*."[44]

Romanticism exerts its force on Cavell too because it is an attempt to solve "the problem of Kant" not simply on the philosophical level (as in Schopenhauer or Hegel) but through and in literary expression. Kant established a context in which literature for the first time could be conscious of itself as enacting answers to deep and troubling philosophical dilemmas. "No man was ever yet a great poet," Coleridge maintained, "without being at the same time a profound philosopher."[45] Ever since "The Avoidance of Love" at least, Cavell has pursued an understanding of skepticism through the reading of literature, and so it becomes a natural extension of his project to examine the Romanticism of Wordsworth and Coleridge, which is at once a literary and a philosophical response to that problem.

The direct impetus for Cavell's turn to literary Romanticism, however, is his discovery in Wordsworth's emphasis on the "common" and the "low" of an analogue to an important aspect of Wittgenstein's "solution" to the problem of skepticism: his call for a return to ordinary language, to some acknowledgment of our "forms of life," and for philosophers' freedom from philosophers' discourse, in which language idles unengaged. "The idea here is that the procedures of ordinary language philosophy do not (as some philosophers have from the beginning attacked and others defended these procedures for doing) defend ordinary or common beliefs, but rather take our words back, or take them on, let me say, to an intimacy with the world which exists before, or after, the expression of beliefs or propositions that may be true or false, certain or nearly certain or doubtful."[46]

The Romantic turn in Cavell's thinking is represented most obviously in such papers as "In Quest of the Ordinary" and "Genteel Responses to Kant? In Emerson's 'Fate' and Coleridge's *Biographia Literaria*," in which he argues that the Romanticism of Wordsworth and Coleridge and later of Emerson and Thoreau – their search for a new intimacy with the world – is a poetic and philosophical response to an intellectual dilemma bequeathed to a new generation of European thinkers at Kant's death. The notion of Romanticism underlying Cavell's own investigations, in turn, is one long since made familiar to students of English and

American literature by the work of such major scholars as Northrop
Frye, M. H. Abrams, and Harold Bloom.[47]

Kant and Coleridge

Kant heralds Romanticism[48] in part because he humanizes the
world, contending that "objects must conform to our knowledge."[49]
The world depicted by Kant is ours in part, not alien to us; this is why
we can know its basic structures of space, time, and causality. Kant's
system is in fact part of the great humanizing movement described by
Frye in his *Study of English Romanticism,* in which European thought began to cast off "an encyclopedic myth, derived mainly from the Bible,"
according to which God was the center of creativity, to work toward
a new myth in which human creativity assumes a central place. "I see
Romanticism," Frye writes, "as the beginning of the first major change
in this [older] pattern of mythology, and as fully comprehensible only
when seen as such."[50]

But the world that Kant envisions us as constituting in the *Critique of
Pure Reason* seems from a Romantic point of view to be cold, dead, and
alien. For a world composed of Newton's meaninglessly moving particles, with only spatial, temporal, and causal relations to one another,
contains nothing fundamentally living and nothing of moral value.[51] Cavell argues that Coleridge is criticizing the world as presented in the first
Critique, the world of the Understanding, when he writes in his *Biographia Literaria* of coming to the realization that "all the products of the
mere reflective faculty partook of DEATH." "I interpret the death, of
which the reflective faculty partakes," Cavell writes, "as of the world
made in our image, or rather through our categories, by Kant's faculty
of the Understanding."[52] According to Cavell, Coleridge depicts that
death in "The Rime of the Ancient Mariner" through the oppressive
heat, cold, and stillness of the world "below the line" and through the
shipful of inspirited corpses with which the Mariner journeys.

The solution Coleridge offers in the poem is not an external influx of
grace but an outflow from the heart of the Mariner. Becalmed and cursed
by the staring eyes of the dead sailors, the Mariner looks down at the
water snakes, "beyond the shadow of the ship":

> O happy living things! no tongue
> Their beauty might declare:
> A spring of love gush'd from my heart,
> And I bless'd them unaware:

The Mariner's reaction is elicited by the world, by its life and beauty,
but that reaction then has its own effect on the world to which it is a
reaction: The albatross falls off the Mariner's neck, the "upper air" bursts

into life, rain falls, and the world becomes reanimated. The Mariner's blessing brings the world to life.

The world is dead, the poem is saying, if we are dead, or death, to it. The world we inhabit, as Cavell puts it, is one "that has died at our hands."[53] But we have the power – through something like the Mariner's "love" – to revive the world, to change the forms we give it. Speaking in this way of the death and animation of the world seems like a mere metaphor or projection rather than a literal description of the world. Cavell calls this position "something like animism"[54] and interprets it as a revision of Kant's landscape in the first *Critique,* an attempt to bring the thing-in-itself – where freedom and value lie – into the phenomenal world, the world of experience. He thus describes "the Kantian bargain with skepticism (buying back the knowledge of objects by giving up things in themselves) and Romanticism's bargain with the Kantian (bringing back the thing in itself by taking on animism)."[55] Animism in this sense is the claim that the world's life and meaning, not only its spatiotemporal and causal structure, are made possible by humanity. Unlike the latter structures, which we have no choice but to encounter because of the automatic operation of our sensibility and understanding, the animation of the world is understood as under our control, subject in some sense to our will. If Romanticism (as so interpreted) is correct, we live a kind of skepticism not just concerning other minds but also concerning the world.

Coleridge's solution to the (Kantian) "death of the world" is parallel to Cavell's solutions to external world and other minds skepticism: Other minds, Cavell asserts, are to be "acknowledged" and the world "accepted." The problem of self–world relation – the "central Romantic question," as Sharon Cameron defines it – is our problem in a deep sense, not just a feature of the situation we happen to be in.[56] The responsibility is ours, and the solution is an act or attitude of our own. ("The ruin or the blank, that we see when we look at nature," Emerson observed, "is in our own eye.")[57]

But our adjustment is not just our own. It is in some sense mutual. Many Romantics, following their predecessor Plotinus, seek an end to alienation or separation in a union with what is initially "other."[58] Some – Cameron argues that Thoreau is one of them – seek to preserve a sense of the otherness of, the autonomy of, nature. These two goals might seem incompatible. If one thinks of union with nature as requiring the dissolution of mind and nature into an homogeneous One, then the otherness of nature must be discarded, an illusion. On the other hand, one may think that otherness precludes connection: that if two things (say two billiard balls) are truly separated, they are simply not connected, and that if they were connected (say by a string), they would no longer be two things, but one.

Kant's "Refutation of Idealism" in the *Critique of Pure Reason* provides one model for a connection that preserves otherness. Kant connects us to the world by the categories and forms with which we endow reality. But he has a strong sense of that world as other. In the "Refutation" he attacks the subjective or skeptical idealism that seems to threaten his transcendental idealism by showing that our ability to be conscious of ourselves requires the existence of the world: We exist as selves, he argues, only on the condition that the world exists too. The idea on which Kant's refutation rests is that our existence as conscious beings requires a framework of space, time, and the objects within them. Without such a framework, he maintains, our consciousness could not take place in time, nor could our ego be assigned a position in time.[59]

Although Kant connects us to, by placing us in, the world via the transcendental structures of space, time, and causality, the world to which he joins us is, as we have seen, not all that appealing. It is the "inanimate, cold world" Coleridge depicts in "Dejection," a world lacking freedom, concealing the (noumenal) basis for the "respect" that, according to Kant's moral theory, human beings deserve. We can only know phenomena, Kant holds: "We cannot *know* . . . objects as things in themselves."[60] But then as Cavell points out, Kant ends up denying "that you can experience the world as world, things as things, face to face as it were, call this the life of things." And about defeating skepticism by negotiating away things in themselves "one will sometimes feel: Thanks for nothing."[61]

Marriage

An important expression of an alternative view of our relation to the world can be found in lines, themselves lying near the center of literary Romanticism, occurring near the end of Wordsworth's *Recluse:*

> . . . Paradise and groves
> Elysian, Fortunate Fields – like those of old
> Sought in the Atlantic Main – why should they be
> A history only of departed things,
> Or a mere fiction of what never was?
> For the discerning intellect of Man,
> When wedded to his goodly universe
> In love and holy passion, shall find these
> A simple produce of the common day.[62]

"Paradise" becomes "common." "Man" achieves "holy passion." This is no longer a world in which the noumenal and the phenomenal are separated. It is the world of "natural supernaturalism" described by

Thomas Carlyle and later by M. H. Abrams, in which the supernatural is naturalized and the divine is humanized.[63] Wordsworth tells us that his "high argument," that is, his subject, is "the creation (by no lower name / Can it be called) which [mind and world] Accomplish."[64] He embraces the traditional force of the word "creation" but naturalizes it, ascribing creation to the mind–world interaction. God is simply not in this picture, although "paradise" and "groves Elysian" are. For Wordsworth, paradise can be a human achievement.

The marriage of self and world that Wordsworth depicts has three elements: the "discerning intellect of Man," the "goodly universe" to which the mind is wedded, and the "love and holy passion" that joins the two. (The third element, neither simply human nor simply worldly, is perhaps the "motion" or "spirit," which in "Tintern Abbey," "rolls through all things.") This structure, so common in Romantic writing, expresses the closeness of the mind–world relationship, the "fitness" of the partners for each other. But it acknowledges their separateness as well. The mind–world wedding that Wordsworth describes is a relationship, not a homogeneous unity. The marriage does not dissolve the differences between the partners. According to Abrams: "Unlike the German idealists . . . Wordsworth does not posit an initial One, or absolute, which subdivides into the knowing mind and the object known, but instead begins, as he says in the Prospectus, with a 'Mind' which is fitted to 'the external World' and an 'external World' which is 'fitted to the mind.' "[65]

Wordsworth expresses the intimacy and fitting of nature and mind, but in a way that develops our sense of each. He has a strong feeling for place, for the Wye valley celebrated in "Tintern Abbey" for example, which Bloom calls "the scene of instruction."[66] That there is such a scene is significant, for Wordsworth develops his poetic and philosophical genius in league with nature, and with nature not in the general or abstract but in the concrete. "Once again / Do I behold these steep and lofty cliffs," he writes in "Tintern Abbey." These cliffs and the "quiet of the sky" exert their force on the solitary thinker, who remembers his last visit to this place together with the "five long winters" between. Wordsworth does ultimately inquire into "the mind of Man," what he calls in the *Prelude* "my haunt / And the main region of my song." But the inquiry occurs in a partnership with the world *in concreto*. In much of his poetry, Wordsworth offers what Kenneth Johnston characterizes as "a definition of poetic inspiration in terms of the *places* which nurture it and which it must in turn minister to."[67]

Wordsworth sees nature as akin to us in its "passion" but as separate nonetheless. He describes the valley at Grasmere, for example, as "a haunt / Of pure affections" and maintains in the *Prelude* that "the forms /

Of Nature have a passion in themselves / That intermingles with those
works of man / To which she summons him."[68] The world is akin to us
in its "passions" and "affections," so that our human feelings, no less
than our conceptions of size or velocity, correspond to the world's nature. But the world is nevertheless distinct: Nature's forms have a passion in themselves, not just on the basis of our human projection.

So much does Wordsworth's vision involve a sense of an objective
world, separate from ourselves, that it is possible to argue that Wordsworth's hoped-for marriage actually expresses a sense of dispersion and
alienation.[69] And there are certainly moments in his poetry when he expresses not only the separateness of nature but also its alienness. The
imagined grandeur of Mont Blanc, which had sustained him during the
long Alpine journey he records in the *Prelude,* proves a poor anticipation
of the actual sight: "a soulless image on the eye / That had usurped upon
a living thought / That never more could be."[70] And although the imagination is predominantly a power reconciling and deepening the relationship between mind and nature,[71] it sometimes appears as an alienating
and disorienting force. Learning from a peasant that he had already
crossed the Simplon Pass without so much as noticing it, Wordsworth
experiences some moments of imaginative vertigo: "Imagination – . . .
That awful Power rose from the mind's abyss / Like an unfathered va-
pour that enwraps, / At once, some lonely traveller. I was lost; / Halted
without an effort to break through."[72]

Such moments of being "lost" rather than at home (as he is, for instance, in "Home at Grasmere") in nature give a sense of contingency
to Wordsworth's claim that the mind is "fitted" to the world. Such fitting does not necessarily take place. Mind and world are – sometimes
quite frighteningly – distinct. Hartman, who stresses this "apocalyptic
imagination," describes "the precarious separateness of Wordsworth's
imagination, and the fact that true reciprocity – mind meeting world
with equal flame – was realized at only two periods in Wordsworth's
life, and is mainly a hope, and faith, and desire."[73]

The Mont Blanc and Simplon Pass episodes give us a sense of the
rarity of those "gleaming moments" of connection that Wordsworth
seeks. They also provide a way of incorporating moments of radical
doubt and disorientation – skepticism about the metaphysical foundations of things – into the account of the "growth of a poet's mind" that
he offers in the *Prelude.* Some philosophers try to defeat or avoid such
radical doubt by maintaining its uselessness or (as in positivism) its
meaninglessness. Others – Descartes and Hume are classical cases – try
to meet doubt head on, hoping to confine it after it has had its full play.
The problem for them is that doubting has a tendency to get out of hand,
to become unstoppable (or only minimally so if one accepts Descartes's

proof of his own existence as a stopping point). Once the genie is fully out of the bottle, it is hard to put it back.

Wordsworth follows a strategy (pursued in their various ways by Austin, Wittgenstein, and the American writers to whom we shall be turning) of accepting doubt in some way but, as it were, confining it, preventing it from generalizing. One concedes something to the skeptic – areas of uncertainty – but does not concede that such areas throw doubt on everything else. Wordsworth makes his loss of bearings merely a stage or a mood in a life characterized as one of growth or progress. Mont Blanc is superseded by Mount Snowdon in the *Prelude's* concluding book, in which the poet finds his "mind sustained / By recognitions of transcendent power" and "a world of life."[74]

Coleridge's version of the marriage of mind and nature is more idealistic than that of Wordsworth. He writes in "Dejection":

> . . . we receive but what we give,
> And in our life alone does Nature live:
> Ours is her wedding garment, ours her shroud!
> . . . from the soul itself must issue forth
> A light, a glory, a fair luminous cloud
> . . . A sweet and potent voice, of its own birth,
> Of all sweet sounds the life and element!

But even here nature is separate: We give it life, not existence. Later in the poem, Coleridge offers this well-known formulation:

> Joy, Lady! is the spirit and the power,
> Which wedding Nature to us gives in dower
> A new Earth and new Heaven,
> Undreamt of by the sensual and the proud –
> Joy is the sweet voice, Joy the luminous cloud

Here, as in Wordsworth, we are the key ("joy . . . is the power") to the union of self and world. Again, we don't, through our joy, so much produce nature (as in a simple form of idealism) as give it to ourselves in a new form, modifying it. We receive, in fact, a new earth. (We also receive a new heaven, evidence for the correctness of Cavell's suggestion that Coleridge envisions an alteration not only of the worldly or phenomenal but of the noumenal or spiritual as well, that he is trying to "recover, or recover from, the thing-in-itself.")[75]

Idealist though he may be, Coleridge is clearly committed to some version of realism. This is no doubt one of the reasons that he was attracted to Kant, who offered an "empirical realism" as part of his "transcendental idealism."[76] Coleridge contrasts his experientially based realism with a realism of inference, such as Locke's representative realism. He in effect accuses certain empiricists of being unempirical. "Wherein," he asks in the *Biographia Literaria,* "does the realism of mankind properly consist?" Not, he replies, "in the assertion that there exists a something without them, what, or how, or where they know not, which occasions the objects of their perceptions." Rather, the "realism common to all mankind is far elder and lies infinitely deeper than this hypothetical explanation of the origin of our perceptions, an explanation skimmed from the mere surface of mechanical philosophy. It is the table itself, which the man of common sense believes himself to see, not the phantom of a table, from which he may argumentatively deduce the reality of a table."[77] But Coleridge's realism is inseparable from his idealism: "In every act of conscious perception, we at once identify our being with that of the world without us, and yet place ourselves in contradistinction to that world."[78]

There is no doubt a strong mystical streak in Coleridge: "I never find myself alone within the embracement of rocks and hills . . . but my spirit courses, drives, and eddies like a Leaf in Autumn: a wild activity, of thoughts, imaginations, feelings, and impulses of motion, rises up from within me – a sort of *bottom-wind,* that blows to no point of the compass, & comes from I know not whence, but agitates the whole of me."[79] But Coleridge's mysticism is not purely monistic, pantheistic, or Spinozistic, as he thought of it. He had nothing but contempt for Fichte's philosophy, for example, which he claimed "degenerated into a crude egoismus, a boastful and hyperstoic hostility to NATURE."[80] His later, Christian philosophy preserved in the notion of a "Catholic faith of Trinal Unity," a commitment to the union amidst separation that he had earlier expressed in the idea of a marriage of self and world.[81] Indeed, one of the reasons that Coleridge was attracted to Christianity in his later years was its commitment to the body and to the natural world. (Thomas MacFarland calls this Coleridge's commitment to "the dignity of nature" and argues that it separates Coleridge from his heroes Plato and Kant and in part explains his deep, if ambivalent, attraction to Spinoza.)[82] Considered philosophically, Christianity can be said to follow Platonic thought in its notion of a soul separated from the body at death. But it offers a radical departure from Platonism in its doctrine of the resurrection of the body, according to which human bodily forms are essential to our spiritual life.[83] Coleridge did not want to escape earthly forms, but to redeem them.

Coleridge's interest in the worldly side of the self–world relation is suggested by his interest in science. This is the Coleridge who, for instance, as an intimate friend of the chemist Sir Humphry Davy, kept notebooks of detailed observations on electricity and magnetism, chemistry and biology.[84] Like the *Naturphilosophen,* Coleridge was persuaded that the unity of the world (as well as its variety) is revealed by the sciences: in such developments, for example, as Galvan's discovery of "animal electricity" in frogs' legs or Oersted's assimilation of magnetism and electricity.[85] As a recent commentator observed, Coleridge "systematically rejects doctrines that involve a radical denial of the experiential world."[86] Poetry no less than science requires, in his view, a "faithful adherence to the truth of nature."[87] Like others in the Romantic tradition, Coleridge gives the human experience of nature a central place in his theories of knowledge and being.

This is the larger background against which we are to view the Romantics' hostility to science. Wordsworth wrote that "our meddling intellect / Mis-shapes the beauteous forms of things: – / We murder to dissect." But the first line of this stanza from "The Tables Turned" – "Sweet is the lore which Nature brings" – is important, for the poem in fact turns us toward the sense world, urging us to "hear" and to "watch." Wordsworth is hostile to science, not because it focuses on the empirical world, but because, though its pretensions are enormous, its inquiries are limited: It doesn't tell or show us enough about the world that we inhabit. The problem, then, is not empiricism but what Emerson calls "paltry empiricism."[88] Or as Cavell states, "what is wrong with empiricism is not its reliance on experience but its paltry idea of experience."[89] Wordsworth begins the last stanza of "The Tables Turned" with "Enough of Science and of Art, / Close up those barren leaves" but completes it with "Come forth, and bring with you a heart / That watches and receives." He opposes not observation but the "setting" from which our observation normally takes place. "Watching and receiving" may require a readjustment in our basic mode of living.

There is thus no necessary opposition between Romanticism and empiricism. Indeed, according to Robert Langbaum, they are inextricably related to each other. "The essential idea of romanticism," he writes, is a "doctrine of experience. . . . Like the scientist's hypothesis, the romanticist's formulation is evolved out of experience and is continually tested against experience."[90] But Romantics regard experience as containing more than just the atoms of sensation postulated by many empiricist writers.[91] I am "a lover of the meadows and the woods . . . of all the mighty world / Of eye, and ear," Wordsworth writes in "Tintern Abbey." But he speaks there too of "a sense sublime / Of something far more deeply interfused, / Whose dwelling is the light of setting suns, / And the round ocean and the living air, / And the blue sky, and in the mind of man."[92] Sometimes Romantic writers express their expanded notion of human experience by speaking of a blend of thought and feeling, of an originary sense that is a blend of sound and sight, or of the operation of the imagination. In the preface to the *Lyrical Ballads,* for example, Wordsworth states that his principal object is to depict "incidents and situations from common life" in "language really used by men, and, at the same time, to throw over them a certain colouring of imagination, whereby ordinary things should be presented to the mind in an unusual aspect."[93] Romantic empiricism is an imaginative empiricism, conceiving experience not just as given but as something we mold, a directed process. When guided by our "discerning intellect" and "holy passion," this process can be understood as a "quest of the ordinary" in which we seek a "common life," as Wordsworth says, which is nevertheless "unusual."

It can also be conceived as the abandonment of the ordinary described by Coleridge as "the lethargy of custom," the "film of familiarity and selfish solicitude" that covers the events of our lives.[94] That "ordinary" is to be buried, and an "extraordinary ordinary" is to take its place. Like "natural supernaturalism," the notion of an "extraordinary ordinary" can be read in two ways: (1) as a form of religious naturalism, with the emphasis on "natural" or "ordinary," and (2) as a contradictory, or at least dialectically unstable, idea signaling the need for overcoming the distinctions, for example, between the divine and the common, on which it seems to operate.

Feeling

The marriage of self and world, like Romanticism itself, takes as its center feeling or emotion – the "love and holy passion" with which Wordsworth sees us wedded to the universe, for instance, or Coleridge's idea that the mariner transforms the world by learning to love "all creatures both great and small." The philosophical import of emotion considered in this light is suggested by a phrase that Wordsworth uses to describe his own response to the world at certain privileged or heightened moments, when it becomes not merely feeling but also "the sentiment of being." Yet the Romantics neither celebrate emotion in exclusive terms nor devalue intelligence, balance, and other classical virtues. Some Romantics cultivated extremes and tested limits, particularly emotional ones, enough to tempt T. S. Eliot to define Romanticism as "excess in any direction" (one thinks of Rousseau, Berlioz, or Wagner).[95] Other Romantics direct their efforts toward redressing a balance that has been lost rather than toward the excess that Wordsworth rejected in "Hart-leap Well": "The moving accident is not my trade; / To freeze the blood I have no ready arts: / 'T is my delight, alone in summer shade, / To pipe a song for thinking hearts." Wordsworth's handling of emotion is often gentle and restrained, and it is portrayed as calm and ordinary:

> Who doth not love to follow with his eye
> The windings of a public way? the sight,

Familiar object that it is, hath wrought
On my imagination since the morn
Of childhood . . .[96]

The Wordsworth who wrote that "all good poetry is the spontaneous overflow of powerful feelings" also maintained that good poetry was "never produced on any variety of subjects but by a man who, being possessed of more than usual organic sensibility, had also thought long and deeply." For Wordsworth, the poet is someone who both "thinks and feels."[97]

To their opponents, Romantics seem sentimental and adolescent (according to Cavell, "for each one who wants to be a Romantic, there is someone else who wishes them to outgrow it"),[98] but they in turn complain about the deadness or mechanical nature of (what passes) for human thought, our lack of feeling. "We have given our hearts away," Wordsworth laments in "The World Is Too Much with Us":

This sea that bares her bosom to the moon;
    The winds that will be howling at all hours,
    And are up-gather'd now like sleeping flowers;
For this, for everything, we are out of tune;
It moves us not.

Wordsworth's poetry operates in a universe of emotion and its lack. He tries to counter both "listlessness" and "mad endeavor," indeed "all that is at enmity with joy." But often, as in the "Immortality Ode," his poems end with a characteristic mix of sadness, contingency, and reconciliation: "To me the meanest flower that blows can give / Thoughts that do often lie too deep for tears." Wordsworth once defined poetry as "emotion recollected in tranquility." In his mature work, as Hartman says, "emotion, when contemplated, increases like the expanding ripples in a lake, then settles to all-embracing stillness."[99]

In Coleridge's "Dejection," the poet himself suffers from the absence of feeling, from "a grief without a pang." On "a long eve, so balmy and serene," he gazes at the chilly loveliness of the sky and the "thin clouds above, in flakes and bars, / That give away their motion to the stars . . . / I see them all so excellently fair, / I see, not feel, how beautiful they are!"

The emotional opposite of such dejection is the joy of which Wordsworth and Coleridge so often speak. Thus Wordsworth:

I felt the sentiment of Being spread
O'er all that moves, and all that seemeth still . . .
O'er all that leaps, and runs, and shouts, and sings,
Or beats the gladsome air, o'er all that glides
Beneath the wave, yea, in the wave itself

> And mighty depth of waters, Wonder not
> If such my transports were; for in all things
> I saw one life, and felt that it was joy.[100]

Such joy does not dissolve the world but, rather, transforms it. Wordsworth (and Coleridge in calling for a "new *Earth*") seeks a renewal or revitalization of the world and the self rather than a transcendence of our normal forms, thereby making the ordinary extraordinary.

Sometimes Wordsworth writes of reviving our interest rather than our joy, and Cavell highlights that choice:

> When Wordsworth dedicated his poetry, in his preface to *Lyrical Ballads,* to arousing men in a particular way from a "torpor," the way he sought was "to make the incidents of common life interesting," as if he saw us as having withdrawn our interest, or investment, from whatever worlds we have in common, say this one or the next. This seems to me a reasonable description at once of skepticism and of melancholia, as if the human race had suffered some calamity and were now entering, at best, a period of convalescence.[101]

"Withdrawing our interest, or investment" from the world is another way of saying that we don't care about it, and this in turn suggests that we are in the position of Coleridge's Mariner before he finds his love for the water snakes.

Far from representing a turning away or inward from the world, the Romantic concern with feeling turns us toward it. The feeling developed in his poems, Wordsworth writes, "gives importance to the action and situation, and not the action and situation to the feeling."[102] Like traditional empiricists, the Romantics seek to know the world on the basis of human experience. But they have a broader notion of experience than do many empiricists and stress the role of interest or feeling in knowing the world.

Two key questions with which any philosophical development of the Romantic interest in feeling or emotion must contend are (1) What part do and can emotions play in our experience, including that of philosophy, and (2) what cognitive role do our emotions play? Wordsworth and Coleridge engage this latter question more or less explicitly, for example, when Coleridge writes that "deep thinking is attainable only by a man of deep feeling."[103] When he complains in "Dejection" that he stares with "a blank eye" or that "I see, not feel, how beautiful they are," he is talking about his apprehension of the world and blaming its imperfection on a failure of feeling. "Feeling" is here used transitively to describe not a purely subjective event but a cognition, knowing.[104]

This is the context in which, with characteristic daring and penetration, Cavell finds a quasi-Romantic answer to the question of the cognitive status of emotion or feeling in that doyen of the analytic family, Hume. Commenting on the claim (which he regards as mistaken) that knowing the world is knowing some large object, Cavell reconsiders the argument from design so much under attack in Hume's *Dialogues Concerning Natural Religion:*

> Freed from this assumption [that the world is an object], the *experience* of design or purpose in the world (which Cleanthes always begins with and comes back to, and which Philo confirms) has a completely different force. It is no longer a modest surmise about a particular object, for which there is no good evidence . . . but rather, being a natural and *inescapable* response, it has, in terms of Hume's own philosophizing, the same claim to reveal the world as our experience of causation (or of objecthood) has.[105]

Cavell returns to this claim and gives it a specifically Kantian accent when interpreting a passage from *Walden:* "Human forms of feeling, objects of human attraction, our reactions constituted in art, are as universal and necessary, as objective, as revelatory of the world, as the forms of the laws of physics."[106] This is certainly to go beyond Kant (for whom our aesthetic reactions were universal but subjective, not revelatory of the phenomenal world, and who deemphasized the role of emotion both in morality and in knowledge), but not beyond the Kantian picture of a world whose form is determined by the peculiar receptive and organizing principles of human beings.

Will

Romantic accounts of the forms of feeling with which we shape the world always involve an element of choice, of power and will. If "the world is too much with us," the assumption of the poet will be that we have the power to change (our relation to) it. There is clearly an element of willed action in the Romantic idea of marrying self and world. Marriage itself is an act requiring a choice, a commitment of the partners to it. Coleridge, in particular, brings out this willful aspect: "Joy" is a "power" that gives us a "new Earth and new Heaven" by wedding nature to us. A striving and willful vitality is also at the heart of Coleridge's conception of the imagination, which he defines in *Biographia Literaria* as a faculty that "dissolves, diffuses, dissipates, in order to recreate . . . it struggles to realize and to unify. It is essentially *vital,* even as all objects (*as* objects) are essentially fixed and dead."[107] Romantics speak of the world as coming to life (or becoming a paradise or becoming fluid; the terminology varies, but the idea is that the world changes) because of, or as a part of, some action or attitude of the mind, intellect, or person. Wordsworth's words for this action or attitude are "love," "joy," "imagination," or "wise passiveness";[108] Coleridge adds "power" and "will" (Cavell's words are "accepting," "acknowledging," and, following Heidegger, "thanking").

Situations such as the marriage of self with world, in which our passionate and willful natures are responsible for the character of the object or world we then encounter, I shall term "voluntaristic structures" of knowledge and being. In calling them voluntaristic, I am alluding to usages by Kant, Coleridge, Emerson, and others and, more importantly, am thinking broadly of "will," in the way that William James does in *The Will to Believe,* in that our "willing nature" includes not only "deliberate volitions" but "all such factors of belief as fear and hope, prejudice and passion."[109] In thinking of these factors as part of our "willing nature," we take them to be in some way under our control.

The will in this sense is central to Cavell's concept of acknowledgment: "Being human is the power to grant being human."[110] That is, our humanity does not exist if it is not acknowledged, so that acknowledgment is a "power" and acknowledgment is "up to us," not automatically there, so that "humanity" depends on what we will. We have the power, but not necessarily the willingness, to allow others' claims on us, to allow their being in what Kant called the "kingdom of ends."[111] Acknowledgment as "empathic projection" transforms the world, according to Cavell, at least the moral world of our personal interactions. In Wordsworth and Coleridge, love, imagination, or the will transform the world as a whole, so that being human is the power (by no means always or easily exercised) to grant (which does not mean "create" but something more like "allow") the being or existence of "Paradise." "From thyself it comes, that thou must give," Wordsworth wrote in the *Prelude,* "Else never canst receive."[112]

The idea that a passion such as love joins self and world has deep roots in Western thought. St. Augustine, for example, saw in the mind, its knowledge, and love "a kind of image of the Trinity" and wrote that "love itself is nothing but a kind of life which couples together or seeks to couple some two entities, the lover and the loved."[113] Such love, which "seeks" its goal, is a willful love, and Augustine clearly anticipates Coleridge in associating love with the perfection of a "striving" and searching "will."[114]

In looking at will in Coleridge, however, we shall follow Cavell – himself guided by Coleridge's statement that Kant had taken him over "as with a Giant's hand"[115] – in tracing the evident Kantian strains in Coleridge's discussion. Kant maintains that the will is our faculty of acting freely, of recognizing and imposing on ourselves the moral law (and recognizing the humanity of others). This law is not, like the Newtonian laws that govern phenomena, a law that we obey automatically; we obey it only by willing. When we will in accord with the moral law, we put ourselves into what Kant calls "another order of things," the noumenal order: "When he conceives of himself as intelligence endowed with a will," man puts himself "into relation with determining causes of quite another sort . . . than he does when he perceives himself as a phenomenon in the sensible world (which he actually is as well)."[116]

For Coleridge, the will can put us into relation with the "different order of things" he calls the "new Earth." "All true reality," he writes in *The Friend*, "has both its ground and its evidence in the *will*, without which as its complement science itself is but an elaborate game of shadows, begins in abstractions and ends in perplexity."[117] "Science as a game of shadows" is exactly what the skeptic fears. The will (properly functioning) somehow ensures that science will overcome the basis for this fear. But the will puts us in touch with "true reality," and this is moral and religious, not just scientific. Like Kant, Coleridge associates the will (properly employed) with reason, but the world apprehended from within the relationships that this will creates is far from the stern commands of the Categorical Imperative. Rather, "it is an eternal and infinite self-rejoicing . . . neither singly that which affirms, nor that which is affirmed; but the identity and living copula of both."[118]

In understanding the will to be the ground of reality, Coleridge is perhaps responding to the following passage in the *Critique of Pure Reason:*

> What *use* can we make of our understanding, even in respect of experience, if we do not propose ends to ourselves? But the highest ends are those of morality. . . . We cannot make use of the knowledge of nature in any serviceable manner . . . unless nature has itself shown unity of design. . . . But [this unity] is necessary, and founded on the will's own essential nature. . . . And thus the transcendental enlargement of our knowledge, as secured through reason, is not to be regarded as the cause, but merely as the effect of the practical purposiveness which pure reason imposes on us.[119]

Kant is saying not only that we must believe in the unity or purposiveness of nature but also that there is a transcendental ground in our will (and in the rational law that it imposes on itself) for such purposiveness, for the coherence of our theories with the nature we investigate. For Coleridge the will permeates even the synthetic a priori truths of geometry: "In all inevitable Truths, e.g. that the two sides of a triangle are greater than the third, I feel my will active: I seem to will the Truth, as well as to perceive it."[120]

One aspect of the will that becomes increasingly important as our story progresses is its dynamic and forward-looking nature. Hannah Arendt puts this best and most succinctly in her book *Willing*, stating that the will is "an organ for the future."[121] If the will shapes reality, it does so in time, in our actions, but not eternally, once and for all. This point is crucial to our understanding of the development of pragmatism.

III. CAVELL ON MARRIAGE

We have seen that Cavell's work on the relations between minds reveals logical patterns which, from the perspective of Romanticism, apply to our relations with the world generally. Othello, for example, tries to wed himself to Desdemona by the only method he can employ that provides him with certainty: her death at his hands. In his most recent work on Romanticism, Cavell reads this tragedy as an interpretation of external world skepticism, now understanding skepticism as rooted in the desire to make our attachment to something automatic.[122] In fact, Cavell's writings on Shakespeare, Wittgenstein, film, and American philosophy develop in many different registers the idea of knowledge as marriage, or marriage as knowledge, and of skepticism as jealousy or lack of trust.

The Comedy of Remarriage

Cavell focuses on marriage in his book on American film comedy, *Pursuits of Happiness: The Hollywood Comedy of Remarriage*, published in 1981, two years after *The Claim of Reason*. He argues that such Hollywood classics as *The Awful Truth, It Happened One Night, The Philadelphia Story, Bringing up Baby, Adam's Rib*, and *His Girl Friday* reveal and offer instruction in our successful knowledge of others, our acknowledgments rather than our avoidances of them.

These films portray remarriages in several ways and senses. Some of them portray literal remarriages, for example, *The Philadelphia Story*, in which Cary Grant has actually divorced Katherine Hepburn but remarries her in the end. But "remarriage" also expresses the idea that couples are committed to some form of repetition, that they find they must go through "a sort of continuous reaffirmation."[123] The term also signals the idea that for the comedy of marriage, that is, for a happy or successful marriage, a separation is necessary. In his discussion of Cary Grant and Katherine Hepburn in Howard Hawks's 1938 comedy *Bringing up Baby*, Cavell observes:

> The validity of marriage takes a willingness for repetition, the willingness for remarriage. The task of the conclusion is to get the pair back into a particular moment of their past lives together. No new vow is required, merely the picking up of an action which has been, as it were, interrupted; not starting over, but starting again, finding and picking up the thread. Put a bit more metaphysically: only those can genuinely marry who are already married. It is as though you know you are mar-

ried when you come to see that you cannot divorce, that is, when you find that your lives simply will not disentangle. If your love is lucky, this knowledge will be greeted with laughter.[124]

Cavell stresses the ordinary nature of what is repeated, so that the happiness of marriage as these films picture it is a happiness – like that sought by Wordsworth and Coleridge – of daily life. Although the movie couples usually have to go "somewhere else" to find or refind themselves (usually in these films this place is called Connecticut), their marriages are as ordinary as a meal in a restaurant, a home movie, a telephone conversation, or an argument. Marriage in these films is pictured not as physical lovemaking or as a series of profound moments of understanding[125] but as a conversation in which each party appreciates the other's talk, his or her style, more than anyone else does. So it is in *His Girl Friday,* which begins with Hildy's (Rosalind Russell's) divorce from Walter Burns (Cary Grant) and her impending marriage to the awkward and unimaginative Bruce (Ralph Bellamy). Early on, Grant manipulates the engaged couple into having lunch with him and manages to "talk" seriously (and also hilariously) with Hildy even while seeming to make ingratiating small talk with Bruce. The whole tone of Hildy's interaction with Walter is completely different – more knowing and intimate – from the dull formalities she manages with Bruce, the Albany insurance salesman. At lunch, Hildy and Walter surreptitiously (at least for Bruce, but not for each other or for the audience) dispute the new direction she is trying to take, but as Cavell puts it:

> They dispute it within a family agreement – within, I wish to teach us to say, a conversation – of a profundity and complexity the guest cannot begin to fathom. The kicks on the shin Hildy gives Walter under the table are familiar gestures of propriety and intimacy; and the pair communicate not only by way of feet and hand signals but in a lingo and tempo, and about events present and past, that Bruce can have no part in. They simply *appreciate* one another more than either of them appreciates anyone else, and they would rather be appreciated by one another more than by anyone else.[126]

(In this idea of appreciation, as earlier in the idea of "picking up the thread," Cavell echoes the Augustinian idea of a love that "is not extinguished when it reaches its goal" but remains "*steadfast* in order to *enjoy* it.")[127]

These movies contain much talk, often at a breathtaking pace, making all the more reasonable Cavell's suggestion that in them marriage is portrayed as a conversation. Cavell finds a more traditional source than Hollywood comedy for this idea in John Milton's statement that "in God's intention a meet and happy conversation is the chiefest and noblest end of marriage."[128] Whether it is Hildy and Walter Burns talking over "their special distance of the telephone"[129] while following a hot news story, Hepburn's and Tracy's bickering in *Adam's Rib,* or Grant's and Irene Dunne's collusion in covering up her presence in his apartment on the night before their final divorce decree in *The Awful Truth,*[130] in all these films "talking together is fully and plainly being together, a mode of association, a form of life."[131]

Cavell finds a combination of intimacy and alterity in the marriages that these Hollywood comedies depict. The very notion of a conversation connotes this, for if people are in conversation and not just talking past one another, they are connected and responsive, although on the other hand, a conversation (even if with oneself) requires two voices, two centers, a speaker and a listener. Cavell makes explicit this blend of connection and alterity when he understands Dunne saying to Grant near the end of *The Awful Truth:* "What is necessary now is not to estrange ourselves but to recognize, without denying our natural intimacy, that we are also strangers, separate, different."[132] Indeed, Cavell maintains that the separation of divorce (necessary for a remarriage) is an emblem of the freedom that marriage requires. A narcissistic or incestuous intimacy must first be ruptured, he argues, "in order that an intimacy of difference or reciprocity supervene. Marriage is always divorce, always entails rupture from something."[133] Marriages in these comedies, like the Romantic marriages of self and world, are unions that preserve otherness. As Cavell sees it, a marriage is a "scene in which the chance for happiness is shown as the mutual acknowledgment of separateness."[134]

Will

The entanglement of feeling, will, and knowledge in Coleridge's account of the self–world marriage is duplicated in Cavell's treatment of acknowledgment. Cavell's discussion, like Coleridge's, owes much to Kant, not only in regarding acknowledgment as something claimed (via rationality) by each human being from every other human being, but in the explicit identification of acknowledgment with the Kantian concept of respect.[135] Kant writes that "although respect is a feeling, it is not a feeling *received* through outside influence, but one *self-produced* by a rational concept." Kant thus emphasizes the individual's autonomy, the choice or will he or she exercises in respecting another rational being. Respect thus contrasts with such feelings as pain or jealousy. The latter are produced in us, according to Kant, without the operation of our will, as more or less automatic responses. Respect is not just a response, it requires "the activity of a will."[136] There is, then, a moral dimension to acknowledgment. As the title *The Claim of Reason* indicates, "reason" "claims" acknowledgement from us on behalf of the others with whom

we live. We cannot escape this claim: "The alternative to my acknowledgment of the other is not my ignorance of him but my avoidance of
him, call it my denial of him."[137]

Although for Kant respect is a feeling, it has an objective pole. Respect
is willed, but it is also demanded or claimed; it is both subjectively and
objectively determined: "Immediate determination of the will by the law
and consciousness of this determination is called *'respect'*, so that respect
is regarded as the *effect* of the law on the subject and not as the *cause* of
the law. Respect is properly awareness of a value which demolishes my
self-love."[138] Cavell reproduces this objective–subjective structure in his
account of acknowledgment, whose subjective side comes out in his
linking it with feelings, the self, and the will. But its objective side appears in the idea that respecting or acknowledging others is responding
to their claim on us, just by being human. The objectivity of "the claim
of reason" that our feeling of respect acknowledges is expressed by Cavell's contention that the opposite of acknowledgment is not ignorance
but avoidance, and in such concrete claims as that there is an "anxiety"
in the slaveholder's situation – he has to fight off the respect that the
existence of other people demands from him.[139] The Romanticism toward which Cavell sees his work on acknowledgment pointing holds
that the world makes claims on us too and that we mostly live our lives
avoiding these claims.

Cavell departs from Kant, however, in thinking of respect – in the
form of acknowledgment – as our knowledge of other minds. From a
Romantic perspective, such a departure constitutes another step along
the path of bringing into the phenomenal world what Kant treats as noumenal or nonempirical. We know other minds by acknowledging them,
that is, by responding to their claims on us. Cavell also departs from
Kant in treating willing not as an act, for example, an act of resolution,
but as something like a Kierkegaardian sphere of existence, a way of
existing. He connects the will with what Wittgenstein called an attitude.[140] (Coleridge's dejection, the "grief without a pang," is such an
attitude.)

The duck–rabbit figure that Cavell follows Wittgenstein in discussing,
and his general concern with "seeing as"[141] are attempts to furnish analo-
gies for the kind of willing and the kind of apprehension arising in crucial
moral cases. We find our will at work when we control which aspect of
an ambiguous figure appears; we can try to see it as a duck. Such cases
are examples of voluntarist structures in that the will (e.g., to see the
duck aspect) is required in order to see what is "there." Cavell suggests
the analogy that just as we see the duck or the rabbit aspect of the duck–
rabbit figure, so we may see another person restrictedly or fully. People

who can see only one aspect of the duck–rabbit miss what is objectively there to be seen. Our avoidance of the world, including other people, is equally a lack of knowledge.[142]

Reading

The marriage of self and world requires an attitude or feeling that appears sometimes as will, sometimes as acknowledgment or acceptance, but in all cases as a way of apprehending the world. It involves an expansion of experience beyond its narrow or "paltry" forms. Cavell explores domains of human experience untouched by classical empiricism and pragmatism in his writings on film, on Freudian analysis, and on literature.

Cavell can be said to bring literature into empiricism by discovering (or, if one admits the significant cases of Thoreau and Emerson, rediscovering) reading as a form of experience. There is an irony to this discovery in the fact that Wordsworth, the founding father of Cavell's Romanticism, contrasts the narrow experience gleaned from "books" with the fullness of experiencing "nature" in "The Tables Turned": "Close up those barren leaves; / Come forth, and bring with you a heart / That watches and receives." Cavell can be taken as reminding the poet that such a heart can be engaged by a book as easily as by a walk (not all that easily in either case). Like the appreciation of nature that Wordsworth sought all his life but rarely attained, "reading, in a high sense," as Cavell (following Thoreau) sees it, is something that we mostly only strive for.[143]

Cavell takes his cues regarding our experience of literature from *Walden*, which is often taken to be a book about nature but which Cavell convincingly argues is about reading and writing and especially about the reading and writing of itself. In the chapter entitled "Reading," Thoreau writes: "Books must be read as deliberatively and reservedly as they were written." Cavell replies in *The Senses of Walden:*

> My subject is nothing apart from sensing the specific weight of these words as they sink; and that means knowing the specific identities of the writer through his metamorphoses, and defining the audiences in me which those identities address, and so create; and hence understanding who I am that I should be called upon in these ways, and who this writer is that he takes his presumption of intimacy and station upon himself. For someone who cannot yield to Thoreau's words, or does not find them to warrant this power to divide him through, my subject will seem empty, even grotesque.[144]

Cavell seeks an experience of *Walden*, a "sensing" of the "weight of . . . words" that requires analysis of both Thoreau and himself. He reads Thoreau as offering an "epistemology of conscience," an analysis of the calling of a text, something "upon which empiricist philosophy has come to grief."[145] Cavell's position is thus far from structuralist analyses, which attempt to rely only on the "text." Cavell makes explicit his interest in what used to be dismissed as the author's intentions when, in summarizing his ideas about meaning, he writes that writing "must assume responsibility . . . for three of the features it lives upon: (1) that every mark of a language means something in the language . . . (2) that words and their orderings are meant by human beings, that they contain (or conceal) their beliefs, express (or deny) their convictions; and (3) that the saying of something when and as it is said is as significant as the meaning and ordering of the words said."[146]

There is a voluntaristic structure to the experience of a text like *Walden*, as Cavell records and theorizes about it. We must "yield to Thoreau's words" if we are truly to hear them. "Yielding" occupies the place in Cavell's depiction of the structure of reading that "watching" does in Wordsworth's "heart that watches and receives" and that "belief" or "trust" does in James's discussions of the "will to believe." "Yielding" in Cavell names a human act that is necessary for the appearance of something that is nevertheless already there to be observed. The "observation" appropriate to "reading in a high sense" is to a great degree self-observation: Reading what Thoreau calls "classics" cannot be separated from reading or understanding one's self. About *Walden*, Thoreau's attempt at an American "classic," Cavell states: "The quest of this book is for the recovery of the self, as from an illness."[147] (Thoreau characterizes this illness as our "lives of quiet desperation.")[148]

The "deep" reading to which Cavell aspires he finds in Thoreau's images of departure and orientation:

> A deep reading is not one in which you sink away from the surface of the words. Words already engulf us. It is one in which you depart from a given word as from a point of origin; you go deep, as into woods. Understanding is a matter of orientation, of bearings, of the ability to keep to a course and to move in natural paths from any point to any other. The depths of the book are nothing apart from its surfaces. Figurations of language can be thought of as ways of reflecting the surfaces and depths of a word onto one another.[149]

The point of Cavell's explorations, like Thoreau's, is to achieve writing that permits such reading. This is why Cavell so often returns, even in his own texts, to his earlier language, letting it discover new contexts years after its initial formulation. The process of weighing words never ends. Cavell's experience of the philosophy of Thoreau is akin to Wittgenstein's experience of poetry: "A poet's words can pierce us," Wittgenstein wrote, and this is connected with the way "we let our thoughts roam up and down in the familiar surroundings of the words."[150]

The Cognitive Role of Feeling

Cavell maintains in *The Senses of Walden* that our feelings or attitudes either help or hinder our gaining access to the world. Indeed, his
claim is that those feelings help constitute the world that we know. He
extracts an argument for these claims from *Walden:* "Our imagination
or our capacity for images, and for the meaning or phenomenology of
our images – of dawn and day and night, of lower and higher, of straight
and curved, hot and cold, freezing and melting and moulting, of birds
and squirrels and snakes and frogs, of houses and bodies of water and
words, of growth and decay, of mother and father – are as *a priori* as our
other forms of knowledge of the world." Cavell appends in support of
this remark a long quotation from the "Spring" chapter of *Walden,* including Thoreau's description of "the arching and sheaflike top" of the
last summer's woolgrass and concluding with his comment that "many
of the phenomena of Winter are suggestive of an inexpressible tenderness
and fragile delicacy. We are accustomed to hear this king described as a
rude and boisterous tyrant; but with the gentleness of a lover he adorns
the tresses of Summer." Cavell's claim is that here Thoreau is providing
nothing other than a Kantian account of this delicacy and gentleness,
establishing the claim that "human forms of feeling, objects of human
attraction, our reactions constituted in art, are as universal and necessary,
as objective, as revelatory of the world, as the forms of the laws of physics."[151] This claim is both epistemological and ontological: The world is
revealed to us through "human forms of feeling," and in addition, such
forms, like those of space and time, are structures of or in the world.

If our feelings, including our moral feelings like Kant's "respect,"
Wordsworth's "love and holy passion," or Coleridge's "will" and
"joy," help constitute the world, then the world becomes something
valuable in itself, or "ideal." The unknowable noumenal overflow re-
cedes or disappears, becoming part of phenomenal reality, the only reality there is. If "human forms of feeling" reveal the phenomenal world,
then at least part of the noumenal has been recovered, and part of the
supernatural has been naturalized. Human forms of feeling become one
key to the "recovery of, or from, the thing-in-itself" that Cavell takes
to be the Romantic project.

In his movement toward some such revision of Kant, Cavell suggests
in a footnote in *The Senses of Walden* that Kant ought to have provided
a transcendental deduction of the thing in itself. Such a deduction would
presumably show the concept of the noumenal to be legitimate, indeed
necessary for our ordinary "phenomenal" experience. Although Cavell
claims that Thoreau provides such a deduction, he does not amplify or
defend this claim in *The Senses of Walden:* "This is the place, but not the
time, to try to make clearer what I mean by saying that *Walden* provides

a transcendental deduction of the category of the thing-in-itself."[152] Fourteen years later, however, Cavell finds "In Quest of the Ordinary" the occasion for another step along this path. A transcendental deduction of the thing in itself, Cavell maintained in *The Senses of Walden,* would expose "the externality of all objects to us." Now he connects this idea with Heidegger's task of recovering "the thing" and with the Romantic quest for a renewed intimacy with the world. Heidegger wrote that "near to us are what we usually call things. But what is a thing? . . . What is the thing in itself? We shall not reach the thing in itself until our thinking has first reached the thing as a thing." The recovery of the thing in itself is thus equated with the recovery of the "thing as a thing." This in turn is figured as "nearness." But it is a nearness that requires not reaching out but "stepping back," perhaps, Cavell suggests, as Thoreau did at Walden. There, Thoreau found that "next to us the grandest laws are continuously being executed," that "the most innocent and encouraging society may be found in any natural object," and that he could become "suddenly neighbor to the birds."[153] "Neighboring" becomes Cavell's word for Thoreau's way – at once literary, philosophical, and existential – of reaching a new intimacy with the world, of recovering things as things. Romanticism, whether in Wordsworth and Coleridge, Emerson and Thoreau, Heidegger and Wittgenstein, or Cavell himself, seeks to reveal and inculcate "an intimacy with the world."[154]

In the following chapters I shall explore the perspective suggested by Cavell's own general intuition that his work belongs to a line extending back at least to Emerson and Thoreau and that the very meaning of "American" (when the word is used to modify "philosophy") has to do in an essential way with its Romanticism. This brings us to a tradition running through the work of Emerson, James, and Dewey to Cavell himself that is as much "transcendentalist" as "pragmatic," as much "religious" as "scientific," one representing a fundamentally Romantic response to the epistemological problem of the mind–world relation. The divorce between scientific facts and religious facts, wrote William James, "may not necessarily be as eternal as it at first sight seems, nor the personalism and romanticism of the world, as they appear to primitive thinking, be matters so irrevocably outgrown."[155] The perspective in Cavell's work, I shall argue, points to nothing less than the recovery of a philosophical tradition that has so far remained unapparent even to students of American philosophy.

2

RALPH WALDO EMERSON

Emerson's writing will, from the outside, seem vague and inflated, but from inside will acquire a terrible exactness.

Stanley Cavell, "An Emerson Mood"

Emerson is a direct link between American philosophy and European Romanticism. Soon after leaving his ministry in the Unitarian church (in part because he no longer believed in the "divine authority and supernatural efficacy"[1] of the communion he administered), Emerson traveled to Europe where he met his heroes Wordsworth, Coleridge, and Carlyle. There is little doubt of their influence on his thought or of Emerson's founding role in American Romanticism. As Harold Bloom observed, "Emerson is to American Romanticism what Wordsworth is to the British or parent version."[2]

What is less clearly established is Emerson's importance as a philosopher. His thought plays a minor role in many histories and surveys of American philosophy,[3] perhaps because it has no obvious connection with the major American movement of pragmatism. Yet one pragmatist, John Dewey, thought that Emerson was "the one citizen of the New World fit to have his name uttered in the same breath with that of Plato,"[4] and another, William James, thought enough of Emerson to deliver an address to the Emerson centenary celebrations (after rereading his entire corpus), in which he called him a "real seer . . . [who] could perceive the full squalor of the individual fact, but . . . also . . . the transfiguration."[5] In recent years, Stanley Cavell, Barbara Packer, David Van Leer, and Cornel West have worked at establishing Emerson's philosophical credentials.[6]

In this chapter I shall focus on Emerson's philosophical views, particularly on his epistemology and metaphysics.[7] In Emerson's writings, the

34

ideas and projects of the European Romantics – "the feeling intellect,"
the "marriage of self and world," the human mind as a shaper of experience, the criticism and expansion of empiricism, and the naturalization
and humanization of the divine – developed in a philosophically distinctive way on American soil.

Emerson, then, is America's first Romantic philosopher. His relation
to those who follow him is both significant and complex. He actually
met the young William James in the James family home in New York,
where he was a frequent visitor of William's father, Henry James, Sr.
There is, as Richard Poirier has shown us, a deep Emersonian layer in
James's thought. But it was John Dewey and, later, Stanley Cavell who
better enunciated Emerson's philosophical importance.[8] Dewey saw
Emerson as a philosopher of experience, an "idealist" who traced the
existence of ideals not to a transcendental realm but to their sources in
human life. Cavell treats him as an "epistemologist of moods" who
teaches the Romantic doctrine that our feelings are as objective and revelatory of the world as are our thoughts or sensations. All the American
philosophers whom I shall examine criticize and attempt to move beyond what Emerson calls "paltry empiricism."[9]

I. FREEDOM

Emerson's views on the metaphysical topic of freedom serve as
a convenient introduction to his philosophy. In general, Emerson is not
so much interested in analyzing the concept of freedom (though some of
his remarks are relevant to such analyses) as he is in exploring ways in
which human beings are or can be free and, correspondingly, ways in
which we – by either our own wills or the forces of fate – are less free
than we might be. I shall look to Emerson's earlier essays and addresses
for his outlook on freedom and to some of his later ones to show the
severe constraints on freedom that he discerns. This is not to say that he
ignores such constraints in his earlier essays nor that he abandons belief
in or hope for freedom later on. Indeed, most of Emerson's ideas that
concern us in this chapter are expressed throughout his career. Emerson's
vision does darken, however, especially after the death of his son
Waldo,[10] and this fact is reflected in the comparative ease with which one
can find discussions of freedom in the earlier works and discussions of
limitations on freedom in the later ones.

In his first writings, *Nature* (1836) and "The American Scholar"
(1837),[11] Emerson is concerned with our freedom from the traditions and
institutions of the past. It is not that he sees no value in them – books
are of great value if well used – but that valuable as they are, they can
prevent our enjoying what he calls in *Nature* "an original relation to the
universe." Why, he begins that work by asking, should we not enjoy

such a relation? "Why should not we have a poetry and philosophy of insight and not of tradition, and a religion by revelation to us, and not the history of theirs?"[12]

"The American Scholar" amplifies this message. Emerson criticizes traditional scholarship precisely because of its slavishness. He warns against "the restorers of readings, the emendators, the bibliomaniacs of all degrees."[13] These idolizers of books may know all that they contain, page by page, but they lack what Emerson calls "their own sight of principles," the source of all good thinking and writing. (There is an obvious connection here with Wordsworth's injunction to "close up those barren leaves" and "Come forth . . . with . . . a heart / That watches and receives." However, Emerson stresses the active, as opposed to the receptive, powers of humanity more than does Wordsworth.)[14] Emerson criticizes his contemporary "meek young men" who "grow up in libraries" and who feel duty bound to find out and follow the dictates of the works they worship. Such duty is that of the slave: The "guide" has become a "tyrant."[15]

Emerson accordingly puts forward a different conception of the scholar, one that depicts him or her as self-reliant, not dependent, exploratory, not tied to already-discovered truth. The true purpose of books, he tells us, is "to inspire," not to promote imitation or idolization. Their power may be misused: "I had better never see a book than to be warped by its attraction clean out of my own orbit." Emerson is confident that within each man or woman lies a "genius," a unique capacity. As he later stated in "Self-Reliance": "The power which resides in him is new in nature, and none but he knows what that is which he can do, nor does he know until he has tried."[16] True scholarship sets this genius free: discovering, developing, and relying on it.

Emerson's idea of self-reliance, so prominent in his early addresses and essays, is explicitly connected with freedom in "The American Scholar": "In self-trust, all the virtues are comprehended. Free should the scholar be, – free and brave. Free even to the definition of freedom, 'without any hindrance that does not arise out of his own constitution.' Brave; for fear is a thing which a scholar by his very function puts behind him."[17] This passage shows Emerson thinking of freedom as a virtue, like courage. He is not, then, treating freedom or its lack as a metaphysical condition affecting all people equally but as something of which people can have more or less. By enjoining his readers to become self-reliant, Emerson evinces his belief that we can control, to some extent at least, our freedom, that – to use "free" in the more usual philosophical sense – we are free to become more free by becoming more self-reliant.

Although Emerson's aim is toward freedom – forward rather than backward as he says[18] – "The American Scholar" both implicitly and explicitly records our failures to act freely. "We are the cowed," he writes, "the trustless."[19] Using images that remind one of his admirer Nietzsche, he characterizes human existence as like that of bugs or spawn or, as in the following case, as that of a herd: "Men in history, men in the world of to-day . . . are called 'the mass' and 'the herd.' "[20] Yet "The American Scholar" is suffused with confidence that a new day is at hand and that humankind, and particularly Americans, are ready to slough off the past. Emerson writes in the first paragraph that "our day of dependence, our long apprenticeship to the learning of other lands, draws to a close," and in the last paragraph he predicts that "we will walk on our own feet; we will work with our own hands; we will speak our own minds."[21]

If "The American Scholar" urges the abandonment of slavish scholarship for the self-reliant and creative life of "Man Thinking," Emerson's "Divinity School Address" urges the abandonment of slavish religion for the free apprehension of a divinity that "is, not was."[22] As scholars idolize books, so do Christians idolize Christ: "The language that describes Christ to Europe and America is not the style of friendship and enthusiasm to a good and noble heart, but is appropriated and formal, – paints a demigod, as the Orientals or the Greeks would describe Osiris or Apollo."[23] Emerson's shocking moral is that we should try not to imitate Christ but to achieve our own original spiritual relationship to the universe.[24] Each of the Harvard Divinity College graduates to whom he is speaking is "a newborn bard of the Holy Ghost," who must "cast behind you all conformity, and acquaint men at first hand with Deity." The imitator is hopelessly mediocre; he "bereaves himself of his own beauty, to come short of another man's."[25] Once again, one is to be free from all external reliance, even on so good a model as Jesus or Moses. Our religion is characterized by a "soul-destroying slavery to habit." Still, Emerson maintains, "it is not to be doubted, that all men have sublime thoughts; that all men do value the few real hours of life."[26] (Emerson's assertion that all men have sublime thoughts is an indication of the democratic impulse that Dewey so admired in him.[27] Although it might seem to conflict with his portrayal of our domination by herdlike instincts, one should remember that the hours of sublime thought are "few.")

It is these "few real hours" that Emerson constantly seeks. In "Circles," published as one of his first series of essays in 1841, he identifies these hours with those times in our lives when we cast off the old, whether in the form of a model (like Christ or Locke or, a philosopher might add today, Wittgenstein or Husserl or Derrida) or a habit. "Our life is an apprenticeship to the truth, that around every circle another can be drawn."[28] Each new circle represents freedom from the constriction of the old one, but each will harden into a new constriction: "It is the inert effort of each thought, having formed itself into a circular wave of circumstance, – as, for instance, an empire, rules of an art, a local usage, a religious rite, – to heap itself on that ridge, and to solidify, and hem in the life." Our real hours are our original ones, when "the heart refuses to be imprisoned"[29] and we burst through to a new circle, thereby abandoning the old.

In "Circles" this idea of abandoning our old forms begins to assume the status of a metaphysical principle, as when Emerson writes: "The way of life is wonderful: it is by abandonment."[30] Abandonment of the old imprisoning circle is, Emerson asserts, both the way in which "life" actually proceeds (though not the way in which human life is conducted) and an ideal of human conduct, as if we become real (enjoy our few real hours) only in such transitions. Although Emerson's links to the Platonic (including the Neoplatonic) tradition are important, he is not, like Plato, a follower of Pythagoras, who maintained that the real is the unchanging. Emerson is a Heraclitean rather than a Pythagorean on this issue, maintaining that the real is the changing: "In nature, every moment is new; the past is always swallowed and forgotten; the coming only is sacred. Nothing is secure but life, transition, the energizing spirit. . . . No truth so sublime but it may be trivial tomorrow in the light of new thoughts. People wish to be settled: only as far as they are unsettled, is there any hope for them."[31]

Emerson applies his notion of radical human freedom to the moral domain in "Circles," again foreshadowing Nietzsche.[32] "The great man will not be prudent in the popular sense; all his prudence will be so much deduction from his grandeur."[33] In the idea of deducing his virtues from the grandeur of his character, Emerson expresses the thought that the great man is responsible only to himself, that he is, as Nietzsche would say, a creator of values. A consequence of this view is that the great man is not limited even to commonly and deeply accepted virtues (of which prudence is a minor example). For Emerson all virtues are, as he puts it, "initial." "The terror of reform," he continues, "is the discovery that we must cast away our virtues, or what we have always esteemed such, into the same pit that has consumed our grosser vices." Not only may we abandon good; we also may abandon, or transcend, evil: "It is the highest power of divine moments that they abolish our contritions also."[34]

That Emerson's notion of freedom is akin to those of philosophers like Nietzsche, Kierkegaard, and Heidegger is suggested also by Cavell's analysis of a key passage in "Self-Reliance" in his complex and provocative paper "Being Odd, Getting Even: Threats to Individuality."[35] The passage in question is this one: "Man is timid and apologetic; he is no longer upright; he dares not say 'I think,' 'I am,' but quotes some saint or sage."[36] Once he points it out, one must be struck, as Cavell is, by the seeming allusion to Descartes's classical argument in the Second Meditation in which he proves his own existence. Cavell reminds us of the importance in the Cartesian argument of actually saying or thinking "I am, I exist" and examines the ways in which, for Emerson, saying becomes a metaphor for existing, and quoting a metaphor for herdlike, conforming, "ghostly" nonexistence. Just as saying or thinking in Descartes's account is necessary for certain knowledge of my own existence, so for Emerson, saying becomes a metaphor for the enactment of my existence. Here "existence" is used in the existentialists' sense of a way of human life that one does not have merely by virtue of being a live human being but that one must acquire (Kierkegaard's word for this is "choosing").[37] We are beings, Cavell interprets Emerson as meaning, for whom their existence is an issue and who must claim or enact it for it to occur.[38] Quotation, the opposite of saying, is the equivalent of the "warping out of one's orbit" that Emerson warns against in "The American Scholar" and "Divinity School Address." In "Self-Reliance" Emerson is saying that our quotation, our slavery to others (even to our own past sayings and doings), robs us of our existence. The only real existence is a free one (i.e., "without any hindrance that does not arise out of his own constitution"). "Imitation," as he stated, "is suicide."[39]

If Emerson hopes for a constantly renewed "original relation to the universe," he is not unaware of the barriers to, and the general unlikelihood of, such relations taking place. In "Experience," published in his second series of essays in 1844, he records his disenchantment with even those people who seem least conforming and hidebound:

> There is an optical illusion about every person we meet. In truth, they are all creatures of given temperament, which will appear in a given character, whose boundaries they will never pass: but we look at them, they seem alive, and we presume there is impulse in them. In the moment, it seems impulse; in the year, in the lifetime, it turns out to be a certain uniform tune which the revolving barrel of the music-box must play.[40]

Life moves by expanding circles, he had written, but here in "Experience" he pictures people who only "seem alive" (i.e., in Kierkegaardian terms, who seem to exist) and whose "boundaries" will never expand. "Temperament shuts us in a prison of glass,"[41] a prison we cannot even see.

Emerson notes restrictions on our freedom in all his writing, maintaining even in the ebullient "Self-Reliance," for example, that through our conformity to society we are "as it were, clapped into jail by [our] consciousness."[42] In his later essays, however – as in the preceding quotation – he comes to emphasize the extent to which these restrictions are not under our control. Nowhere is this recognition more apparent than in his late essay "Fate," published in 1860 in *The Conduct of Life*. There, fate becomes a name for "whatever limits us,"[43] and Emerson provides a veritable catalogue of forces that limit our ability to find or express ourselves: earthquakes, climatic changes, disease, sex, "organization tyrannizing over character."[44] Emerson seems to be talking about his earlier thought when he explains: "Once we thought positive power was all. Now we learn that negative power, or circumstance, is half. Nature is the tyrannous circumstance, the thick skull, the sheathed snake, the ponderous, rock-like jaw."[45] Even when he stresses our human influence over events, Emerson's moral seems to be that this too is fated and that such influence comes unconsciously, unintelligently, like bodily secretions:

> Each creature puts forth from itself its own condition and sphere, as the slug sweats out its slimy house on the pear leaf, and the woolly aphides on the apple perspire their own bed, and the fish its shell. In youth we clothe ourselves with rainbows and go as brave as the zodiac. In age we put out another sort of perspiration, – gout, fever, rheumatism, caprice, doubt, fretting and avarice. . . . A man will see his character emitted in the events that seem to meet, but which exude from and accompany him.[46]

At the end of "Fate," Emerson offers a "solution to the older knots of fate, freedom, and foreknowledge." But it is difficult to make sense of this. It lies, he tells us, in "the propounding . . . of the double consciousness." His idea seems to be not that the universe is essentially dual – for he speaks of it as a "Blessed Unity"[47] – but that our consciousness of it is. We vary, he explains, in the way we handle the dictates of fate.[48] A person may be "the victim of his fate," but he ought then (and this would presumably be the alternative or double consciousness of which Emerson speaks) "to rally on his relation to the Universe, which his ruin benefits. Leaving the daemon who suffers, he is to take sides with the Deity who secures universal benefit by his pain."[49] Note that "his ruin" remains, and so Emerson is not talking about escape to another (e.g., a transcendental or noumenal) "world." We are stuck with this one, but we can, he seems to hold, accommodate ourselves to it.

So far, this sounds like typical Stoic doctrine. Emerson departs from this position, however, by saying that we can, after all, "offset the drag of temperament," that we are compensated for "taking sides with the Deity" by an access of "sudden power. When a god wishes to ride, any chip or pebble will bud and shoot out winged feet and serve him for a horse."[50] Fate becomes something that we can control. Whether this position makes sense is questionable; a fuller examination of it must await our examination of Emerson's idealism. It is in any case characteristic of

Emerson both to set out the limitations on our power and to testify to their being overcome. Perhaps the fairest summary of Emerson's position is that offered earlier in "Fate" and just quoted: "Circumstance is half," but "positive power" is the other half. And although his talk of "impulse" might make it seem as if Emerson posits a contracausal notion of freedom, it seems just as easy to make him out to be a Humean on this question (if on few others), his list of the forces arrayed against us just a catalogue of those "chains"[51] that we must and can avoid if we wish to be free.

II. IDEALISM

Emerson's idealism is a blend of many elements: Neoplatonic, Hindu, Kantian, Coleridgean, and others. These philosophies share a sense of the immense power of the human mind in determining both reality and our knowledge of it. In this respect, Emerson is an inheritor of Kant, who stressed this power of the mind. Like Kant and his followers (including Coleridge), but unlike Berkeley, Emerson is not a simple idealist. He does not hold that reality is only mental, and he gives substantial play (as in the idea of fate) to the idea that there are objective forces beyond our influence. Emerson's idealism does not come neatly packaged, however, so that our task is to distinguish some of its main parts.

Illusion Versus Reality

We begin with the Platonic/Neoplatonic/Hindu strain, which we met when discussing "Fate." In that essay, Emerson sets out the forces of fate arrayed against us but maintains that by an access of sudden power it can be transcended. In such places in his writing, Emerson comes close to the Platonic view that the world we inhabit is (like the shadows on the wall of Plato's cave) an illusion and that we can transcend that illusion, breaking out to reality. In "Experience," for example, after discussing the limitations brought about by temperament, Emerson writes:

> On its own level . . . temperament is final. . . . But it is impossible that the creative power should exclude itself. Into every intelligence there is a door which is never closed, through which the creator passes. The intellect, seeker of absolute truth, or the heart, lover of absolute good, intervenes for our succor, and at one whisper of these high powers we awake from ineffectual struggles with this nightmare. We hurl it into its own hell, and cannot again contract ourselves to so base a state.[52]

Emerson suggests that the world we see (or the way we see the world) is dreamlike or, worse, nightmarish. It is in any case base and ghostly, not solid or elevated. We may hope to wake up to "reality."

Emerson tends to identify the reality with which we come in touch in the elevated moments he describes as "ours," the "soul's," or that of some cosmic "self." This makes his position similar to the Hindu view that behind all phenomena lies an "atman," or world-soul. The poem with which "Experience" begins, for example, lists the forms of experience Emerson calls the "lords of life" (which include "Temperament," "Dream," "Succession," and "Surprise"), but though these lords appear to tower over the "little man, least of all," they are in fact just his creations or emanations:

> "To-morrow they will wear another face,
> The founder thou! these are thy race!"

More Neoplatonic in tone is Emerson's remark, again in "Experience," that "the consciousness in each man is a sliding scale, which identifies him now with the First Cause, and now with the flesh of his body; life above life, in infinite degrees."[53] Again, "man" can be identified with divinity, with the "First Cause" that created the world.

Although Emerson shares the idea of the soul's waking up to a higher order of things with Hindus and Platonists, there are important differences. The Platonic Ideas are timeless, unchanging, and the soul that ascends to them becomes more steady and settled (as in the *Phaedo*).[54] Emerson offers, however, a Heraclitean rather than a Pythagorean outlook, what he calls a philosophy of "fluxions."[55] "God offers to every mind its choice between truth and repose," he writes in "Intellect." "Take which you please, – you can never have both."[56]

Again, Emerson does not think that one can make a direct assault on truth – as the geometer does in piling up one reliable truth on another, or the yogi by years of meditation. For Emerson reality comes in flashes and gleams, and it is these "few real hours" of our lives for which he searches. These gleaming moments may not be only in the past, as in Wordsworth's poetry, but they are equally rare: "Reason, the prized reality, the Law, is apprehended now and then for a serene and profound moment amidst the hubbub of cares and works which have no direct bearing on it; – is then lost, for months or years, and again found, for an interval, to be lost again. If we compute it in time, we may, in fifty years, have half a dozen reasonable hours."[57]

Finally, we should note that the dualism (of dream and reality) that Emerson seems to embrace is countered by an equally strong sense that this world, the world we experience, contains all the divinity we shall ever need or find. "Life wears to me a visionary face," he reports in "Experience."[58] And earlier, in a passage from "The American Scholar" that Cavell rightly connects with the Wordsworthian (and Wittgensteinian) interest in the "ordinary" or "common," Emerson writes:

> I embrace the common, I explore and sit at the feet of the familiar, the low. Give me insight into today, and you may have the antique and future worlds. . . . The meal in the firkin; the milk in the pan; the ballad

in the street; the news of the boat; the glance of the eye; the form and
the gait of the body; – show me the ultimate reason of these matters;
show me the sublime presence of the highest spiritual cause lurking, as
always it does lurk, in these suburbs and extremities of nature . . . and
the world lies no longer a dull miscellany and lumber-room, but has
form and order.[59]

Although Emerson calls for us to awake from our nightmare, it is not
to a separate, transcendent world that he calls us, but to a vision of "the
sublime presence" at work in the "familiar" phenomena of our lives.

Subjective Idealism

Emerson flirts with the subjective idealism of Berkeley, particularly in *Nature*. According to Berkeley, the world just is our ideas of it,
so that reality is made up entirely of ideas and the selves who experience
them. Emerson clearly has Berkeley in mind when he treats idealism as
the view that "matter is a phenomenon, not a substance." But he criticizes this view: It "leaves me in the splendid labyrinth of my perceptions,
to wander without end. Then the heart resists it, because it baulks the
affections in denying substantive being to men and women. . . . This
theory makes nature foreign to me, and does not account for that consan-
guinity which we acknowledge to it."[60] Berkeley's theory "makes nature
foreign" because it makes it just a set of ideas, whereas I am not a set of
ideas. Emerson insists that on the contrary, nature, including the "men
and women," are consanguineous – of the same blood – with me. The
subjective idealist errs in saying that they are ideas and I am substantial.
For Emerson, we all are equally substantial.

Emerson counters in another way the solipsistic implications of his
flirtation with Berkelian idealism in *Nature,* by speaking of a relationship
between mind and world that, like those depicted in Wordsworth's and
Coleridge's poetry, resembles a marriage. "I am the lover of uncontained
and immortal beauty," he writes at the end of *Nature's* first chapter:

> In the wilderness, I find something more dear and connate than in
> streets or villages. In the tranquil landscape, and especially in the distant
> line of the horizon, man beholds somewhat as beautiful as his own na-
> ture.
> The greatest delight which the fields and woods minister is the sug-
> gestion of an occult relation between man and the vegetable. I am not
> alone and unacknowledged. They nod to me, and I to them. . . . Yet
> it is certain that the power to produce this delight does not reside in
> nature, but in man, or in a harmony of both.[61]

This passage emphasizes our relations with nature, though its vision
is a shifting one. The first paragraph praises the wilderness and opposes
it to the "I" by portraying it as "distant" and by contrasting it with one's
"own nature." But the ultimate praise offered the wilderness is that it is

as beautiful as man's own nature, which suggests a link between it and ourselves. And the first clause of the last sentence veers toward subjectivism in asserting that "this delight" – presumably the beauty of nature – resides "in man." Yet on the other hand, the pronouncement, or phenomenological report, that "I am not alone and unacknowledged" is surely not the language of the solipsist. Further complicating Emerson's view is the alternation contained in the last sentence: The power resides in man and not in nature, its first half tells us, but the second adds, "or in a harmony of both."

Although Emerson is talking about beauty here, and not about the world *in toto,* his suggestions and withdrawals or qualifications of idealism are entirely typical.[62] This same section of *Nature,* in which he asserts the alternatives of the self's dominance over, or harmony with, nature also includes the famous (and in some quarters, infamous)[63] "transparent eyeball" passage, which postulates the disappearance of the self: "Standing on the bare ground – my head bathed by the blithe air, and uplifted into infinite space, – all mean egotism vanishes. I become a transparent eyeball; I am nothing; I see all; the currents of the Universal Being circulate through me; I am part or parcel of God." (Note, however, that it is only "mean" egotism that vanishes.)

Although in *Nature* Emerson rejects idealism, at least of a solipsistic sort, he does admit that it is "a useful introductory hypothesis." In later writings he continues to suggest, if not to assert, the insubstantiality of the "men and women" who surround us: "Let us treat the men and women well," he writes in "Experience," "treat them as if they were real: perhaps they are."[64]

Transcendental Idealism

Emerson wants both to assert the vast powers of the human mind in forming our experience and to acknowledge the objectivity or substantiality of the world that this mind encounters. These two ideas come together in a form of idealism that was available to Emerson through his knowledge of Coleridge, the transcendental idealism developed by Kant.

Stanley Cavell has attempted, beginning with his 1978 paper "Thinking of Emerson" and in later papers, to assess Emerson's place in a Romantic Kantian tradition.[65] (Van Leer's *Emerson's Epistemology* also argues, though in a rather different way than Cavell does, for Emerson's basic Kantianism.)[66] In "Thinking of Emerson" Cavell contends that Emerson revises Kant's scheme of categories beyond Kant's twelve pure concepts of the Understanding, by countenancing more ways of knowing or making the world than did Kant. (This would presumably be part of Emerson's active opposition to what he refers to as "paltry" empiricisms.)[67] Just as Kant is trying to justify our claims to necessary knowledge of geometry, arithmetic, and Newtonian physics, so Emerson is trying to justify claims to other necessary knowledge, for example, that centering on our moods. "Experience," Cavell maintains, "is about the epistemology, or say the logic, of moods."[68]

For moods to deserve a transcendental deduction or exploration, they would have to constitute a form of knowledge, just as geometry, arithmetic, or physics is knowledge. That they do is a point Cavell wants to confirm: "The idea is roughly that moods must be taken as having at least as sound a role in advising us of reality as sense-experience has."[69]

But should we take moods as revelatory? There is no established science of moods as there is a science of physics or geometry. Here it must be said that Emerson is as much interested in discovering as in justifying the truths about moods he treats; his essay contains penetrating observations about the operation of moods in our knowledge of the world. In this respect, he does more than Kant does in the *Critique of Pure Reason*. There Kant relies on Euclid and Newton to provide his sciences of geometry and physics (though in the moral and political realms, Kant has a greater claim to be a discoverer of truth, for example, the Categorical Imperative). Many of the most important laws on which Emerson relies are those he has observed himself (which is not to say that he does not look to science or literature for such laws). Emerson is at once an empiricist (insofar as he relies on observations), a transcendental idealist (insofar as he attempts to justify their validity by invoking some structure in us), and an experimenter (insofar as he discovers truths).

What truths, then, does Emerson investigate? In "Experience," he observes that it "depends on the mood of the man whether he shall see the sunset or the fine poem"[70] and adds that the universe "inevitably . . . wear[s] our color. . . . As I am, so I see."[71] (The word "inevitably" marks the truth as necessary, thus signaling the need for a transcendental explanation.) Emerson indicates an area of experience about which Wittgenstein wrote in the *Tractatus* when he said that "the world of the happy man is a different one from that of the unhappy man."[72] Wittgenstein's way of phrasing it coheres with Emerson's in stressing the global (and hence for a Kantian categorial or formal) extent of such "moody" structures: The whole world is "colored." In his treatment, Cavell maintains that "sense-experience is to objects what moods are to the world."[73] This means, first, that moods reveal the world (as our senses reveal objects) but, second, that "the world" is to be distinguished from "objects." "The world" is to be understood as indicated by our whole sense of things, what William James calls those "dumb responses" or "*consents*," which seemed to him, as they did to Emerson, to be "our deepest organs of communication with the nature of things."[74] "Mood" in this context is much like "will," as discussed in Chapter 1: It is both subjective and revelatory. Coleridge wrote that "all true reality has both its ground and its evidence in the *will*," thereby regarding the will as having both the metaphysical ("ground") and epistemological force ("evidence") that Emerson and Cavell ascribe to mood. Kant sets the stage for these claims with his view that other (if less obviously) subjective structures – such as space, time, and causality – both determine and furnish us with knowledge of the world.

Another candidate for a synthetic a priori truth about moods is Emerson's remark in "Circles," that "our moods do not believe in each other."[75] It is not just that our moods vary but that they affect what Emerson calls the whole "tissue of facts and beliefs"[76] we encounter, so that (as in the difference between Wittgenstein's happy and unhappy world) they bring about a radical discontinuity of outlook and being. Our problems look different in the middle of a sleepless night than they do in the bright morning. "Our life is March weather," Emerson notes in "Montaigne," "savage and serene in one hour. We go forth . . . believing in the iron links of Destiny . . . but a book . . . or only the sound of a name, shoots a spark through the nerves, and we suddenly believe in will. . . . All is possible to the resolved mind. Presently, a new experience gives a new turn to our thoughts; common sense resumes its tyranny."[77]

To the extent that Emerson is a Kantian, he would want to stress not only our (subjective) role in experience but also the objectivity of the knowledge with which experience furnishes us. Cavell admits that many of Emerson's remarks (e.g., that the universe "wears our color") sound subjective but responds that "whether you take this to be subjective or objective depends upon whether you take the successive colors or moods of the universe to be subjective or objective." Emerson, Cavell argues, "is out to destroy the ground on which such a problem takes itself seriously, I mean interprets itself as a metaphysical fixture. The universe is as separate from me, but as intimately part of me, as one on whose behalf I contest, and who therefore wears my color. We are in a state of 'romance' with the universe (to use a word from the last sentence of ["Experience"])."[78] This "intimate separation" between ourselves and the universe is what Wordsworth and Coleridge call a "marriage" of self and world. Some such vision is characteristic of each of the American Romantic philosophers.

Another way in which Emerson incorporates objectivity into his epistemology of mood is to stress the receptive, rather than the active, element in knowing. The treatment of our organizing powers as receptive rather than active is, according to Cavell, Emerson's "most explicit reversal of Kant," for in Kant one knows by synthesizing – gathering together and shaping. But at the end of "Experience" Emerson concludes: "All I know is reception; I am and I have: but I do not get, and when I have fancied I had gotten anything, I found I did not. I worship with wonder the great Fortune."[79] Emerson here describes a mode of apprehending the world that is receptive, not active (not "getting"), but also subjectively influenced, "moody" in its "worship" and "wonder." Cavell links this receptive mode of apprehension with the thought of Heidegger, who stresses "listening" and who connects truth with an attitude he calls "thinking," but equally "thanking."

The Lords of Life

If one follows up Cavell's suggestion that one can "hear Kant working throughout Emerson's essay 'Experience,' "[80] then one must be struck by the "lords of life" that are the essay's ostensible subject. Emerson lists them in the essay's last section – "Illusion, Temperament, Succession, Surface, Surprise, Reality, Subjectiveness" – and speaks of them as "threads on the loom of time." The metaphor suggests that they are woven into time, just as Kant's categories weave objects by synthesizing, weaving together, the temporalized material furnished through our faculty of sensibility. Each lord, then, would be a way of weaving temporalized material, a Kantian category.[81]

There is much that is attractive about this view, though there are important problems with it as well. One problem is that some of the lords seem more plausible as categories than do others. For example, because Temperament is subjective yet also yields us knowledge (of a person, of the world as seen through or responding to a person), it is a plausible candidate for a category. But Illusion seems distinctly implausible, for it seems on its face not to give us knowledge, something a category must do. Again, Reality seems hard to construe as a category both because it is not an epistemological notion but a metaphysical one and because it seems, especially as Emerson uses it, too objective, not subjective enough to be traced to a faculty of our mind. That is, Emerson seems at times to mean by Reality something nonphenomenal.

Another problem with the list of lords is that moods – for which Cavell provides the compelling argument that they function as Kantian categories and which, because of their shifting nature, are clearly temporalized – are not on Emerson's list of lords, even though they are a dominant subject of "Experience" and other of Emerson's essays. We can handle this problem by noting that Emerson's list is only an approximate one, that moods do concern him, and that the case for moods as categories is as strong as that produced for any named lord. Indeed, the list at the end of "Experience" does not match the list given in the poem that begins the essay. Van Leer sees the list of seven lords at the end as corresponding to the essay's seven sections, and there is some textual evidence for this, but there is also evidence against it. For example, Emerson makes the important general claim that "life is a series of surprises" not in the section Van Leer identifies as being about surprise but in the one that he takes to be about Surface.[82] Again, Emerson remarks that "our friends early appear to us as representative of certain ideas which they never pass or exceed," a remark about character in the section Van Leer regards as about succession,[83] and all sections of the essay treat Reality in some way. Sharon Cameron seems to be on more solid ground in claiming that "these designations seem divorced from, and seem only arbitrarily to apply to, discrete portions of the essay."[84] In any case, it is instructive to treat at least some of the lords of life as Emerson's extensions of Kantian categories and to look not just to "Experience" but to other of Emerson's essays for help in understanding how this is so.

Temperament. In connection with Emerson's views on freedom, we discussed temperament and its associated notion of character. Like the category of causality or the form of space, temperament provides limits to reality, boundaries that a person "will never pass," a "uniform tune which the revolving barrel of the music-box must play." (As with moods, Emerson indicates necessity here by his use of the word "must.")[85] In an inversion that we can now recognize as characteristic, Emerson does allow that "it is impossible that the creative power should exclude itself,"[86] but temperament is clearly a powerful force hemming it in.

Sometimes temperament issues in the kind of potent character Emerson discusses in the essay of that title. A hero or genius like Napoleon or Washington is "destined" to organize events: "He encloses the world, as the patriot does his country, as a material basis for his character, and a theatre for action."[87] The unswerving force of temperament is as effectual in the world as a law of physics: "It is of no use to ape it, or to contend with it. . . . The hero sees that the event is ancillary: it must follow *him*."[88]

Emerson's talent for observation is at work in his many reports of the pervasive force of character in human life. To one person – but to no one else we have ever met – we will reveal secrets that normally make us "wretched either to keep or to betray."[89] To others we cannot speak at all; our bodies "seem to lose their cartilage." Our friends exert a positive force on us just by their characters, refreshing and energizing us just by their presence: "The entrance of a friend adds grace, boldness, and eloquence."

Temperament and the character in which it issues are forces for Emerson, but like gravity, they both shackle and enable us to act. Temperament is responsible for "the power and furniture of man" and makes possible that "profound good understanding"[90] that arises between friends. But it operates implacably even when we wish it would not, so that we become the prey of our personalities or temperaments. "Character teaches above our wills. Men imagine that they communicate their virtue or vice only by overt actions and do not see that virtue or vice emit a breath every moment."[91]

Surface. We "emit" our characters constantly, Emerson holds, in the ways we sit or walk, respond or ignore, talk or laugh: We lie exposed to view. But that exposure does not reveal all there is to know about us. We may be able to tell that "this or that man is fortunate" just by meeting him, but we cannot discover "the reason why."[92] Indeed, just at the point a person is most self-reliant, most himself or herself, Emerson sees a mystery: "A man will not be observed in doing that which he can do best. There is a certain magic about his properest action, which stupefies your powers of observation, so that though it is done before you, you wist not of it."[93] (Think of Wittgenstein "doing philosophy," of Larry Bird playing basketball.)

Emerson finds such hiddenness or obliqueness, which can be assigned to the lord Surface but also in some respects to Dream and Illusion, to be a characteristic of all human experience: "Nature does not like to be observed, and likes that we should be her fools and playmates. We may have the sphere for our cricket-ball, but not a berry for our philosophy. Direct strokes she never gave us power to make; all our blows glance, all our hits are accidents. Our relations to each other are oblique and casual." We can give a cricket ball a good whack, but we cannot touch – except by accident – any of our philosophical berries, cannot grasp or understand life. The context for this remark, as indeed for the entire essay in which it appears, is the death of Emerson's son Waldo.

> It does not touch me: something which I fancied was a part of me, which could not be torn away without tearing me, nor enlarged without enriching me, falls off from me, and leaves no scar. . . . The Indian who was laid under a curse, that the wind should not blow on him, nor water flow to him, nor fire burn him, is a type of us all. The dearest events are summer-rain, and we the Para coats that shed every drop."[94]

Although the inaccessibility of, or our obliqueness to, experience takes on a deeply personal tone in "Experience," Emerson in fact uses Waldo's death to register a more general complaint, about the essential "evanescence and lubricity" of all phenomena. This is the dark side, the darker mood of the inaccessibility praised when it was manifested in the form of the genius, doing what "he can do best." Now, in "Experience," Emerson laments that the tendency for things to "slip through our fingers then when we clutch hardest [is] the most unhandsome part of our condition."[95]

Surface, Illusion, and Dream thus emerge in Emerson's account as phenomenal, or phenomenological terms, describing not something arrived at as a conclusion from an argument (as in Plato or Descartes) but a characteristic of human experience. Descartes argued that dreams do not have a dreamlike quality, for if they did, we could tell them from waking experiences and refute radical skepticism.[96] But Emerson is saying that waking experiences have a dreamlike quality: "Dream delivers us to dream, and there is no end to illusion."[97]

Surprise. There is still, as always in Emerson, another mood, another side to the play of surfaces: "In liberated moments, we know that a new picture of life and duty is already possible."[98] Such moments, which must also be recognized as part of the "succession of moods or objects," come as surprises to us. Emerson records some of them in *Nature:* "The waving of the boughs in the storm, is new to me and old. It takes me by surprise, and yet is not unknown."[99] Again, in a famous passage employed by both James and Dewey:[100] "Crossing a bare common, in snow puddles, at twilight, under a clouded sky, without having in my thoughts any occurrence of special good fortune, I have enjoyed a perfect exhilaration. I am glad to the brink of fear."[101] These surprising insights may be brought about by a person, by art rather than nature: "In the thought of genius there is always a surprise." Or they may come about for no clearly assignable reason, with the mere passage of time: "The results of life are uncalculated and uncalculable. The years teach much which the days never know. The persons who compose our company, converse, and come and go, and design and execute many things, and somewhat comes of it all, but an unlooked for result. . . . It turns out somewhat new."[102]

Surprise is essential to Emerson's conception of life as a set of concentric circles, around every one of which another can be drawn. When it is drawn, the limitations and possibilities of life take on an entirely different aspect. Emerson concludes "Circles" in his hopeful voice, stressing the surprise of overcoming rather than the routine of confinement:

> Life is a series of surprises. We do not guess to-day the mood, the pleasure, the power of to-morrow, when we are building up our being. . . . The masterpieces of God, the total growths and universal movements of the soul, he hideth; they are incalculable. . . . The one thing which we seek with insatiable desire, is to forget ourselves, to be surprised out of our propriety, to lose our sempiternal memory, and to do something without knowing how or why; in short, to draw a new circle.[103]

The last sentence here portrays surprise not as a limitation that, as it were, causes us to lose our way by disorienting us but, rather, as something that is helpful in forming our expanding series of circles and so leads us on our way to what we desire. (The last sentence is interesting too for its blending of the Platonic and Neoplatonic image of desire – felt by the soul for the Ideas in Plato's *Phaedo* and *Symposium,* for example – with the Romantic and Kantian idea that knowledge and the reality it discloses (Emerson's new circle) are constructed by us, are things that we draw.)[104]

The form of experience Emerson wants to explain by positing a category of Surprise is expressed not only in such general pronouncements as "life is a series of surprises"[105] but also in his frequently stated thought that what we know comes, as it were, in our side glances, by the wayside. Emerson writes in "Intellect," for example: "You cannot, with your best deliberation and heed, come so close to any question as your spontaneous glance shall bring you, whilst you rise from your bed, or walk abroad in the morning after meditating the matter before sleep, on the previous night."[106] Truth comes in glimpses, for Emerson, not in a total and finished product. He searches widely for these genuinely new ideas or insights, finding "every surmise and vatication of the mind . . . entitled to a certain respect. . . . We learn to prefer imperfect theories, and sentences which contain glimpses of truth, to digested systems which have no one valuable suggestion."[107] The surprising and indirect character of truth requires the special epistemological attitude that Emerson sees in his self-reliant heroes: "A man should learn to detect and watch that gleam of light which flashes across his mind from within, more than the lustre of the firmament of bards and sages." But there is a darker, even tragic side to the claim that truth comes only by surprise: We cannot be surprised twice by the same object. One must thus, Emerson advises, leave a picture forever, after seeing it well once: "You shall never see it again." This is a painful discovery, one that "murmurs" a "plaint of tragedy" to us "in regard to persons, to friendship and love."[108]

With Surprise, we reach a feature of experience that is problematic when seen as a category. For although one might say there are synthetic a priori truths about surprise (e.g., that life is a series of surprises), it is implausible to say that those surprises come from us. Indeed, the surprises of life give us the sense of how much we do not determine, how much of our experience is not up to us.[109] Nevertheless, no matter how Emerson wishes to account for the surprising newness we find from time to time in our experience, he clearly wishes to record his strong sense of it. More than Wordsworth (who wrote in *The Prelude* of a "gentle shock of mild surprise") or Dewey, with whom he shares it, Emerson has a vast appreciation for the role that the unexpected or novel plays in our life and thought.

III. EMERSON'S EXPERIMENTALISM

Even when he lists the lords of life, Emerson is careful to put them forward tentatively or experimentally:

Illusion, Temperament, Succession, Surface, Surprise, Reality, Subjectiveness, – these are threads on the loom of time, these are the lords of
life. I dare not assume to give their order, but I name them as I find
them in my way. I know better than to claim any completeness for my
picture. I am a fragment, and this is a fragment of me. I can very confi-
dently announce one or another law, which throws itself into relief and
form, but I am too young yet by some ages to compile a code. I gossip
for my hour concerning the eternal politics."[110]

Emerson shares an open-ended, experimental attitude with the pragmatists James and Dewey. They all leave room for the possibility that the
true account of a given matter is quite different even from what they are
convinced of. James distinguishes himself from Hegel on this point, for
example, by finding the "completed" Hegelian system "suffocating"
(see Chapter 3). Because he is an "idealist," it might seem that Emerson
must be committed to the idea, which attracted Hegel and Plato, of a
completed and unchanging account of the world. But Emerson is committed to experimentation; his idealism is, as Dewey's was to be, experimental.

The idea of testing is essential both to the meaning of the words "experience" and "experiment" and to Emerson's use of them. The English
word "experience," deriving from the French *expérience* (the word used
by Montaigne in his essay on experience), in turn comes from the Latin
verb meaning "to try, to put to the test." ("Experiment" is derived from
the same verb.) It may seem odd to think of Emerson as a tester rather
than a speculator, spinning ideas out of his head, but that is perhaps
because we associate experience with the Lockean (and Humean, Russel-
lian, etc.) account, according to which experience consists primarily of
sensation.

Like traditional empiricists, Emerson values the senses and the natural
world they reveal. As a young man he was excited more by the discoveries of geologists or botanists than by the world of art. In Paris in 1833
(on the trip during which he met Wordsworth, Coleridge, and Carlyle)
he was "only mildly excited" by the Louvre but had "memorable experiences in the Musée Nationale d'Histoire Naturelle and the Jardin des
Plantes." There he confronted what he called in his journal "the inexhaustible riches of nature."[111] When he returned from Europe he contin-
ued his study of astronomy, thermodynamics, and geology and gave
lectures on these topics.[112] "I have no hostility to nature, but a child's
love to it," he writes in *Nature*. "I expand and live in the warm day like
corn and melons."[113] But Emerson does want to "expand and live" in
that nature, not to be confined in his experience of it. He complains in
"The Poet" that "too feeble fall the impressions of nature on us to make
us artists." The word "impressions" here marks his awareness of his

connection with the experiential philosophy of Locke and Hume, whereas his search for an artistic way through the world marks his Romantic criticism of their unimaginative account of human life.

Emerson enacts his commitment to observation and experiment by his use of the essay form, a form invented by his hero Montaigne. An essay is, etymologically, a trial or test of something, an examination. Such an inquiry need not present the final and unrevisable word on some issue, as so many philosophical and religious texts (e.g., Hegel's *Logic*, Wittgenstein's *Tractatus*) claim to do. Emerson pays homage to the spirit of open inquiry that he finds in Montaigne's essays in his own essay "Montaigne; or the Skeptic," published in 1850 as part of *Representative Men:*

> I weary of these dogmatizers. I tire of these hacks of routine, who deny the dogmas. I neither affirm nor deny. I stand here to try the case. I am here to consider, σκέπτειν, to consider how it is. . . . Why pretend that life is so simple a game, when we know how subtle and elusive the Proteus is? Why think to shut up all things in your narrow coop, when we think there are not one or two only, but ten, twenty, a thousand things, and unlike? Why fancy that you have all the truth in your keeping? There is much to say on all sides.[114]

Skepticism is not Emerson's most considered stance: He sees it as something to be incorporated but also transcended in a larger truth: "The new philosophy must take [skepticisms] in and make affirmations outside of them."[115] But in "Montaigne," Emerson gives voice to a part of his outlook that, because of its naturalistic sense of uncertainty and risk combined with its emphasis on our great human powers, coheres especially well with the pragmatic projects of James and Dewey. Emerson values Montaigne's sense that the uncertainty of the universe is a spur to do better, not a reason for resignation. The following passage from Montaigne's great essay "On Experience" captures – as it surely inspired – the spirit in which Emerson conducts his inquiries: "There is no end to our investigations. . . . No generous spirit stays within itself. . . . If it does not advance and push forward . . . it is only half alive. Its pursuits have no bounds or rules; its food is wonder, search, and ambiguity."[116] Emerson accepts "the clamor and jangle of contrary tendencies," but he finds among them patches and places of insight: "The seer's hour of vision is short and rare," and the "authentic utterances of the oracle" are sparingly distributed even among the works of Plato and Shakespeare. But these are what the experimenter seeks.[117]

Emerson's incipient pragmatism emerges in such early essays as "Man the Reformer," in which he holds that "manual labor is the study of the external world," and in "The American Scholar," in which he maintains that without action "thought can never ripen into truth." "Only so much do I know," he continues, "as I have lived."[118] When Dewey defines knowing as "a form of doing" and holds that we in part constitute the objects we know by the actions we take in knowing them, he takes a path prepared by Emerson.[119]

The dwarflike, still-emerging man that Emerson describes in *Nature* is just learning to guide the changes of nature: "We do not know the uses of more than a few plants, as corn and the apple, the potato and the vine."[120] In the chapters "Commodity" and "Discipline" Emerson sets out the project of understanding nature by influencing it. And even though he follows his Romantic forebears Wordsworth and Coleridge in giving a primary role to the imagination, he gives it a practical cast: "The imagination may be defined to be, the use which the Reason makes of the material world."[121] In later essays, Emerson continues to ascribe not only insight to his heroes but power as well: "the thought and the publication."[122]

Emerson extends his experimentalism to our reading, anticipating Cavell's development of the thought that our experience takes special and important forms in the realm of literature. Books can speak to us, although they may, depending on our attitude or background, be entirely mute. Emerson aspires to write such telling books. "There is some awe mixed with the joy of our surprise," he writes in "The American Scholar," "when this poet, who lived in some past world . . . says that which lies close to my own soul, that which I also had well-nigh thought and said." But, he warns, "one must be an inventor to read well," a creative reader as well as a creative writer. Emerson's wide-ranging discussions of the classics of East and West are as much records of his experience as is Hume's discussion of the collision of two billiard balls. In commenting on Emerson, John Dewey was surely correct in stressing the basic experientialism of his philosophy: "I fancy he reads the so-called eclecticism of Emerson wrongly who does not see that it is a reduction of all the philosophers of the race, even the prophets like Plato and Proclus, whom Emerson holds most dear, to the test of trial by the service of the present and immediate experience."[123]

Emerson's experimentalism infiltrates not only his religion, epistemology, and metaphysics but also, as Poirier and West have seen, his philosophy of language. "All symbols are fluxional," he states in "The Poet," indicating the impermanence he sees even in those instruments with which we order change. Furthermore, he believes that "all language is vehicular and transitive, and is good, as ferries and horses are, for conveyance, not as farms and houses are, for homestead." He thus treats language as an instrument needed for some result, not as mirroring some preexisting reality. Emerson's position anticipates those of the pragmatists: James's view, for example, that truth is what we can "ride" and that "essences" are not "the copying, but the enrichment of the previous world," or Dewey's claims that ideas are operations and that "essences are provisional."[124]

In concluding "Circles," Emerson writes:

> But lest I should mislead any when I have my own head, and obey my own whims, let me remind the reader that I am only an experimenter. Do not set the least value on what I do, or the least discredit on what I do not, as if I pretended to settle any thing as true or false. I unsettle all things. No facts are to me sacred; none are profane; I simply experiment, an endless seeker with no Past at my back.[125]

Emerson here gives us a rule for interpreting all of his pronouncements. He does not lack conviction or passion, but he commits himself to the possible overturning of even those convictions that he feels most strongly. Emerson is open to phenomena. He embraces the surprises that experience brings. Yet he is a "seeker" of truth, even as he claims to "settle" nothing.

IV. HUMANISM

> There was only one thought which could set him aflame, and that was the unfathomed might of man.

John Jay Chapman

Emerson's heroes are experimenters, confident, as he remarked in "The American Scholar," "in the unsearched might of man."[126] If Emerson was a "transcendentalist," his transcendentalism was, as Firkins states, "in essence, a disclosure of possibilities; it showed vistas within man."[127] The Unitarianism of Emerson's day postulated a supernatural rather than a deified Christ, an intrusion or eruption from beyond the human and natural.[128] But Emerson advances a natural and human supernaturalism in "The Divinity School Address," stressing not the divinity but the humanity of Christ. He argues that "we degrade" Christ's life and dialogues by making them transcendental and that we should rather "let them lie as they befel, alive and warm, part of human life, and of the landscape, and of the cheerful day."[129] He understands religion to be in partnership with the natural world, maintaining (in language clearly reminiscent of "Tintern Abbey") that "faith should blend with the light of rising and of setting suns, with the flying cloud, the singing bird, and the breath of flowers." Where in this divine natural world, he asks, "sounds the persuasion, that by its very melody imparadises my heart, and so affirms its own origin in heaven?"[130]

Emerson's experiments require a human contribution, as in his idea that to be a good reader one must also be a creative one. Here Emerson embraces what we called in Chapter 1 a voluntarist picture of knowledge: To know something (in this case, the book one is reading) one must do something (read creatively), take a special attitude or stance. Coleridge took such attitudes to be produced by the will, and some of Emerson's language describing the power of the human mind clearly derives from Coleridge. For example, he writes: "Such is the constitution of all things, or such the plastic power of the human eye, that the primary forms, as the sky, the mountain, the tree, the animal, give us a delight *in and for themselves.*"[131] The "plastic power" of the human eye echoes Coleridge's account of the imagination as an "esemplastic power," that is, as a power of shaping.[132] Coleridge's idea of the human mind "giving form to a yielding material" (which is the first Oxford English Dictionary meaning of "plastic") derives from Kant, whose forms and categories do just that. But Coleridge and, following him, Emerson depict such shaping not as automatic operations of the faculties of sensibility, imagination, and understanding, as in Kant, but as, to some degree at least, under our control, subject to our will. Emerson follows Coleridge in complaining of "the wintry light of the understanding" and in placing redemptive hopes in an "educated Will."[133]

In "Experience" Emerson asserts that the universe "inevitably wear[s] our color," that character and mood determine the world we experience. These ideas and some of the same language go back to *Nature,* in which Emerson claims: "Nature always wears the colors of the spirit." Some of Emerson's most Coleridgean expressions of the mind's plastic powers occur in *Nature:* "The sensual man conforms thoughts to things; the poet conforms things to his thoughts. The one esteems nature as rooted and fast; the other, as fluid, and impresses his being thereon. To him, the refractory world is ductile and flexible; he invests dust and stones with humanity, and makes them the words of the Reason."[134] From the standpoint of someone who believes that there are things–in–themselves, a possibly inaccessible set of facts or truths against which our human "facts" or "truths" are measured, Emerson's talk of ductility and fluidity will seem like a glorification of illusion and of the poetic embroidery of illusion. But it is important to see that Emerson associates such ductility with truth. Like Kant, who defends the reality of the humanized or phenomenal, or James, who writes that "the trail of the human serpent is . . . over everything," Emerson denies that we can separate the human from the real.[135] When properly employed, the plastic powers of the human mind gain us access to, as they shape, the only world about which we can possibly gain truth.

A great part of what seems idealistic in Emerson is his development of this Romantic doctrine of the shaping power of the individual mind. It is easy to take him as being some sort of solipsist, with the Oversoul perhaps as the single cosmic entity, spinning off the world from itself or creating it *ex nihilo*. The shaping metaphor, on the contrary, suggests that the mind works on and with its material. "We want men and women," he states in "Self-Reliance," "who shall renovate life and our social state."[136] Although Emerson clearly glorifies the individual, he does not call for isolation. He envisions a society reconstituted, not eliminated, in which men and women will "sit apart as the gods, talking from peak to peak all round Olympus." But he warns of the dangers of "an excess of fellowship" and counsels "lovers" to "guard their strangeness."[137]

Emerson's claim is that we are not sufficiently aware of our powers, not sufficiently noble. "Man," he notes in *Nature*, "is the dwarf of himself." This striving and transformative man emerges further in the work of William James and John Dewey, who participate in the formation of the new human-oriented Romantic myth described by Frye and in "the act of discovery that is also a making" which Bloom sees as essential to Romanticism.[138] Dewey's theory of education, for example, is a recipe for producing an active and imaginative human being, not the narrow and skulking "dwarf" diagnosed by Emerson. Both James and Dewey follow Emerson in focusing on the shaping power of the human mind, holding that the world we know is a malleable product of our pragmatically determined concepts. James particularly stresses the role of temperament in forming our vision of things, especially our philosophical visions. James and Dewey follow Emerson in criticizing the paltry notion of experience with which empiricism traditionally operates. Whether through their interest in feeling, in religious experience, in imagination, or in the shaping powers of the mind, the American Romantic philosophers seek to expand the narrow focus of classical empiricism while retaining the empiricist commitment to human experience for our knowledge of the world.

3

WILLIAM JAMES

Unlike Emerson, William James was a professional philosopher. Nevertheless, he kept his distance from the profession. He maintained that "*technical* writing on *philosophical* subjects is certainly a crime against the human race!"[1] And from his summer home in New Hampshire he wrote that he was "one unfit to be a philosopher because at bottom he hates philosophy, especially at the beginning of a vacation, with the fragrance of the spruces and sweet ferns all soaking him through with the conviction that it is better to *be* than to define your being."[2] (Of course this is a philosophical statement.)

James was always "a man speaking to men," as Wordsworth wrote of the poet, and nowhere more so than in his philosophy. Indeed, it is almost as if Wordsworth were forecasting the character of William James when he described the poet as

> "a man . . . endowed with more lively sensibility, more enthusiasm and tenderness, who has a greater knowledge of human nature, and a more comprehensive soul, than are supposed to be common among mankind; a man pleased with his own passions and volitions, and who rejoices more than other men in the spirit of life that is in him; delighting to contemplate similar volitions and passions as manifested in the goings-on of the Universe, and habitually impelled to create them where he does not find them."[3]

In fact, Wordsworth played a major role in William James's life and thought. As a young man, James struggled with depression, but he came out of it by the spring of 1873, at which time his father wrote to his younger brother Henry of the change:

> "What a difference there is between me now and me last spring this time: then so hypochondriacal" (he used that word, though perhaps in substantive form) "and now feeling my mind so cleared up and restored to sanity. It is the difference between death and life." He had a great

effusion. I was afraid of interfering with it, or possibly checking it, but I ventured to ask what specially in his opinion had promoted the change. He said several things: the reading of Renouvier (specially his vindication of freedom of the will) and Wordsworth, whom he has been feeding upon now for a good while; but especially his having given up the notion that all mental disorder required to have a physical basis.[4]

Wordsworth figures prominently in some of James's writing, for example, in an essay entitled "On a Certain Blindness in Human Beings," versions of which James gave many times as a talk to students. In that essay, James cites the sense that Wordsworth and Shelley, Emerson and Whitman, had "of a limitless significance in natural things."[5] Wordsworth tramped the fields, "responsive . . . to the secret life of nature round about him," while his neighbors remained "tightly and narrowly intent upon their own affairs," blind to the character of his experience.[6] Whitman rode the bus or the ferry through New York, "refresh'd by the gladness of the river and the bright flow,"[7] while around him scurried the "ordinary Brooklynite or New Yorker," obsessed with cares, failing to realize what James calls

> the indisputable fact that this world never did anywhere or at any time contain more of essential divinity, or of eternal meaning, than is embodied in the fields of vision over which his eyes so carelessly pass. . . . There is the only kind of beauty there ever was. . . . There is the text and the sermon, the real and the ideal in one. But to the jaded and unquickened eye it is all dead and common, pure vulgarism, flatness, and disgust."[8]

Wordsworth's inner life, James writes, "carried the burden of a significance that has fed the souls of others, and fills them to this day with inner joy."[9]

Wordsworth is, of course, just one of many writers who influenced James – a man who could think in German, French, and Italian, as well as in English. But the Wordsworthian influence is, by his own testimony, a strong one, and Wordsworth's ideas, such as the naturalization of the spiritual, the "feeling intellect," and the marriage of self and world, are useful headings under which to consider some of the Romantic aspects of James's thought. James once wrote that the central vision of a philosopher is the important fact about him and that this vision is a matter not of reasoning but of basic attitude.[10] James was a doctor and psychologist, a man of science, but he was at the same time – and his "feeding" on Wordsworth is just one sign of this – a Romantic in his basic vision.

II. UNITING EMPIRICISM WITH SPIRITUALISM

One thing James discovered, from writers like Wordsworth and Emerson and from his own life, was a range and variety of experience that the professionals of psychology and philosophy as well as ordinary people either ignored or failed to acknowledge. His interest in such experience is both descriptive and evaluative: He describes the phenomena of human thought and behavior, but he also questions their epistemological and moral adequacy. He examines the wide range of human experience and particularly its spiritual side, both because of what it shows about the kind of creatures we are and because of what it might reveal about the world.

James was throughout his life an empiricist,[11] a believer in experience as the basic source of knowledge. But although he admired Locke, Hume, and Mill for their empirical methods, he found them not thorough or "radical" enough as empiricists, neglectful of the full range of human experience. He wrote in 1905 that he wanted "to unite empiricism with spiritualism,"[12] and his work both before and after bears this out. His reports of and thinking about the "gleaming moments"[13] of Wordsworth and others are an attempt to place spiritual phenomena in the natural world, the world that contains the smell of a flower or the buzzing of a mosquito. There is a sense of mystery and wonder about such moments, but the mystery comes within human awareness itself, not from divine intervention and not from what Emerson called a "foreign addition."[14] In combining empiricism with spiritualism, James thus expresses the Romantic perspective that Carlyle and Abrams call "natural supernaturalism": the idea that our human encounters with the natural world can be wide and deep enough to contain the experiences traditionally ascribed to the influx from abroad of a divine power. There is, then, no "outside" in James's picture of human experience, no "external," but only "internal" or experiential standards of truth, reality, or spirit. All " 'homes'," as he puts it, "are in finite experience. . . . Nothing outside of the flux secures the issue of it."[15]

As a theorist of knowledge, James frequently asks what credence we should place in reports like those of Wordsworth and Emerson. The answer to this question is not easy, and James is no dogmatist. In his "Blindness" talk, he urges that we "tolerate, respect, and indulge those whom we see harmlessly interested and happy in their own ways, however unintelligible these may be to us." But his reason for this injunction is not so much moral as epistemological: "Neither the whole of truth nor the whole of good is revealed to any single observer. . . . Even prisons and sick-rooms have their special revelations."[16] Again, discussing Whitman's "loafing" away his afternoon riding down Broadway on the top of an omnibus, James comments: "Truly a futile way of passing the time, some of you may say, and not altogether creditable to a grown-up man. And yet, from the deepest point of view, who knows the more of truth, and who knows the less, – Whitman on his omnibus-top, full of the inner joy with which the spectacle inspires him, or you, full of the disdain which the futility of his occupation excites?"[17] James's rhetoric supports Whitman. "Some of you," but presumably not James, think his is not a creditable way of living. James suggests here the common Romantic epistemological claim that there is a link between joy and truth, on the one hand, and disdain (Coleridge would say dejection) and falsehood or shallowness on the other.

James's intellectual career was astonishingly diverse. He was the first great American psychologist, a pioneer in the study of religion, and, of course, a major American philosopher, a founder of pragmatism. We shall look at each of these aspects of James's career as they bear on his project of developing an empiricism broad enough to be united with spiritualism. James explicitly identifies this broader empiricism with what he calls the "romantic" as opposed to the "classic–academic" type of imagination. The Romantics, according to James, show the "world of mind" to be "something infinitely more complex than was suspected."[18]

"The Principles of Psychology" (1890)

James's almost constant preoccupation in the Principles is to place within experience what other writers see as outside it. He opposes the idealist tradition stemming from Kant, which places the unifying Self behind the empirical, "phenomenal," scenes; yet he disagrees with traditional empiricists, who give no account of the unity of experience. Searching for a middle way, James maintains that unity is directly experienced, that each pulse of consciousness finds warm and intimate some of its predecessors, and that it knows these as part of the self. Self-unity is experienced from moment to moment, James observes. It is "the hook from which the chain of past selves dangles, planted firmly in the Present, which alone passes for real, and thus keeping the chain from being a purely ideal thing."[19]

James's discussion of relations provides another example of the richness he sees in experience. Again, he tries to find a middle position between traditional empiricists, represented by Hume, who "have for the most part denied that feelings of relations exist,"[20] and the "intellectualists," who maintain that such relations are known, but "by something that lies on an entirely different plane, by an actus purus of Thought, Intellect, or Reason, all written with capitals and considered to mean something unutterably superior to any fact of sensibility whatever."[21] James asserts that we do experience such relations and (taking a position that anticipates those developed by such early twentieth-century analytic philosophers as Russell and Wittgenstein) that we are prevented from noticing this in part by our language. The empiricists demonstrate that just because we have a word, it does not follow that some entity corresponds to it, but they have failed to consider the "obverse error" of holding that if there is no word for it there is no object or feature of experience.[22]

Consider trying to remember a person's name. There is a gap in our consciousness, but it is "no mere gap," for if totally wrong names are proposed to us, "the gap" will reject them, because "they do not fit into its mold." We have no word to describe the gap (the gap in fact being a word's absence), but this absence is nevertheless unlike others: "When I vainly try to recall the name of Spaulding my consciousness is far removed from what it is when I vainly try to recall the name of Bowles." Such cases show, James argues, that "our psychological vocabulary is wholly inadequate to name the differences that exist, even such strong differences as these."[23]

James's basic picture of human experience is of a field, a spread, or, as he describes it, a "stream." Experience is originally chaotic, so that a "baby, assailed by eyes, ears, nose, skin, and entrails at once, feels it all as one great blooming, buzzing confusion."[24] Discrimination between one thing and another comes with interest, without which "the consciousness of every creature would be a gray chaotic indiscriminateness, impossible for us even to conceive."[25]

If I am working on my car or on a book, I am interested in the task at hand and discriminate as much detail as I need (a screw holding a hose clamp, the last sentence I wrote), but many other things remain in the background. They have some order of their own, but not the precise ordering that my discriminating attention brings: "The sound of the brook near which I write, the odor of the cedars, the comfort with which my breakfast has filled me, and my interest in this paragraph, all lie distinct in my consciousness, but in no sense outside or alongside of each other. Their spaces are interfused and at most fill the same vaguely objective world."[26] I may need to make determinate part of this "vaguely objective world," as when I hear the splash of a horse in the brook and try to locate it in relation to the trees I am smelling. Until such need arises, however, my awareness does not have to be demarcated any more than it is. James calls "ridiculous" the theory of Hume and Berkeley that consciousness is composed only of definite, sharp-edged, separated bits of experience (ideas, sensations, or sense-data). The elements of the stream of consciousness may be so vague as to be unnameable, but "it is . . . the re-instatement of the vague to its proper place in our mental life which [James] is so anxious to press on the attention."[27]

The vaguer elements of our consciousness can be more important than the clear-cut color or shape of a horse or tree. They make the difference between the feeling that the world we encounter is interesting and vital and "the feeling that everything is hollow, unreal, dead."[28] They include what James calls our *"consents,"* the "dumb responses" that we make minute by minute to the question "will you have it so?" and that "seem our deepest organs of communication with the nature of things."[29] James thus suggests, here in the *Psychology,* that these vaguer aspects of consciousness are epistemologically superior to the more definite colors and shapes or meter readings of traditional empiricism.

These more vague or, as James also calls them, "fringe" elements are the stock in trade of Wordsworth's poetry, which characteristically treats the loss and recovery of such "consents." In "Tintern Abbey," for example, he writes that he is "still / A lover of the meadows and the woods" but also that "I have learned / To look on nature, not as in the hour / Of thoughtless youth; but hearing oftentimes / The still, sad music of humanity." Such blendings of thoughts and feelings with sensation are what lead James to say that we rarely get an identical sensation from an identical object. "We feel things differently," he observes, "according as we are sleepy or awake, hungry or full, fresh or tired; differently at night and in the morning, differently in summer and in winter, and above all things differently in childhood, manhood, and old age."[30]

This is one of the many points at which James's work anticipates that of phenomenologists such as Husserl, Merleau-Ponty, and Heidegger.[31] But it is also a place in which what Poirier calls James's "enormous and largely unadmitted debt to Emerson" is apparent,[32] as in his use of the word "mood" to describe these phenomena: "The difference of the sensibility is shown by the difference of emotion about the things from one age to another, or when we are in different organic moods." A bit later in the "stream of thought" chapter, James writes that "we wonder how we ever could have opined as we did last month about a certain matter" and that "from one year to another we see things in new lights," illustrating these mood changes with the example of "books": "What *was* there to find so mysteriously significant in Goethe, or in John Mill so full of weight?"[33] There are echoes here of Emerson's description of his encounter with books in "Experience": "Once I took such delight in Montaigne, that I thought I should not need any other book; before that, in Shakespeare; then in Plutarch; then in Plotinus; at one time in Bacon; afterwards in Goethe; even in Bettine; but now I turn the pages of either of them languidly, whilst I still cherish their genius."[34]

James's stress on the synthesis and interpenetration of the elements of consciousness sometimes has the sound of the German idealists, whose thought he generally opposes.[35] Take a cross section of a thought at a time, James argues in a passage that Hegel would have nodded approvingly over, and "you will find, not the bald word in process of utterance, but that word suffused with the whole idea."[36] Indeed, he maintains that "the fundamental *facts* of consciousness have been, on the whole, more accurately reported by the spiritualistic writers" than by those of the empirical school.[37] James finds that all the elements of consciousness interpenetrate: "Colors, sounds, smells, are just as much entangled with other matter as are more formal elements of experience, such as extension."[38] But rather than requiring some hidden, ghostly agency to put together our atomistic ideas, James sees such fusion as the natural condition and discrimination as secondary, though obviously important. We build up our awareness of self and objects in the world by separating an initial coalescence, not by joining discrete ideas.[39]

In the *Principles of Psychology,* James offers an account of human experience that is broad and varied enough to encompass the experiences of Wordsworth or Emerson and that explores the continuities between their lives and the common experience of humanity. James does not have the "fear of experience" that Cavell diagnoses in so much philosophy.[40] He is not embarrassed by Whitman's bus ride or Wordsworth's "blessed mood, / In which the affections gently lead us on."[41] Rather, it is as if his pychological theory were made to fit them. "When very fresh," James writes, "our minds carry an immense horizon with them. . . . Under ordinary conditions the halo of felt relations is much more circumscribed. And in states of extreme brain-fag the horizon is narrowed almost to the passing word."[42] James thus employs the idea of a halo or fringe of consciousness to describe the contrast between what Coleridge called "the sense of novelty and freshness" and the "lethargy of custom."[43]

"Varieties of Religious Experience" (1902)

Though the James family did not belong to a church – William's brother Henry describes their "pewless state"[44] growing up in New York – there was nevertheless a strong religious interest in the family, especially on the part of William's and Henry's father, Henry James, Sr., a follower of Swedenborg and close friend of Emerson (who was a frequent visitor in their home). As we have seen, James had a strong feeling for those "responses" to the universe as a whole that are so important to both traditional religion and Romantics like Wordsworth and Coleridge. James's philosophical, psychological, and personal interest in the wide range of human experience led him quite naturally to an exploration of religious experience.

Varieties of Religious Experience tells us by its title that in it James is looking not at religious dogma or ceremony but at religion as a part of human life. He finds the source of religion in human experience, not in its later refinements: "When a religion has become an orthodoxy, its day of inwardness is over; the spring is dry; the faithful live at second hand exclusively and stone the prophets in their turn."[45] But James's definition of religion is wide enough to cover what he calls the "a theistic" outlooks of Emerson or the Buddhists, as well as traditional Judeo-Christian perspectives: "Religion . . . shall mean for us *the feelings, acts, and experiences of individual men in their solitude, so far as they apprehend themselves to stand in relation to whatever they may consider the divine.*"[46] With this conception of his area of study, James finds it as reasonable to look at Thoreau as at St. Theresa.

In his *Psychology*, James stated that our self is defined by what we take an interest in.[47] His major work on religious experience and his numerous uses of such experiences throughout his writings define the kind of empiricist he is. Empiricists have their almost obsessionally maintained sets of examples, what Wittgenstein called a one-sided diet. Often these are visual, like the appearance of a tomato or a table, or the meter readings of logical positivism. James too has his obsessions (e.g., the psychic phenomena associated with the activities of "mediums"), but he casts his net widely. As Ralph Barton Perry remarked, "philosophy, for James, was not an attempt to secure universality, coherence, definiteness, or any other such intellectual end, but to *see* the world as it is in all its fullness."[48]

Varieties of Religious Experience furnishes a basis for James's project of uniting "empiricism with spiritualism" by focusing on the undeniable facts of human religious experience. James's treatment of religion is empirical and humanistic: He examines not God but humanity, not a supernatural phenomenon but a natural human development, a form of natural supernaturalism. The regeneration that religious experience often includes, James writes, may "possibly be a strictly natural process, divine in its fruits, of course . . . neither more nor less divine in its mere causation and mechanism than any other process, high or low, of man's interior life."[49]

The "dumb responses" or "consents" whose epistemological validity James had affirmed in the *Psychology* become, in *Varieties,* the essence of religion, which at bottom is concerned "with the manner of our acceptance of the universe."[50] Religion is "a man's total reaction upon life," and to get at such a reaction one "must go behind the foreground of existence and reach down to that curious sense of the whole residual cosmos as an everlasting presence, intimate or alien, terrible or amusing, lovable or odious, which in some degree every one possesses."[51] Like other Romantics, James associates these total responses to the world, what we called attitudes in Chapter 1, with our "willing nature."

There are, of course, different religious responses to the universe, varieties of religious experience. For example, the "resignation" of the Stoics and "the passionate happiness of Christian saints" are so different that in looking at them "two discontinuous psychological universes confront you."[52] James divides basic religious responses according to their treatment of evil. What he calls the religion of healthy mindedness "looks on all things and sees that they are good." On the other hand, the "sick soul," even amidst its religious enthusiasm, preserves an awareness of the world's widespread and horrible imperfections. Healthy mindedness, which James sees in Whitman and in the mind-cure movement, embraces the basic positive and expansive emotion that is essential to religion, but (like Kierkegaard's aesthetic sphere of existence)[53] it "breaks down impotently as soon as melancholy comes." Buddhism and Christianity, which recognize evil and suffering, range over a "wider scale of experience" and are therefore the "completest" religious outlooks.[54] James regards Bunyan and Tolstoy (and one could add both Wordsworth and Emerson)[55] as having such an outlook: "They had drunk too deeply of the cup of bitterness ever to forget its taste, and their redemption is into a universe two stories deep. Each of them realized a good which broke the effective edge of his sadness; yet the sadness was preserved as a minor ingredient in the heart of the faith by which it was overcome."[56] Though he once called the pragmatist "a happy-go-lucky anarchistic sort of creature,"[57] James is not a happy-go-lucky Romantic. Like Wordsworth, Coleridge, and Emerson, James appreciates the harmony and disharmony, the joy and the despondency, that human experience records.

To describe these deep attitudes or responses to the universe, James continues to find the idea of "the entire wave of consciousness or field of objects" superior to the "ideas" of traditional psychology. Some fields are narrow and oppressive, whereas others are wide and expansive. "Usually when we have a wide field we rejoice, for we then see masses of truth together, and often get glimpses of relations which we divine rather than see."[58] Whether healthy or morbid minded, religious experience tends to be of this wider sort. (James here anticipates Heidegger's and Cavell's distinction between moods and sense.)

As befits his empiricist leanings, James favors those whose religious experience engages the world. He paints a fairly repellent picture, for example, of St. Louis of Gonzaga, who "systematically refused to notice his surroundings" and was so wary of pleasure that he avoided touching or smelling flowers.[59] On the other hand, he is full of enthusiasm for that "excellent little illiterate English evangelist" Billy Bray, who upon his conversion reported, as James phrases it, "a sense of newness." " 'Everything looked new to me,' " James quotes him as saying, " 'the people, the fields, the cattle, the trees. I was like a new man in a new world.' "[60] According to James, this experience is not "a vision," either in the head or projected on the sense world, but a fresh way through the old world. It is the manifestation of a state of "religious assurance," in which the world appears to undergo an "objective change."[61]

James continually wrestled with the question of what these experiences reveal about the world. He tended to believe (and, at times, needed to believe)[62] that they are in some way veridical, offering glimpses of reality denied to us in our more ordinary experiences. The pluralism that James develops – according to which there are many ways of knowing the world, as well as many ways the world is – provides a framework for these varieties in insight.[63] In *Varieties,* for example, he discusses the differences between the "psychopathic temper," often susceptible to religious experiences, and "your robust Philistine type of nervous system, forever offering its biceps to be felt." He speculates that if "there were such a thing as inspiration from a higher realm, it might well be that the neurotic temperament would furnish the chief condition of the requisite receptivity."[64] He reminds us of the power that tears, or what he frequently calls "the melting mood," have to "open" us.[65] And in his discussion of the "sick soul," he notes that "pity, pain, and fear, and the sentiment of human helplessness may . . . open a profounder view" than does the religion of healthy mindedness.[66] Elsewhere in *Varieties* he suggests that alcohol, drugs, and dreams open up relatively uncharted areas of reality: "The hubbub of the waking life might close a door which in the dreamy Subliminal might remain ajar or open."[67]

Finally, toward the end of the book, in his chapter on mysticism, he comes to the conclusion (based substantially on his own experiences with nitrous oxide) that

> our normal waking consciousness, rational consciousness as we call it, is but one special type of consciousness, whilst all about it, parted from it by the filmiest of screens, there lie potential forms of consciousness entirely different. We may go through life without suspecting their existence; but apply the requisite stimulus, and at a touch they are there in all their completeness, definite types of mentality which probably somewhere have their field of application and adaptation.[68]

Pragmatism (1907)

"Pragmatism" has meant different things to different people.[69] James did "not like the name" and insisted that it is "a new name for some old ways of thinking." His discussion of "the pragmatic movement, so-called,"[70] is informed by a pragmatic sense of language that, like Emerson's, sees ideas as means of conveyance. The term "pragmatism," and the related "rationalism" and "empiricism," are, for James, "to a certain extent arbitrary," denoting "types of combination that nature offers very frequently, but by no means uniformly."[71] But these terms may be "ridden on" nevertheless. James uses "pragmatism" as he uses such other terms as "radical empiricism" and "pluralism," to get some work done and specifically to get a handle on certain tendencies in philosophy and in his own evolving outlook.

"Pragmatism" in James's hands becomes a name for his Romantic project of naturalizing the supernatural, of "uniting spiritualism with empiricism," for he construes the pragmatist as a mediator between empiricism and idealism. Pragmatism is a form of empiricism but quite distinct, James holds, from the "hardheaded" or "materialistic" empiricisms of his (or our) day. "Rationalism usually considers itself more religious than empiricism," he writes, but this is a true claim only "when the individual rationalist is what is called a man of feeling, and when the individual empiricist prides himself on being hard-headed."[72] Rationalists or empiricists, that is, may be hardheaded. James's pragmatism is part of a tradition, stretching from Wordsworth through Emerson and leading to Dewey and Cavell, that opposes what Emerson calls "paltry empiricism." It was James's particular task not merely to oppose such empiricism but also to develop alternatives to it.

James speaks of "the pragmatic openness of mind" and maintains that pragmatism "has no dogmas, and no doctrines save its method." He characterizes that method as "*the attitude of looking away from first things, principles, 'categories,' supposed necessities; and of looking towards last things, fruits, consequences, facts.*"[73] Accordingly, James maintains that pragmatism has "no *a priori* prejudices against theology"[74] but that religious beliefs, like all others, must be validated through human experience and must accord with "other truths that also have to be acknowledged."[75]

> [Pragmatism] is completely genial. She will entertain any hypothesis, she will consider any evidence. It follows that in the religious field she is at a great advantage both over positivistic empiricism, with its antitheological bias, and over religious rationalism, with its exclusive interest in the remote, the noble, the simple, and the abstract. . . . In short, she widens the field of search for God. Rationalism sticks to logic and the empyrean, Empiricism sticks to the external senses. Pragmatism is willing to take anything, to follow either logic or the senses, and to count the humblest and most personal experiences.[76]

(Note James's use of the feminine pronoun for his way of uniting the hardheaded and the tender-minded.)

It is in this context that one must see James's activities in the area of psychical research.[77] He was a respected and sober critic of the claims made by various "spiritualists" to enjoy a nonbodily existence,[78] but he was hopeful that some link to the other areas of consciousness of which he speaks in his religious writings would be forthcoming from studying alleged paranormal phenomena. James became actively involved in the British Society for Psychical Research (which investigated clairvoyance, thought transmission, and other such alleged phenomena), serving as its president, and he was a founder of the corresponding American Society. Toward the end of his life, he made a pact with Frederic Myers, according to which the first of them to die would attempt to contact the other.

Alex Munthe, who, along with James, was present at Myers's death, describes James sitting by Myers's bedside, "his open note-book still on his knees. The page was blank."[79]

James was not a man who suppressed his internal conflicts. A chemist, naturalist, and physiologist, the founder of the first psychological laboratory in America, he nonetheless flirted with the idea of an entirely "other" world, inaccessible to science's investigations.[80] Occasionally he maintains that religion requires such a world, as when in "Is Life Worth Living?" he writes that he will treat religion in a "supernaturalist sense, as declaring that the so-called order of nature, which constitutes this world's experience, is only one portion of the total universe. . . . A man's religious faith . . . means for me essentially his faith in the existence of an unseen order of some kind in which the riddles of the natural order may be found explained."[81] In his 1897 lecture entitled "Human Immortality," he speculates that the brain merely transmits consciousness rather than produces it, just as a prism transmits light. If so, then consciousness does not require the brain to exist, and the transmitted consciousness might encompass that order in which solutions to the problems of this world could be found.[82] Though James had a need, as he once put it, "to fall on our father's neck, and be absorbed into the absolute life,"[83] he did not rest content with faith; he expected the truth of any hypothesis, whether religious or not, to make a difference in human experience.

In *Varieties,* as we have seen, James gives a natural rather than a supernatural sense to religion, defining it as "the experiences of individual men." This illustrates his most characteristic approach to any problem: to come at it via human experience (the subtitle of *Varieties* is "A Study in Human Nature"). The validation for any claim about the divine must come, James ultimately held, not from faith, tradition, or miraculous interventions, not from the deductions of some pretentious logic, but from the difference its truth makes in human life.[84] In this way, James's supernaturalism is natural. In the major work on metaphysics on which he was at work until a few weeks before his death, James wrote that "the deeper features of reality [including time, freedom, and novelty] are found only in perceptual experience."[85] Although the idea of an "absolute consciousness" had some appeal for James, his main tendency was to agree with Wordsworth in focusing on, as his subject, "the mind of Man" and, as his setting, the natural world "in which . . . we find our happiness, or not at all."[86]

III. THE FEELING INTELLECT

A renowned writer, teacher, and lecturer, James succeeded in large part because he was, as Wordsworth put it, a man who "thinks and feels."[87] James tended, as his friend Dickenson Miller writes, to "*feel* ideas." He was "not argumentative, not inclined to dialectic or pertinacious debate of any sort. . . . He almost never, even in private conversation, contended for his own opinion. He had a way of often falling back on the language of perception, insight, sensibility, vision of possibilities." "That theory's not a warm reality to me yet," James once told Miller, "still a cold conception."[88]

James points to the "problematic thrill"[89] we feel in doing philosophy. "Pretend what we may," he writes in *The Will to Believe*, "the whole man within us is at work when we form our philosophical opinions."[90] True as this statement may be in general, of no philosopher is it more clearly true than William James. James is a Romantic philosopher in incorporating feeling into his writing, as an important topic in his psychology and epistemology and as a part of his style. His psychology is adequate to the Wordsworthian insight that the complete human being "thinks and feels." His epistemology defends the claim that the feeling part of our "feeling intellect" (again the phrase is Wordsworth's) is as significant to our apprehension of the world as is its "colder" intellectual aspect.[91]

Although he does not carefully distinguish them, James makes four different claims about the feeling intellect that he discerns: (1) the *phenomenological* claim that thoughts are inseparable from feelings, (2) the *causal* claim that feelings produce or determine our thoughts and beliefs, (3) the *epistemological* claim (so common in Romanticism) that we know the world as much through feeling as through thought or sensation, and (4) the *metaphysical* or *existential* claim that in certain circumstances our feelings produce not thoughts but the objects that our thoughts or feelings posit, anticipate, or acknowledge. As we examine the important role of feelings in James's account of human experience and knowledge, we shall try to sort out these claims.

Causal and Phenomenological Claims in the "Principles of Psychology"

"Feeling" covers much ground in the *Principles*, from sensation, to the halo or fringe, to interest, to emotions like love or aversion. Although James does not always distinguish these applications of the word (he has not, as he might put it, a passion for distinctions, as does Lovejoy or Chisholm), his discussion amounts to a powerful demonstration of how great a role all of these feelings play in our human life.

Interest is a case in point. In contrast with the empiricist tradition of Locke, Hume, and Mill – to which he generally conceives himself as belonging – James sees our experience as active at its basis, not passively received, and interest is the key factor in it. As he explains, "Millions of items of the outward order are present to my senses which never properly enter into my experience. Why? Because they have no *interest* for me. *My experience is what I agree to attend to.*"[92] Interest is a cause of my experience. Years later, he described the process even more aggressively and willfully, writing in *Pragmatism* that "we carve out everything, just as we carve out constellations, to suit our human purposes."[93]

The self that is depicted in the *Principles* is no more passively received than is our experience. It has a focus, an organizing principle that it itself provides: its own interests and excitements.[94] Certain things "appeal to primitive and instinctive impulses of our nature, and . . . we follow their destinies with an excitement that owes nothing to a reflective source. These objects our consciousness treats as the primordial constituents of its Me."[95] (A few years later, Dewey reconceived education as the directed utilization of such "excitement.") James pictures the human being as a builder of experience, an artist: "The mind . . . works on the data it receives very much as a sculptor works on his block of stone."[96] We feel as well as think our way through life.

Philosophy and Temperament

From the *Principles of Psychology* through *The Will to Believe* to *Pragmatism* and *Essays in Radical Empiricism,* James insists that philosophy is largely a matter of temperament. Sometimes he seems to be expressing the causal claim that one's temperament leads one to the kind of philosophy one expresses. At other times he seems to stress the phenomenological claim that philosophical views cannot be disentangled from, or that they just are, human temperamental outlooks. James also broaches the third view, that feelings, in the form of temperament, lead us to philosophical truth.

In James's day, the primary opposition was between empiricists such as Mill or Spencer and rationalists like Hegel or Green, but the temperaments in terms of which he analyzes these schools – "tough-minded" for the empiricists, "tender-minded" for the rationalists – constantly recur in philosophy. The rationalists, James holds, are idealistic, optimistic, religious, freewillist, monistic, and dogmatic, whereas the empiricists are materialistic, pessimistic, irreligious, fatalistic, pluralistic, and skeptical.[97] The rationalists think of the empiricists as "unrefined, callous or brutal," and "the tough think of the tender as sentimentalists and softheads."[98] James is sometimes taken to be advocating the tough-minded approach. He certainly is antipathetic to absolute idealism and labels his own system "radical empiricism." Others see him as an excessive sentimentalist wallowing in impression and imprecision. In fact, James finds both outlooks unsatisfactory, offering "the oddly-named thing pragmatism as a philosophy that can satisfy both kinds of demand."[99]

This temperamental approach to philosophy is responsible for a great deal of the charm and interest of James's writing (unless one is an Hegelian). In the *Principles*, for example, he characterizes nominalists as those who "despise the reverential mood," whereas their opponents, believers in universals, "invent" an absolute Ego, "whose function is treated as quasi-miraculous and nothing if not awe-inspiring, and which it is a sort of blasphemy to approach with the intent to explain and make common."[100] In *Pragmatism*, he describes the pragmatist as "a happy-go-lucky anarchistic sort of creature" who, if he had to live in a tub as Diogenes did, "wouldn't mind at all if the hoops were loose and the staves let in the sun" (one thinks of the open windows in Thoreau's summer cabin at Walden). To the rationalist, for whom "the belly-band of [the] universe must be tight," the "loose universe" of the pragmatists produces the effect that freedom of the press does on "a veteran official in the Russian bureau of censorship."[101] In the posthumously published *Essays in Radical Empiricism*, James writes that "likes and dislikes *must* be among the ultimate factors of . . . philosophy"[102] and tries to find the source of idealism's hostility to empirical facts. A fact may have a certain integrity (like the surprising photos of Uranus's moons), an independence from our preexisting picture or system. Such indeterminacy and "external" (in the sense of being outside our system of expectations) determination of truth make some people anxious: "Fact holds out blankly, brutally and blindly, against that universal deliquescence of everything into logical relations which the Absolutist Logic demands. . . . It simply says *to outsiders:* 'Hands off!' " And some people have "a fantastic dislike to letting *anything* say 'Hands off'."[103]

These characterizations stick with you, they make reading James fun, and they show James's sensitivity to the human temperaments that philosophy expresses, but do they really establish anything? It might seem as if James launches an ad hominem, and hence fallacious, argument, claiming that because a person's position is determined by his or her emotions or temperament, that position is in error. James is clearly not advancing such an argument, however, as he admits that his own position – pluralism, or pragmatism, or radical empiricism – is also based on temperament. Rather than debunking those positions that temperament plays a major role in determining, James wants to show how widespread they are and is the first to admit that this applies to his own case:

> I feel sure that likes and dislikes *must* be among the ultimate factors of their philosophy as well as of mine. Would they but admit it! How sweetly we then could hold converse together! There is *something* finite about us both, as we now stand. We do not know the Absolute Whole yet. . . . We might go on and frankly confess to each other the motives for our several faiths. I frankly confess mine – I cannot but think that at bottom they are of an aesthetic and not of a logical sort. The

"through-and-through" universe seems to suffocate me with its infallible impeccable all-pervasiveness. Its necessity, with no possibilities; its
relations, with no subjects, make me feel . . . as if I had to live in a large
seaside boarding-house with no private bed-room in which I might take
refuge from the society of the place. . . . Certainly, to my personal
knowledge, all Hegelians are not prigs, but I somehow feel as if all prigs
ought to end, if developed, by becoming Hegelians. . . . Again I know
I am exhibiting my mental grossness. But again, *Ich kann nicht anders.*
I show my feelings; why *will* they not show theirs? I know they have
a personal feeling about the through-and-through universe, which is
entirely different from mine, and which I should very likely be much
the better for gaining if they would only show me how. . . . The one
fundamental quarrel Empiricism has with Absolutism is over this repudi-
ation by Absolutism of the personal and aesthetic factor in the construction of philosophy. That we all of us have feelings, Empiricism feels
quite sure. That they may be as prophetic and anticipatory of truth as
anything else we have, and some of them more so than others, cannot
possibly be denied.[104]

A key claim James makes in this powerful but also perplexing statement is that our emotional as well as our logical faculties lead us to truth
(claim 3). If it were not clear already, this certainly would establish that
James does not consider the emotional determination of a belief to invali-
date it. On the contrary, he holds that we are guided in life and in philosophical thought by the temperaments of great men and women. "The
books of all the great philosophers," James writes in *Pragmatism,* "are
like so many men. Our sense of an essential personal flavor in each one
of them, typical but indescribable, is the finest fruit of our own accomplished philosophic education. What the system pretends to be is a picture of the great universe of God. What it is – and oh so flagrantly! – is
the revelation of how intensely odd the personal flavor of some fellow
creature is."[105] According to this picture, philosophy is not the construction of an ideal system in some vast cooperative effort – whether Tho-
mistic, Kantian, phenomenological, or analytic – but, rather, the personal and pungent expression of partially but interestingly true outlooks
on the universe.

James brings the human into philosophy, as in their different ways
Socrates, Kierkegaard, and Emerson did before him. "If we take the
whole history of philosophy, the systems reduce themselves to a few
main types which, under all the technical verbiage in which the ingenious
intellect of man envelopes them, are just so many visions, modes of feeling the whole push, and seeing the whole drift of life, forced on one by
one's total character and experience, and on the whole *preferred* – there
is no other truthful word – as one's best working attitude."[106] Our sense
of these "modes of feeling" rather than our ability to "build the system"
or tear one apart is "the finest fruit of our philosophic education." With

this vision of philosophy, it is not surprising that James would find the one unpardonable sin in a philosopher to be the failure to admit the human and emotional components of his outlook. That would be to lose touch with that "finest fruit" of his education and hence to be an uneducated philosopher, one who failed (as Socrates enjoined) to know himself.

What is perplexing about James's statement in *Essays in Radical Empiricism* is that he embraces a free competition among outlooks, while finding fault, a priori, with any outlook that does not concede the temperamental determinations of outlooks generally. This problem may be based on a misreading of James's statement, however. Perhaps he is only making the pragmatic point that one cannot hope to see what others are talking about if they do not "hold parley on this common ground" of feeling. This view seems doubtful, but it is not incoherent. It is doubtful because even without such acknowledgment of feeling by its proponents, James himself has a good sense of the feeling behind Absolutism, as when he writes in an essay in *Pragmatism* entitled "Pragmatism and Religion," that in the moments of discouragement that we all sometimes face, "we want a universe where we can just give up, fall on our father's neck, and be absorbed into the absolute life as a drop of water melts into the river or the sea."[107]

James did not need a pluralistic Hegelian to show him the temperamental source of the belief in an Absolute. Indeed, James plays out a precise feeling-dialectic within the pages of his own essay. He understands the absolutist search for security, but he asks, again in emotional and aesthetic terms, "may not the notion of a world already saved *in toto* anyhow, be too saccharine to stand? May not religious optimism be too idyllic? Must *all* be saved?" He essentially criticizes the absolutists not for logical error but for temperamental failure, for being "afraid of more experience, afraid of life."[108] His own outlook is expressed in the form of a confession: "I find myself willing to take the universe to be really dangerous and adventurous, without therefore backing out and crying 'no play!' "[109]

However one evaluates the consistency of James's position, one may still find it applicable to current philosophical thinking. For consider how much passion and taste there is in fundamental philosophical allegiances. Some people – like my undergraduate teacher Glenn Morrow – just love Plato and find later developments incomplete or less noble or beautiful than Plato's own system, however flawed. Others see Plato only as a predecessor, not as a model or teacher, and are excited more by the precise crackle of contemporary disputes about such Platonic topics as the third-man argument. Many philosophers find that reading Heidegger or Husserl makes their flesh crawl; others are fascinated by the glimmerings and reverberations that Heidegger's language engenders and find the clean lines of analytic philosophy sterile or inhumane. These are not just intellectual differences. The opponent is often seen not just as mistaken but also as both morally and cognitively deficient. Even within a tradition like the analytic one, likes and dislikes play a larger role than is usually acknowledged: Grice or Wittgenstein do not just convince, they captivate, but they have no charm for a "committed" positivist.

The Sentiment of Rationality

In his paper "The Sentiment of Rationality," published as part of *The Will to Believe,* James carries the assault against one kind of absolutist – the rationalists – onto their home ground. Even in the hallowed territory of argument and inference, James contends, our sentiments are at work: We recognize the rational by a feeling of peace or sufficiency, an absence of need to explain or justify. James calls this feeling the "Sentiment of Rationality."[110] He is presumably thinking of the pleasure attendant on grasping something like a Euclidean proof, the sense of its cleverness, economy, or revelatory character. He wants to make the phenomenological claim that this feeling is inseparable from the rationality of it, that rationality is (as intuitionists believe) a matter inextricably human, not separable from the way proofs strike us or are apprehended by us. These feelings, he often seems to be saying, are what make it a proof.

It can no doubt be stated against James that he confuses our feeling upon recognizing something rational with rationality itself. A proof, it will be said, gives us the "sentiment of rationality" because it is rational. James would presumably want to reply that the feeling is indistinguishable from the rationality, that one grasps or understands the proof only if one has that specific sense of satisfaction or rest.

James never does claim to define rationality in his essay, but only the sentiment of rationality, and it is noteworthy, when trying to figure out what he is doing, that instead of abstract terms like "rational" or "rationality," he tends to use empirical or experiential language like "sentiment of rationality." The sentiment is our response to the satisfaction of a need, akin to an aesthetic need: "The facts of the world in their sensible diversity are always before us, but our theoretic need is that they should be conceived in a way that reduces their manifoldness to simplicity. Our pleasure at finding that a chaos of facts is the expression of a single underlying fact is like the relief of the musician at resolving a confused mass of sound into melodic or harmonic order."[111]

James believes that the satisfaction of the sentiment of rationality comes in part because the rational banishes or diminishes uncertainty, particularly about the future. But the diminution of uncertainty is not the supreme virtue of beliefs. Some such diminutions (e.g., those that occurred for people who believed the world was going to be destroyed in 1780) are erroneous. This means that to be effective in diminishing uncertainty over the long term, one needs a healthy dose of criticism or skepticism. James recognizes this, holding that there is a "vulgarly optimistic" mind to which skepticism acts as a corrective. But he at once adds that "considered as anything else than as reactions against an opposite excess," skepticism is "unacceptable," for "the general mind will fail to come to rest in [its] presence, and will seek for solutions of a more reassuring kind."[112] One may regard this as an empirical remark about what in fact we will accept in our theories, but it has a transcendental aspect too: It is a remark about what any theory we count as rational will be like.

By "reassuring," James means a philosophy that, like Emerson's or Wordsworth's, recognizes failures and surprises but also cultivates an attitude of hope. James rejects any philosophy that would deny ultimate meaning to our human impulses or interests. He observes that "materialism will always fail of universal adoption, however well it may fuse things into an atomistic unity, however clearly it may prophesy the future eternity. For materialism denies reality to the objects of almost all the impulses which we most cherish." According to the reductive materialism of which James is speaking here, a lovely rose, like a heap of garbage, is only a collection of atoms in the void. Its properties – color or form, and our responses – our "hope, rapture, admiration," all are reduced to the level of, portrayed as nothing more than, motions of particles or arrangements of energy. To James, such a philosophy "leaves the mind with little to care or act for. This is the opposite condition from that of nightmare, but when acutely brought home to consciousness it produces a kindred horror. In nightmare we have motives to act, but no power; here we have powers, but no motives."[113]

James is hostile to materialism but not to empiricism. He stresses the novelty that the course of experience brings and the possibility of explanations of the world radically different from those we now have. But there is a limit to any such explanatory scheme: It will not be one "whose principle is so incommensurate with our most intimate powers as to deny them all relevancy in universal affairs."[114]

Sentiment and Objectivity

It might appear that James is an idealist of the sentiments, holding everything we believe to depend on them, and one may then wonder where in all this mass of seeming subjectivity is the position of the medical doctor and scientist William James, instructor in physiology and comparative anatomy at Harvard and author of the *Principles of Psychology*. But James counters the tendencies to idealism in his positions in

three main ways. First, he pictures schemes that contend with one another even if they are emotionally determined. Second, he considers that
feelings are tools of inquiry and do not so much create as reveal their
objects. Third, he embraces a healthy skepticism, frequently pressing the
"pluralistic" point that no one has the whole truth.

In his justly famous essay "The Will to Believe," often interpreted as
defending the view that truth is whatever we need to believe or that we
should believe whatever we wish, James in fact presents a carefully balanced depiction of the relation between the objective world and the potent emotional side of our intellect. He denies, for example, that "our
passional and volitional nature" lies at the root of all our convictions and
gives a number of examples to prove his point. No matter what we
wish, we cannot believe "that Abraham Lincoln's existence is a myth,"
that we are "well and about when we are roaring with rheumatism in
bed, or . . . that the sum of the two one-dollar bills in our pocket must
be a hundred dollars. We can *say* any of these things, but we are abso-
lutely impotent to believe them; and of just such things is the whole
fabric of the truths that we do believe in made up."[115] A few pages later,
James derides any talk of belief on the basis of volition as either silly or
perverse.[116]

Yet, if "simple wishing" appears often to have no effect, it does not
follow that our opinions are settled by "pure reason." It is only with
respect to "dead hypotheses" – those that we have no inclination to believe or no reason for believing at all, like the nonexistence of Lincoln –
that will or sentiment plays no role. For others, will does operate, but
will is understood more broadly than just simple wishing, so as to include "all such factors of belief as fear and hope, prejudice and passion,
imitation and partisanship, the circumpressure of our caste and sect."
Our beliefs in molecules, or in democracy (two of James's examples) are
not based on pure reason but on imitation or faith. Few of us have seen
a molecule of any sort, but we believe someone who believes that she or
he has seen one, as this person in turn believes that a tube looked into is
a microscope, and so forth. "Our faith is faith in someone else's faith."
Even our belief in truth is just "a passionate affirmation of desire, in
which our social system backs us up."[117]

When there are several live possibilities in science, as is often the case,
scientists, like other human beings, believe to some degree in what they
want to be the case or in what is most simple, exciting, or comfortable.
"The greatest empiricists among us are only empiricists on reflection:
when left to their instincts they dogmatize like infallible popes."[118] Is
this not a deplorable situation, though, and should we not strive to be
"empiricists on reflection"? Yes, James answers, the tendency to dogmatize is "a weakness of our nature from which we must free ourselves, if

we can."[119] As he observed in a letter to Dickenson Miller, men should "take their faiths out for an airing into the howling wilderness of nature."[120] A passionate conviction can be of help to someone in discovering scientific truth, but it is best balanced by "an equally keen nervousness lest he become deceived."[121] Rather than embracing such traditional and limited criteria of truth as reason or sensation, James simply and openly says that "we must go on experiencing and thinking over our experience, for only thus can our opinions grow more true."[122] He rejects dogmatism, not sentiment; "experiencing and thinking" counter the former but will not eliminate the latter.

Our passions, interests, faiths, and prejudices are involved in science as everywhere else, but this does not mean that there are no standards or evidence or that we may not exercise special caution in affirming scientific conclusions. James wants to stress, however, that there is no "pure" reason or logic – unimpassioned and uninterested – by means of which we can assess things. We cannot escape our human nature. "Everything we know and are," James wrote in an early letter to Thomas Ward, his companion in Brazil, "is through men. We have no revelation but through man."[123] Later, in *Pragmatism,* he put the point in the form of "the humanistic principle: you can't weed out the human contribution."[124]

The Will to Believe

The discussion of science is only a prelude to James's main point in "The Will to Believe," that some situations are unlike scientific ones in that they do not afford the leisure to withhold belief; they are, in his terminology, "momentous." They are like a once-in-a-lifetime chance to climb Mount Everest, something to be seized immediately or lost forever. As an example, consider the question of what I should believe you to feel about me, a common problem that James renders in the form "Do you like me or not?" Now I can no doubt take a detached attitude, waiting for the evidence to come in, for a smile or a handshake or an invitation to lunch. But while waiting, I may lose both the chance to know whether you like me and the chance for you to like me at all. For whether you do like me may depend on whether I manage to believe that you do (this is an example of the fourth sort of claim that James distinguished). So your liking me

> depends, in countless instances, on whether I meet you half-way, am willing to assume that you must like me, and show you trust and expectation. The previous faith on my part in your liking's existence is in such cases what makes your liking come. . . . How many women's hearts are vanquished by the mere sanguine insistence of some man that they *must* love him! he will not consent to the hypothesis that they cannot. The desire for a certain kind of truth here brings about that

special truth's existence; and so it is in innumerable cases of other sorts. . . . A government, an army, a commercial system, a ship, a college, an athletic team, all exist on this condition, without which not only is nothing achieved, but nothing is even attempted.[125]

Notice how widely extending James sees these attitudes of trust, these non–fully founded beliefs. They are not isolated phenomena but integral to much of what we recognize as human life. Many commentators have assumed James's main point in "The Will to Believe" to be a religious one. But the kinds of beliefs he considers are as common in our secular as in our religious lives.[126]

James wants to provide a "justification" for these beliefs or "faiths" in "The Will to Believe." Indeed, he suggests later that he should have called the paper "The Right to Believe,"[127] emphasizing his justificatory intent. What right do I have to believe that my teammates are also doing their best, that my colleagues love ideas and books, or that someone I meet bears me goodwill? One justification for such faith is that it is often required for the existence of, or the desired relation to, the object of our faith. Another is that – as Sartre later stressed – not to choose is itself a form of choice. Not to believe in my colleagues' integrity or in my own powers to, say, traverse a difficult mountain route for which I have trained is to make a decision or commitment as momentous as its opposite. Because we cannot always escape decision or commitment and because our decisions have consequences that cannot be produced in any other way (i.e., for which those decisions, at a point in time, are necessary) we sometimes have the right to choose one way rather than another, even on an unsatisfactory basis.

James writes that a philosophy is a reflection of "a man's intimate character,"[128] and it is certainly plausible to see James's position on the will, or right, to believe as a justification for his own life, particularly as it unfolded during his recovery from the depression of his early manhood. As we have seen, the writings of Wordsworth played a key role in that recovery. Presumably, Wordsworth's sense of finding "strength in what remains behind" appealed to James.[129] In fact, James uses Wordsworth in another essay he wrote around the time of "The Will to Believe," entitled "Is Life Worth Living?" (printed as the second essay in *The Will to Believe*). He again maintains that in "an enormous class" of cases "the part of wisdom as well as of courage is to *believe what is in the line of your needs.*" The question of whether life is worth living is of this sort: One confirms one's hypothesis by the very holding of it. As James puts it, "If you surrender to the nightmare view and crown the evil edifice by your own suicide, you have indeed made a picture totally black"; but on the other hand, "suppose you find yourself a very well-spring, as Wordsworth says, of

Zeal, and the virtue to exist by faith
As soldiers live by courage; as, by strength
Of heart, the sailor fights with roaring seas . . .
Have you not now made life worth living on these terms?"[130]

James uses words like "decision" and "choice" (as did Kierkegaard) in describing our relation to the beliefs we hold. Yet as he is well aware, one cannot just choose beliefs like clothes on a rack. The Wordsworthian passage that James quotes is helpful here because of phrases like "strength of heart," Wordsworth's words for what James calls "will." Will, as conceived by James, is not a phenomenon (such as an act of wishing) but, rather, as in Wittgenstein and Cavell, an attitude toward phenomena, "a perspective which I may or may not be able to take upon myself."[131] It was just such a changed perspective on things that James appears, by his own testimony, to have garnered from his self-reflective reading of Wordsworth and Renouvier. Thinking of the will as a perspective or attitude brings out another difference between what James means by will and by "simple wishing." Although attitudes are our own, they do not come at our bidding. We cannot wish ourselves into zeal or courage or serenity. "As a matter of fact we find ourselves believing," James writes; "we hardly know how or why."[132]

In his psychological writings from *Principles of Psychology* to *Varieties of Religious Experience,* James shows the great role that our "passional natures" play in our intelligent lives. In epistemological and moral works such as *The Will to Believe* and *Pragmatism,* he not only shows their role in science, philosophy, and daily life, but he also argues that our sentiments are legitimate and valuable instruments for comprehending and, in some cases, creating the world. Like other Romantics, James takes our passions to be a key not only in redeeming ourselves but in redeeming the world as well. Life

> *feels* like a real fight, – as if there were something really wild in the universe which we, with all our idealities and faithfulnesses, are needed to redeem; and first of all to redeem our own hearts from atheisms and fears. . . . The deepest thing in our nature is this *Binnenleben* (as a German doctor lately has called it), this dumb region of the heart in which we dwell alone with our willingnesses and unwillingnesses, our faiths and fears. . . . Here is our deepest organ of communication with the nature of things; and compared with these concrete movements of our soul all abstract statements and scientific arguments . . . sound to us like mere chatterings of the teeth."[133]

IV. INTIMACY AND ALTERITY: THE MARRIAGE OF SELF AND WORLD

James feels the universe to be a receptive and even friendly place, a place where our "most intimate powers" have some relevancy.[134] But he also has a sense of a universe that is "wild," a place where genuine novelty and surprise exists. From his work leading to the *Principles of Psychology,* through the development of his radical empiricism, his humanist pragmatism, and his pluralist panpsychism, James searches for a middle ground between two unpalatable alternatives – an *alien,* that is, not intimately known, and a *suffocating,* or idealistic, world. In doing so, he develops a psychological and philosophical language that conveys the sense of the "self–world relation" that Wordsworth and Coleridge express when they portray us as married to the world: intimate with it, but separate. "The forms / Of nature have a passion in themselves," Wordsworth observes, that "intermingles" with the "works of man."[135] James wants to attribute passion to nature, to speak of "the personalism and romanticism of the world."[136]

My current task is to set out James's basic sense of the self–world relation, his own mode of "feeling the whole push of things."[137] This requires a detailed discussion of his theories of experience and knowledge. But my basic aim will be to show that James's particular vision is a Romantic one in that he seeks to portray our "intimacy"[138] with the world and also the world's otherness, its surprisingness and encounterability.

Materialism and Dualism

James was a player in the world. His brother Henry remembers that during their youthful days on West 14th Street in New York "on my once offering him my company in conditions, those of some planned excursion, in which it wasn't desired, his putting the question of our difference at rest, with the minimum of explanation, by the responsible remark: 'I play with boys who curse and swear!' "[139] The young William James had his bunsen burners and "vials of mysterious liquids";[140] he proudly turned a handkerchief into sugar one day.[141] Materialism came naturally to him. As a student at Harvard, he was inspired by the zoologist and geologist Louis Agassiz, who was fond of quoting Goethe's lines:

> All theory is gray, dear friend,
> But the golden tree of life is green.

Agassiz's enthusiasm for science, conceived as the direct study of nature, convinced James to interrupt his medical studies and journey to Brazil for a year and a half. Although he eventually concluded that he was more a "lover of landscape" than a classifier,[142] James remained a medical student and became a teacher of anatomy and physiology. James saw an alliance, not a conflict, between science and his interest in the world.

There is a strong materialistic strain in the *Principles of Psychology.* James opens with several chapters of physiology (e.g., Chapter 2, "The Functions of the Brain") and throughout the book looks for psychical phenomena that can be explained physiologically. He notes, for example, that a thread tied around one's finger will seem to be there long after it has been removed and explains this by claiming that "profound rearrangements and slow settlings into a new equilibrium are going on in the neural substance."[143] Again, he explains such associations as between snow and cold or movie theaters and popcorn "by a merely quantitative variation in the elementary brain-processes momentarily at work under the law of habit, so that *psychic* contiguity, similarity, etc., are derivatives of a single profounder kind of fact."[144] James's use of "derivatives" and "profounder" suggests some sort of reductive materialism, but this is as close as he comes to espousing such a view, according to which we would be linked to the world, however unsatisfactorily, by our being made of the same stuff.

At other points in the *Psychology* (even with 1 a few pages of the preceding passage), James writes as if he is a dualist of some sort: "*The psychological law of association* of objects thought of through their previous contiguity in thought or experience *would thus be an effect, within the mind, of the physical fact that nerve-currents propagate themselves easiest through those tracts of conduction which have been already most in use.*"[145] The phrase "within the mind," contrasted with "the physical fact" that causes it, seems to indicate a separate mental area. In fact, the *Principles* is a deeply ambivalent work. As Bruce Wilshire notes, "the possibility of a thoroughgoing materialism both attracts and repels [James] throughout the book."[146]

James's interest in the world bifurcates in the *Principles*. He observes his human subjects in the physiology laboratory but also through his own introspection, his observation of what he called "the stream of thought." He shows no hostility to the material world but, like Emerson, has "a child's love" for it (one thinks of his lifetime interest in drawing and painting, of his long walks in the New Hampshire mountains);[147] yet he finds the self-proclaimed interpreters of the natural world – the materialists – offering too bleak a vision to sustain his sense of the world's kinship with humanity. In the *Principles,* James swings toward materialism and back toward dualism, but his course is between them, and it is there that much that is original and anticipatory in the book lies.

Radical Empiricism

In the opening pages of the second volume of the *Principles,* James writes from the perspective of the position he later called radical empiricism, stating that consciousness is not in any place, neither in a transcendental self nor in the brain. It has "dynamic relations" with the brain, but it is not in the brain any more than it is in the objects that it knows. We may say that a sensation is in the brain, "if we like," but we may just as truly say that it is "in the same place with whatever qualities it may be cognizing."[148] "Where then," James asks,

> do we feel the objects of our original sensations to be?
>
> Certainly a child newly born in Boston, who gets a sensation from the candle flame which lights the bedroom, or from his diaper-pin, does not feel either of these objects to be situated in longitude 71 W. and latitude 42 N. He does not feel them to be in the third story of the house. He does not even feel them in any distinct manner to be to the right or the left of any of the other sensations which he may be getting from other objects in the room at the same time. He does not, in short, know anything *about* their space-relations to anything else in the world. The flame fills its own place, the pain fills its own place; but as yet these places are neither identified with, nor discriminated from, any other places. That comes later. For the places thus first sensibly known are elements of the child's space-world which remain with him all his life; and by memory and later experience he learns a vast number of things *about* those places which at first he did not know. But to the end of time certain places of the world remain defined for him as the places *where those sensations were;* and his only possible answer to the question *where anything is* will be to say *"there,"* and to name some sensation or other like those first ones, which shall identify the spot. . . . Our sensations . . . *bring* space and all its places to our intellect, and do not derive it thence.
>
>   . . . by the outer world the child means nothing more than *that place where* the candle-flame and a lot of other sensations like it are felt. He no more locates the candle in the outer world than he locates the outer world in the candle. . . . He does both; for the candle is part of what he *means* by "outer world."[149]

James speaks in terms of a child's awareness, but the point he is making concerns human consciousness generally. Later experience teaches us about the original, primordial place of the candle flame, grafting on to it but not eliminating it. This original place of experience is not apart from the world but is the world itself; we are, on the basis of our sensational life, as much spatial as psychical creatures. Our sensations "bring space" rather than just representing it. "Pain fills its own place," and in the many such places of which our stream of consciousness is composed, there occurs an original union of self and world.

In many places in the *Principles,* James takes pains to clarify the connections among things. He criticizes traditional empiricists for atomizing the world, for missing connections disclosed by experience. And he attacks the rationalists and idealists who make those connections transcendental rather than empirical. If experience contains connections, perhaps it contains the connection between self and world that the skeptic questions. To someone who argues that "the world" is possibly only "the world in our heads," the world as perceived from the isolated standpoint at which sensations appear to the Cartesian ego, James replies in effect that by "experience" he does not mean something so confined.[150] He accuses those operating with the Cartesian picture (this includes standard empiricists like Locke and Hume) of working with an abstraction, rather than with experience as it actually exists: "The 'simple impression' of Hume, the 'simple idea' of Locke, are both abstractions, never realized in experience. Experience, from the very first, presents us with concreted objects, vaguely continuous with the rest of the world which envelops them in space and time."[151] The veil of ideas behind which Descartes's (or Hume's, or Russell's) doubting self remains is, according to James, an intellectual invention. We may, by doing philosophy, convince ourselves that we are such selves, but this is to confuse what at best is an extraordinary and attenuated form of consciousness with the fundamental form that our experience of the world takes. This would be a particularly ironic error for an empiricist to make. "Our earliest most instinctive, least developed consciousness is the objective kind, and only as reflection becomes developed do we become aware of an inner world at all."[152]

James's *Psychology* – more than a thousand pages in the Harvard edition – is a compendium of physiology, psychology, and philosophy. James's solution to the philosophical problem of skepticism, of our relation to the world, is to contend that experience discloses the world. Rather than joining self and world by a transcendental synthesis, as in Kant (or, for that matter, in Emerson), James finds that an investigation of our ordinary experience discloses that they are already joined.[153]

In his later philosophical writing, especially *Essays in Radical Empiricism* – mostly composed in an eight-month burst of enthusiasm in 1904–5 – James sharpens his search for a nondualistic account of our relation to the world while retaining his empiricist presumption that human experience itself is the source from which such an account must be drawn and validated. He coins a new term in the *Essays*, "pure experience," to describe the place where experience occurs: "The instant field of the present is always experience in its 'pure' state, plain unqualified actuality, a simple *that*, as yet undifferentiated into thing and thought, and only virtually classifiable as objective fact or as someone's opinion about fact."[154] He speaks of "a primitive stage of perception in which discriminations afterwards needful have not yet been made. . . . Motion originally simply *is*; only later is it confined to this thing or that. Something like this is true of every experience, however complex, at the moment of its actual presence."[155] When James says that "motion originally simply is" in 1905, he is echoing his 1890 statement that "the flame fills its own place, the pain fills its own place." According to his "radical empiricism," this experiential level of "plain actuality" is primary, truer to our situation in the world than the traditional empiricist veil of ideas.[156]

Consistently enough, James labels as "experience" too the worldly objects that fall out (or are carved out)[157] from the originary pure experience: "If we start with the supposition that there is only one primal stuff or material in the world, a stuff of which everything is composed, and if we call that stuff 'pure experience,' then knowing can easily be explained as a . . . relation . . . into which portions of pure experience may enter."[158] In such relations one "experience *knows*" another; "experiences are cognitive of one another."[159]

Despite maintaining that the "stage" of pure experience precedes the division into self and world, James gives it a subjective tinge by calling it "pure experience." This reflects his resolute attempt to answer the question of self–world relationship within experience, and it shows his kinship with Berkeley and Whitehead, who stress that all we know are experienced things, things *qua* experienced.[160] James follows Hume rather than Berkeley, however, in denying that experiences occur in selves or subjects: Selves or subjects are precipitates from or aspects of, pure experience. So although pure experience sounds subjective and although James does use it to imply that reality generally consists of some form of awareness (panpsychism), he is not committed to a plurality of mental substances, each one excluding the other. He thus attempts to sidestep the traditional standpoint from which skepticism since Descartes has started.[161]

James was well aware of the charges of idealism and subjectivism to which his views were subject. One of the *Essays in Radical Empiricism,* "Is Radical Empiricism Solipsistic?" is his response to the objections to this theory published by B. H. Bode. James there shows himself to be capable of a spirited attack on his own position. He considers the accusation that with his doctrine of pure experience he commits "the fallacy of attaching a bilateral relation to a term *a quo,* as if it could stick out substantively and maintain itself in existence in advance of the term *ad quem* which is equally required for it to be a concretely experienced fact." But he maintains that Bode misses "the doctrine of the reality of conjunctive relations" that is essential to radical empiricism. Some of these relations are momentary, some take time to develop, but they all occur within experience, James insists, and Bode performs on them "the usual rationalistic act of substitution," taking them "not as they are given in their first intention, as parts constitutive of experience's living flow, but only as they appear in retrospect, each fixed as a determinate object of conception, static, therefore, and contained within itself."[162]

Whether this appeal to "experience's living flow" (which comes also in *A Pluralistic Universe,* in which Bergson's influence is prominent) ever completely satisfied James is doubtful. In the years after the publication of the *Essays in Radical Empiricism,* James kept a notebook of over three hundred pages devoted to countering the suggestions of idealism in his system. But he keeps coming back to the basic "fact" of relations on which his radical empiricism is built. As he stated in 1908: "The most general peculiarity of fact is that it consists of things in environments."[163]

Although James's radical empiricism stresses our connections with the world, it also credits the world's otherness. This point emerges from James's discussion in his 1909 work entitled *The Meaning of Truth,* of a fundamental "fact" on which radical empiricism is based: that "the relations between things, conjunctive as well as disjunctive, are just as much matters of direct particular experience, neither more so nor less so, than the things themselves."[164] For James, experience discloses foreignness and alterity as well as intimacy and kinship, disjuncts as well as conjuncts. Although experience gives us relations, they all are not of the same type, and some, (e.g., spatial ones) show us our distance from as well as our proximity to, other things.

As generally in his work, in the *Essays in Radical Empiricism* James castigates the absolute idealists for the obsessively tight universe they picture. He compares their universe to a goldfish bowl, neatly containing its beautiful prisoners, and contrasts it with "the empiricist universe," which is more like

> one of those dried human heads with which the Dyaks of Borneo deck their lodges. The skull forms a solid nucleus; but innumerable feathers, leaves, strings, beads, and loose appendices of every description float and dangle from it, and save that they terminate in it, seem to have nothing to do with one another. . . . This imperfect intimacy, this bare relation of *withness* between some parts of the sum total of experience and other parts, is the fact that ordinary empiricism over-emphasizes against rationalism, the latter always tending to ignore it unduly. Radical empiricism, on the contrary, is fair to both the unity and the disconnexion.[165]

"Pragmatism"

James's attempt to marry self to world in a way that avoids idealism and acknowledges otherness is played out again in a chapter of *Pragmatism* entitled "Pragmatism and Humanism." The main message there is that we are wedded to reality by shaping or constructing it. James's activist metaphors recall the shaping power of the human intellect emphasized by Emerson, who wrote: "Nature is thoroughly mediate. . . . It receives the dominion of man as meekly as the ass on which the Saviour rode."[166] James writes that "in our cognitive as well as in our active life we are creative. . . . The world stands really malleable, waiting to receive its final touches at our hands. Like the kingdom of heaven, it suffers human violence willingly. Man *engenders* truths upon it."[167] James's pragmatic inquirer manifests the creativity of Emerson's poet, for whom "the refractory world is ductile and flexible" and who "conforms things to his thoughts . . . invest[ing] dust and stones with humanity."[168] Like Emerson, James is a Heraclitean, a process philosopher. "For rationalism, reality is ready-made and complete from all eternity, while for pragmatism it is still in the making."[169] James's language looks ahead to Kuhn's *Structure of Scientific Revolutions:* "How plastic even the oldest truths . . . really are has been vividly shown in our day by the transformation of logical and mathematical ideas, a transformation which seems even to be invading physics. The ancient formulas are reinterpreted as special expressions of much wider principles, principles that our ancestors never got a glimpse of in their present shape and formulation."[170] But with his use of "plastic" and the idea of a reinterpretation by "wider principles," James again recalls Emerson, who wrote in "Circles" that "the result of to-day which haunts the mind and cannot be escaped, will presently be abridged into a word, and the principle that seemed to explain nature, will itself be included as one example of a bolder generalization."[171]

If James wants to assert that "we carve out everything, just as we carve out constellations, to suit our human purposes,"[172] he does not mean (any more than Emerson did) that we just create, or make up, truth. He cites the "presence of resisting factors in every actual experience of truth-making"[173] and credits part of our experience – sensation and relations – as coming "without the human touch." But this fraction "has immediately to become humanized in the sense of being squared, assimilated, or in some way adapted, to the humanized mass already there."[174] If one tried to dig down to find, for example, by speaking about, this nonhumanized core, one would not find anything: "altho the stubborn fact remains that there *is* a sensible flux, what is *true of it* seems from first to last to be largely [note this qualification] a matter of our own creation."[175] Reality is not just made up by us, but the part that is our contribution and the part that is not can no more be separated than a river and its banks.[176]

James notes the similarity between his picture – in which the world is akin to and knowable by us because we help form it – and Kant's position but maintains the importance of the distinction between "categories fulminated before nature began, and categories gradually forming themselves in nature's presence."[177] Although James's humanism or pragmatism is clearly related to Kant's transcendental idealism, it is, as James points out, more thoroughly empirical. James is not attached to a pre-constituted set of categories but, like Emerson, finds his categories as he finds the material they organize: experimentally.

"A Pluralistic Universe"

James's concern with an intimate but not suffocatingly tight bond between self and world is perhaps most explicit in *A Pluralistic Universe*, which he delivered to overflow audiences at Oxford in the spring of 1908 as the Hibbert lectures entitled "The Present Situation in Philosophy." James begins by attacking the "over-technicality and consequent dreariness of the younger disciples at our American universities," arguing that "it comes from too much following of German models and manners." He expresses the hope that "you will hark back to the more humane English tradition. . . . In a subject like philosophy, it is really fatal to lose connexion with the open air of human nature, and to think in terms of shop-tradition only."[178]

James's pursuit of this more humane and original form of philosophy leads him to classify and evaluate philosophical theories according to the intimacy that they record between self and world. He attacks absolute idealism, with its picture of the universe as "one vast instantaneous coimplicated completeness," because it leaves no room for otherness, autonomy, or spontaneity.[179] Such a view assumes "that the universe has exhausted its spontaneity in one act," whereas there is in the world "genuine individuality, something to *respect* in each thing, something sacred from without, *taboo*."[180] But if monistic idealism is suffocating in its intimacy, materialism offers no intimacy at all. It defines "the world so as to leave man's soul upon it as a sort of outside passenger or alien."

James is an empiricist but not a materialist. He rejects what he takes to be materialism's picture of a world of meaninglessly moving matter. It "sends us to a lonely corner with our intimacy. . . . From a pragmatic point of view the difference between living against a background of foreignness and one of intimacy means the difference between a general habit of wariness and one of trust. . . . If materialistic, we must be suspicious . . . cautious, tense, on guard. If spiritualistic, we may give way, embrace, and keep no ultimate fear."[181]

James embraces what he calls "spiritualism," which "insists that the intimate and human must surround and underlie the brutal."[182] But there are various forms of spiritualism. The dualistic form, common in scholastic philosophy, pictures us as the caretakers of creation but "still leaves the human subject outside of the deepest reality in the universe" by postulating a transcendent God.[183] "The place of the divine in the world," James maintains, "must be more organic and intimate."[184] A seemingly more intimate, monistic form of spiritualism – absolute idealism – claims that we are so intimate with the universe "as to be substantially fused into it."[185] But like Emerson, James criticizes the idealist picture for lacking intimacy. The Absolute is timeless, eternal, whereas "we humans are incurably rooted in the temporal point of view." So a new "bar to intimacy"[186] breaks out in absolute idealism. We are connected to the universe through an Absolute whose existence we are constitutionally unprepared to recognize and that, timeless and static, is alien to us.

Absolute idealism, as James understands it, sacrifices alterity in its search for connection, evading the problem of relationship that it sets out to solve: "The whole question of how 'one' thing can know 'another' would cease to be a real one at all in a world where otherness itself was an illusion."[187] James stresses the alterity and evasiveness of the world we encounter: "Pluralism or the doctrine that [the universe] is many means only that the sundry parts of reality *may be externally related*. Everything you can think of, however vast or inclusive, has on the pluralistic view a genuinely 'external' environment of some sort or amount. Things are 'with' one another in many ways, but nothing includes everything, or dominates over everything. The word 'and' trails along after every sentence. Something always escapes."[188] Even God is an "other," a part of the universe like ourselves.[189] Pluralism allows room for our human and partial intimacies with the universe, rather than denying them in the name of a transcendent union.

It is explicitly on the basis of human experience that James posits "the wider spiritual environment"[190] in which these intimacies occur. Spiritualism is consistent with empiricism.[191] But James distinguishes between "thick" and "thin" treatments of experience, insisting on the validity of his own "thicker and more radical empiricism," which takes as a basic fact that our awareness of relations is as direct and primary as is our awareness of the things they relate.[192] Pluralism stems from a "thicker" basis than does the "materialism" or "intellectualism" that he found (and no doubt would today find) entrenched at Oxford. But it is not so thick or heavy as idealism is, the Absolute of which "drags the whole universe along with itself and drops nothing." By taking our experiences of intimacy seriously but also admitting their partiality, James produces a system without excess baggage, one that "lets things really exist in the each-form."[193] It pictures our relations with the universe not as frozen in a perfect Oneness but, as in a good marriage or a good conversation, "fluent and congruous with [our] own nature's chief demands."[194]

4

JOHN DEWEY

I

"Who was John Dewey?" John McDermott opened the preface to his influential collection *The Philosophy of John Dewey* with that question, and it is still pertinent. McDermott's query expresses an all-too-common puzzlement when faced with the phenomenon of John Dewey: "Despite a staggering output of lectures, articles and books, an incredibly long career of almost a century, an engendering of fascination, controversy, and widespread influence in many areas of human activity, the question is difficult to answer in any depth. No modern philosopher has exerted such influence while being hidden from view."[1] Interestingly, Dewey himself comes to this conclusion in "From Absolutism to Experimentalism," the short autobiography he wrote in 1929. After reviewing his early life and his philosophical career through his "Hegelian" period, he observed:

> I envy, up to a certain point, those who can write their intellectual biography in a unified pattern, woven out of a few distinctly discernible strands of interest and influence. By contrast, I seem to be unstable, chameleon-like, yielding one after another to many diverse and even incompatible influences. . . . Upon the whole, the forces that have influenced me have come from persons and from situations more than from books – not that I have not, I hope, learned a great deal from philosophical writings, but that what I have learned from them has been technical in comparison with what I have been forced to think upon and about because of some experience in which I found myself entangled.[2]

The focus on experience here is quintessentially Deweyan. His philosophy, like that of Emerson and James, is a philosophy of experience, of its riches and possible transformation. Given the chameleonlike aspects that Dewey in particular presents, I shall not claim to discern the "key to Dewey's philosophy" in tracing his Romantic interests. But I do want to claim that his affection for Romantic writers – Keats, Coleridge, Emerson, Rousseau, and others – reveals and characterizes his basic philosophical vision.

Two main themes dominate Dewey's work: reconciliation and reconstruction. Under the former comes his interest in something akin to James's project of uniting empiricism and spiritualism: Dewey thinks of it as reconciling "ideals" and experience. In general, he attacks oppositions that are traditional in Western philosophy: self and world, thought and action, facts and values, feeling and cognition. As for reconstruction, Dewey is an activist philosopher and portrays an active, constructive human animal who knows the world by transforming it. Dewey's emphasis on reconstruction is particularly pronounced in his theory of education (he once defined education as the continual reconstruction of experience)[3] and in his theory of inquiry.

These twin themes of reconciliation and reconstruction connect Dewey to the Romantics, who, as we saw in Chapter 1, are concerned with connecting self and world, feeling and thought, and the natural and the supernatural or spiritual. They also are concerned with the transformation of the world, with its redemption, as in Wordsworth, Coleridge, and Emerson, and specifically with the power of humanity to bring about that redemption. Romantics stress what Bloom calls "the constructive power of the mind"; they seek "an act of discovery that is also a making."[4] These are exactly Dewey's concerns. Dewey's philosophy is a culmination of the Romantic movement toward the imaginative transformation of the world, a movement including Coleridge's and Emerson's actively transformative will, as well as James's pragmatic "making of truth."

My discussion is divided into three main parts, corresponding to Dewey's early, middle, and late writings. In the first, I stress his development of a natural supernaturalism, a reconciliation of the claims of science, poetry, and religion, paying particular attention to the influence of Coleridge, Hegel, and Browning on his thinking. In the second part, I examine the reconstructive and reconciling aspects of the mature philosophy that Dewey developed in the first three decades of this century, particularly the sense in which Dewey remains an idealist and also the respects in which he, like James, incorporates a strong element of realism into his idealism. Dewey's favorable evaluation of Emerson – whom he called "the one citizen of the New World fit to have his name uttered in the same breath with that of Plato"[5] – falls into place here. Finally, the third part considers Dewey's late and comprehensive work, *Art as Experience,* in which he plumbs artistic experience for its use in transforming human experience generally and in which his commitment to such Romantic writers as Keats and Coleridge is prominent. In *Art as Experience,* the "ideals" that the young Dewey found in the thought of Coleridge and Hegel become possibilities for poetically inspired human construction.

Dewey complained in his autobiography that although "*Democracy and Education* was for many years [the book] in which my philosophy, such as it is, was most fully expounded, I do not know that philosophic critics, as distinct from teachers, have ever had recourse to it."[6] I incorporate Dewey's educational views in my discussion, showing their role in achieving the distinctive Romantic goal of a vitalized and deepened experience, an extraordinary ordinary.

Reading Dewey's works presents problems unlike those encountered in reading Emerson's or James's. Dewey wrote volumes – those who lived with and near him testify to the almost continuous clacking of his old typewriter – but he did not have the natural facility with language that James or Russell did (the latter, for example, wrote his very readable *Our Knowledge of the External World* en route from England to America, where he delivered it as the Lowell lectures), nor did he spend time revising and polishing his work. Dewey is addicted to the passive voice and favors ponderous sentences. Whereas James was famous for his electrifying performances, students testify to Dewey's boring lectures and tell stories of those whom he put to sleep.[7] "Yes, you had to take notes to keep awake," Ernest Nagel reminisced. But what notes they were. As Herbert Schneider, another of Dewey's pupils pointed out: "If we stayed awake enough to take notes, the notes that we got were wonderful to read."[8] Dewey had ideas, whose force becomes apparent with reflection.

Dewey's life and thought had an unpretentious integrity, a force and soundness that are impressive still. And there are times, for example, in his essay on Emerson or in parts of *Art as Experience,* when an eloquent and passionate Dewey speaks out. In "The American Scholar," Emerson wrote that "as the seer's hour of vision is short and rare among heavy days and months, so is its record, perchance, the least part of his volume. The discerning will read, in his Plato or Shakespeare, only that least part, – only the authentic utterances of the oracle."[9] It is these parts of Dewey for which we shall search.

II. DEWEY'S EARLY PHILOSOPHY

The critical literature presents numerous interpretations of Dewey. The excellent study by Sleeper highlights the importance of the logical and metaphysical strands of Dewey's thinking; those by Coughlan and Kuklick highlight his religious orientations.[10] Older commentaries treat Dewey as a theorist of inquiry, as a "philosopher of science and freedom" (to use the title of a classic collection by Sidney Hook). Whether one examines Dewey's religious or his naturalistic outlook, it becomes apparent how much each is involved in the other, that Dewey's naturalism has a religious coloring, and his religion a naturalistic orientation. Kuklick notes, for example, Dewey's attack on "traditional supernaturalism" in *A Common Faith* and rightly concludes that "Dewey's religious attitude conceived of humanity in a world that was the locus and support of its aspiration."[11] My claim is that although Dewey rejected "traditional supernaturalism" because it placed ideals apart from human experience and control, he accepted the natural and humanized supernaturalism of the Romantics. Dewey was raised in a religious home. Until he was well into his thirties, he was a churchgoer, Sunday school teacher, and writer for religiously oriented journals such as the *Andover Review*. But his tendencies were toward rationalizing and naturalizing religion, and in this he was guided by thinkers in the Romantic wing of the Kantian tradition, from Samuel Taylor Coleridge to the English Hegelian Thomas Hill Green.

Coleridge and Marsh

There is little information on Dewey's earliest years. Although his friends found it difficult to get Dewey to reminisce, on one occasion, a birthday dinner, he was given a copy of James Marsh's edition of Coleridge's *Aids to Reflection* (Marsh had been the president of the University of Vermont, and his edition of Coleridge's book was an important influence on the Transcendentalists).[12] When asked what memories the book evoked, Dewey, as his friend and student Herbert Schneider tells it,

> opened up, and said, "Yes, I remember very well that this was our spiritual emancipation in Vermont. Coleridge's idea of the spirit came to us as a real relief, because we could be both liberal and pious; and this *Aids to Reflection* book, especially Marsh's edition, was my first Bible." . . . And then we said, "Well, when did you get over Coleridge?" He said, "I never did. Coleridge represents pretty much my religious views still, but I quit talking about them because nobody else is interested in them."[13]

What did Dewey see in Marsh and Coleridge? Fortunately, we have Dewey's own backward-looking testimony on the matter, in an article entitled "James Marsh and American Philosophy," published in the *Journal of the History of Ideas* in 1941. Marsh, Dewey wrote, was not interested in "the fate or the spread of a particular philosophical system" but in the "re-awakening of a truly spiritual religion which had been obscured and depressed under the influence of the prevalent philosophies of John Locke and the Scottish school."[14] This nondogmatic, indeed nondoctrinal interpretation of religion was what Dewey meant by a "liberal" one.

Although *Aids to Reflection* is a late work of Coleridge, one in which –

in contrast with his earlier writing – he argues for the inherent rationality of the Christian religion, Dewey depicts Coleridge as a radical wanting to replace the existing hollow or dead ways of worship with something entirely different, more vital:

> The more obvious phase of the radicalism of Coleridge in religion is found in his attack on what he called its Bibliolatry. He condemned the doctrine of literal inspiration as a superstition; he urged the acceptance of the teachings of Scripture on the ground that they "find" one in the deepest and most spiritual part of one's nature. Faith was a state of the will and the affections, not a merely intellectual assent to doctrinal and historical propositions."[15]

This "finding," analogous to many religious states that James described in *Varieties of Religious Experience,* is, as he noted, a variety of religious experience. The experiential side of Coleridge that Dewey finds appealing comes, in Coleridge's phrase, as "a state of the will and the affections" rather than as an allegiance to doctrines. Scripture's importance, he reads Coleridge as meaning, is not in the history of its production but in the inspiration it provides to human experience. (This outlook is close to Emerson's doctrines in "The American Scholar" and "The Divinity School Address.") Dewey's focus on a "truly spiritual religion," a religion of experience, is compatible with his constant emphasis on the reconstructive possibilities of human life. For such a religion, being in part "a state of the will," is not just something passively perceived but something that we human beings have the power to develop.

Dewey calls Marsh a "Romantic philosopher" and defends the positive rather than the pejorative sense of the term[16] by noting that for Marsh it did not connote an opposition to realism but, rather, the modern spirit as against the classic. Dewey sees (what our examination of Wordsworth, Emerson, and James has shown) that a Romantic may be a realist. Indeed, he speaks of the "Aristotelianism" of Marsh's position. (Sleeper stresses the strong Aristotelian or realist streak in Dewey's writing.)[17] Although Marsh embraced the Kantian framework of sense, understanding, and rational will, "he did not isolate this ascending series . . . from the natural universe as did Kant, but rather saw in it a progressive realization of the conditions and potentialities found in nature itself."[18] Dewey is in some respects a Kantian,[19] but he consistently portrays Kant as the enemy of reconciliation between self and world, ideals and facts, and, for that reason, rejects his philosophy.

It is remarkable how many traits of his own philosophy Dewey sees in Marsh. Aside from his "Aristotelian" realism, Dewey finds also a kind of pragmatism or instrumentalism in Marsh, similar to Dewey's own: Marsh "held that reason can realize itself and be truly aware or conscious of its own intrinsic nature only as it operates to make over the world, whether physical or social, into an embodiment of its own principles."[20] This "making over the world" – a Kantian, then a post-Kantian and Romantic notion (as in Coleridge's discussion of the transformative will) – becomes fully naturalized and humanized in Dewey's ideas of inquiry as intelligent interaction, of education as transformation, and of "reconstruction in philosophy."

Hegel

Hegel was another important influence on Dewey. He was not for Dewey the suffocating dogmatist that he was for James but, rather, a scientist and a religious philosopher at the same time, a breath of fresh air in the empiricist chamber. While studying Hegel at Johns Hopkins University under George Sylvester Morris, Dewey found what he calls an "immense release." He had been oppressed by a "sense of divisions and separations . . . of self from the world, of soul from body, of nature from God." In Hegel and his disciples, Dewey found "the . . . dissolution of hard-and-fast dividing walls," an intellectual solution to "an intense emotional craving."[21] Hegel was a great reconciler for Dewey, an empiricist who admitted into his system not just a reductionistic domain of ideas but a full range of experience from sensation to scientific law, from the culture of Greece and Rome to the French Revolution.

By understanding Hegel to be an empiricist, Dewey was able to minimize the tension between the approaches of his two most significant teachers at Hopkins, Morris and the psychologist G. Stanley Hall. Dewey wrote as an Hegelian – in what was the lingua franca for expressing spiritual principles to a secular world of university professionals[22] – but he nevertheless thought of himself as a scientist. When Dewey came to teach at the University of Michigan in 1884, it was as an exponent of the new empirical methods being taught at Johns Hopkins. But although he came as an empiricist, he saw no conflict between science and what he called "ideals." Coughlan describes him as a "theistic idealist" with an "empiricist bent."[23] (One could say that he later became an experimentalist with an idealist bent or that he always remained both.) Dewey eventually gave up the Hegelian terminology that he used in the 1880s and 1890s, but he never gave up being both an idealist and an empiricist.

A representative sample of Dewey's Hegelian period is the paper "The Philosophy of Thomas Hill Green," published in the *Andover Review* in 1889. Green was an Oxford professor and the foremost living exponent of an Hegelian system, whom Dewey praises as "a prophet" for trying to "reconcile science and religion."[24] Green maintained that science is not erroneous but that it presupposes an ideal or spiritual principle. When criticizing the isolated skepticism of the British empirical tradition from

Locke through Hume, he argues, for example (as Kant had), that empirical experience requires relations.[25] But according to Dewey, Green possesses just that virtue that James finds him not at all to have: a sense of otherness. Rather than "bare identity and absorption," there are "two sides" to every relation, each side being "an object to itself."[26]

Dewey never ceased to be an idealist. He was, of course, never a Berkelian idealist, as his desire for integration was against the isolated spirits and ideas that Berkeley pictured. But he found in Hegelian idealism an intellectual position that made sense of his feeling for reconciliation, especially between the spiritual and the experiential. Although he valued idealism for its sense that experience embodies "ideals," he came to find its method of proving that the world is ideal an escape from the real task of making it more so. Moreover, Dewey was never attracted to Hegel's (or anyone else's) idea of an all-encompassing Absolute inherent in the nature of the universe.

Yet as commentators have frequently noted, there are many traces of Hegel even in Dewey's later writings. He remains, like Hegel, a process philosopher and one who integrates contrary features of experience in an ongoing drama with – potentially at least – a progressive movement. That movement in Hegel is powered by negation, a "restlessness [of] the ground of Being" that Arendt traces to the Will, the "organ for the future." In Dewey, that movement is one of growth and reconstruction. Hegel wrote that "time finds its truth in the future since it is the future that will furnish and accomplish Being." Truth lies ahead of us, not behind in some preestablished, complete Being; it must be worked up, "accomplished."[27]

This essentially constructive side of Hegel (as well a similar orientation in James) lies behind Dewey's theory that the significance of our "ideas at work" lies in their various outcomes and his general emphasis on intelligent and imaginative reconstruction. Hegel saw spirit – what Dewey called "ideals" – as not a given but an outcome. But Hegel saw it as a necessary outcome, whereas Dewey takes it to be contingent, the product of an intelligent, imaginative, impassioned, and active human animal.

Poetry and Philosophy

For many Romantic writers, philosophy and poetry are closely allied. Coleridge thought of himself as neither a poet nor a philosopher but as a combination, a "Poet-philosopher." Novalis wrote that "the separation of poet and thinker is only apparent – and to the disadvantage of both," and Friedrich Schlegel held that "poetry and philosophy should be made one."[28] As we have seen, Cavell defines Romanticism itself as "the redemption of philosophy and poetry by one another."[29] Dewey's

concern with the affinity of these often-opposed practices is evident
throughout his career; in his 1903 essay on Emerson, in his climactic
vision of 1935, *Art as Experience,* and in his 1890 paper "Poetry and Philosophy," to which we shall now turn.[30]

"Poetry and Philosophy" begins with a paragraph from Matthew Arnold's introduction to *The English Poets,* in which Arnold observes that
poetry is a consolation in an age of shaken creeds and questionable dogmas. In this scientific age, Arnold maintains, we believe in facts, but the
facts do not inspire us: "Our religion . . . has attached its emotion to the
fact, and now the fact is failing it." Arnold views poetry as providing a
refuge from this unpleasant situation: "We have to turn to poetry to
interpret life for us, to console us, to sustain us." Poetry does not have
to be true. Rather, poetic ideas take the place of facts, so that for poetry
"the idea *is* the fact."[31]

Dewey's belief in the spiritual possibilities of the natural (including the
human) world means that for him the facts do or can inspire, that the
natural or factual world itself provides the refuge Arnold seeks. Dewey
immediately questions Arnold's position, then, wondering whether in
spite of "the clear insight of this great critic . . . his insight was essentially limited in range." His main attack on Arnold's theory of poetry
concerns Arnold's separation of poetry from truth: understanding
"truth" not just honorifically but as connoting the incorporation of scientific with logical and philosophical truth. "How can poetry preserve
its genuineness and its sustaining force, if it cut loose from all verifiable
account of the universe? . . . I confess I do not understand how that can
be true for the imagination, for the emotions, which is not also true
for intelligence." Poetry requires feeling, Dewey is saying – its "true
province" is "the emotional kindling of reality" – but it is directed toward, as well as springing from, reality as revealed through human experience, including science. If poetry loses the "belief in the meaning and
worthiness of experience," it becomes nothing but "the tricking out of
illusions, the devising of artifices."[32] Poetry, as Dewey sees it, cannot be
separate from daily life; it is not "transcendental" but, rather, this-
worldly: "the life which the poet presents to us as throbbing, as preg-
nant, ever new from God, is . . . the genuine revelation of the ordinary
day-by-day life of man."[33] Dewey here embraces the key Romantic idea
of a spiritualized commonplace, achieved by or in poetry.

If the poet is in touch with his world, Dewey continues, he will be
influenced by current ideas and theories, drawing "his sustenance from
the intelligence of his time." Contemporary poets then would, Dewey
reasons, have to confront what he politely (if one contrasts Nietzsche's
thundering announcement of the death of God) calls "our agnosticism."
It is for "their attitude toward the agnosticism, the doubt, the pessimism,

of the present day" that Dewey considers the poetry of two then recently deceased poets – Robert Browning and Matthew Arnold.

Dewey observes that Arnold the poet incorporates Arnold the critic: "Translated from the impersonal narrative of prose into the warmth of poetry it is the same lesson" – a sense of loss, a "sad backward glance at the departure of old faiths and ideals . . . the shapeless, hopeless hope for the dawn of a new joy, new faith."[34] For Arnold, all we can do is to make the best of conditions that we cannot alter; poetry may be of help in accommodating, or deadening, us to our condition. Dewey does not see how what Arnold admits is an illusion can be a comfort, how it can satisfy us when it conflicts with something else – the theories of the world for which we have empirical support and in which we deeply believe. A poet, Dewey believes, can succeed only when he has the facts on his side: "I cannot rid myself of the conviction that the weight and the humanity of the message of the poet are proportionate to the weighty and human ideas which he develops; that these ideas must be capable of verification to the intelligence, – must be true in that system of knowledge which is science, in that discussion of the meaning of experience which is philosophy."[35]

Dewey could have gone on to say that the world is as empty of meaning as Arnold claims and that neither poetry nor philosophy nor anything else can replace our losses. This would have brought him roughly to the position of Camus's Meursault in *The Stranger,* or Sartre's Roquentin in *Nausea.* But this is not at all the direction that Dewey takes. He suggests instead that Arnold has his facts wrong, or at least incomplete: "What if Mr. Arnold's interpretation of life be partial? What if a completer account of experience, a deeper and more adventurous love of wisdom, should find community below all isolation? . . . This is the question that comes to me when I put Mr. Arnold's poetry, with all its nobility, beside the poetry of Robert Browning."[36]

Dewey responds to the "warmth" of Browning, as contrasted with Arnold's cold serenity, to his "triumphant hope," and to his joyful embracing of the world. His joy and hope rest on the same reconciliation that attracted Dewey to Hegel: the fact that "Browning knows and tells of no isolation of man from nature, of man from man." According to this view, we do not look to nature for help in bearing the world's burden (as if the world confirms us in our sufferings) but, rather, for a "response" to our "aspiration[s]."[37]

Given that Dewey is attracted to Browning's picture, does he simply assume that it is true? His position is not quite so simple. He emphatically questions the truth of Browning's vision, asking whether his ideas are just the "sporadic outbursts of a fancy which has no root in the nature of things" or, rather, whether they are "the revelations of an imagination

which is but another name for insight." The thrust of the remarks with
which Dewey closes "Poetry and Philosophy" is that Browning's poems
are in some sense true and that philosophy must capture and systematize
"retrospectively" what the poet "flashes home" to us more or less spo-
radically. But Dewey does not really offer any proof, only a picture of
our cultural situation. Part of that picture is his basic position – expressed
earlier in the essay – that if poetry does have any hold on us it is "just
because of the truth, the rendering of the reality of affairs, which poetry
gives us." He claims more specifically that poetry – particularly Romantic poetry – captures something about reality that modern philosophy
has missed:

> In the last few centuries the onward movement of life, of experience,
> has been so rapid, its diversification of regions and methods so wide,
> that it has outrun the slower step of reflective thought. Philosophy has
> not as yet caught the rhythmic swing of this onward movement. . . .
> The deeper and wider spiritual life which makes this movement has
> found an expression in Wordsworth and Shelley, in Browning and in
> Mr. Arnold himself, which has, as yet, been denied to it in English
> philosophy. That which seemed to Mr. Arnold a flight from philoso-
> phy into poetry was in reality but a flight from a hard and partial philos-
> ophy to a fuller and freer one. It is not because poetry is divorced from
> science that it gave Mr. Arnold's nature such satisfaction, but because
> his philosophic instinct was so deep and real that he revolted from the
> professional philosophy of the day as he found it in Great Britain, and
> sought refuge in the unnamed, unprofessed philosophy of the great po-
> ets of England and of all time.[38]

Dewey rebelled in many ways and for many reasons against the British
empirical tradition; clearly part of that rebellion was a Romantic one.
Dewey searched for a "fuller and freer," a more spiritual and poetic philosophy than traditional empiricism and "professional philosophy" had
been able to achieve. Dewey did not reject philosophy or empiricism;
instead, as he later explained, he wanted to "reconstruct" them. His notion of poetry, like his notions of philosophy, inquiry, logic, or religious
experience, is an essentially constructive one, part of his project – which
achieved its climax with the publication of *Art as Experience* more than
forty years later – of widening and deepening human experience.

Education
Wordsworth portrayed the child as the "best Philosopher . . .
On whom truths do rest, / Which we are toiling all our lives to find."[39]
Emerson spoke of the autonomy, wisdom, and freedom of children:
"Their mind being whole, their eye is as yet unconquered, and when we
look in their faces we are disconcerted. Infancy conforms to nobody; all
conform to it; so that one babe commonly makes four or five out of the

adults who prattle and play to it."[40] As depicted by Romantic writers, children have something adults do not: a self-reliant interest in and enthusiasm for the world. The child, "glorious in the might / Of heaven-born freedom," soon however succumbs to "the inevitable yoke" of maturity:

> Full soon thy Soul shall have her earthly freight
> And custom lie upon thee with a weight,
> Heavy as frost, and deep almost as life![41]

Wordsworth dedicated his poetry to "making the incidents of common life interesting." This call for a union of the ordinary and the interesting implies, as Cavell puts it, that "the common world, the world common to us, is as it stands of no interest to us, that it is no longer ours, that we are as if bored quite to death, and that poetry has nominated itself to bring us back from this 'torpor'."[42] Dewey writes from this Romantic perspective in his work on education. He respects the child for his or her integrity and original wisdom, and he tries to employ the child's spontaneous powers rather than weighing down him or her with an externally imposed "yoke." His goal, like Wordsworth's, is to recover, or preserve, the child's "interest" in the world.

In a paper entitled "Interest in Relation to Training of the Will," published in 1896, Dewey writes that when things "have to be *made* interesting it is because interest itself is wanting." He criticizes the "split consciousness" that results when interest is not developed or satisfied: The child will follow his or her own interest internally while outwardly manifesting compliance with the school's externally imposed dictates. In anticipation of the worldwide television habit, Dewey writes of a situation in which children (i.e., people) enjoy (for it is a kind of pleasure) a condition of passive receptivity, an "isolated" form of pleasure that "arises from external stimulation." This type of pleasure, Dewey asserts, comes into play when objects are "*made* interesting." In such environments the child "alternates between periods of over-stimulation and of inertness. It is a condition realized in some so-called kindergartens. . . . Some kindergarten children are as dependent upon the recurrent presence of bright colors or agreeable sounds as the drunkard is upon his dram. It is this which accounts for the distraction and dissipation of energy so characteristic of such children, and for their dependence upon external suggestion."[43]

Interest then is crucial to education if one wants to avoid the condition of split and "drunk" consciousness that Dewey describes. The child's own concerns must be respected, if for no other reason than that "the spontaneous power of the child, his demand for self-expression, can not by any possibility be suppressed."[44] In fact, self-expression is the ground of Dewey's injunctions concerning interest. We become ourselves by fol-

lowing our interests. "Self-expression in which the psychical energy as-
similates material because of the recognized value of this material in aid-
ing the self to reach its end, does not find it necessary to oppose interest
to effort."[45] Such self-expression is encouraged by what Dewey calls a
"moral" "training of will," but the morally trained will is far from the
"willed effort" common in schools' efforts to "make things interesting."
Such an externally generated interest is to be rejected, and self-expressive
and self-motivated effort is to take its place

> because the object lies outside the sphere of self . . . the sheer power of
> "will," the putting forth of effort without interest, has to be appealed
> to. . . . But as a matter of fact, the moral exercise of the will is not
> found in the external assumption of any posture, and the formation of
> moral habit cannot be identified with the ability to show up results at
> the demand of another. The exercise of the will is manifest in the direc-
> tion of attention, and depends upon the spirit, the motive, the disposi-
> tion in which work is carried on.[46]

Dewey's later "instrumentalism" and pragmatism are presaged in his
emphasis here on interest as active. As he puts it, when contrasting the
passive, distracted sort of pleasure with the active enjoyment of interest,
"we take interest; we get pleasure."[47] Interest, he tells us, is "active,
projective, or propulsive. We take interest. . . . The mere feeling regarding a subject may be static or inert, but interest is dynamic." The dyna-
mism of interest means that when we take interest we take action too;
in this sense our interest in something is a reconstruction or working
over of it. Interest is both subjective and objective: "We say a man has
many interests to care for or look after. . . . Interest does not end simply
in itself as bare feelings may, but always has some object, end, or aim
to which it attaches itself." But interest is also "subjective; it signifies an
internal realization, or feeling, of worth. It has its emotional, as well as
its active and objective sides. Wherever there is interest there is response
in the way of feeling."[48] Dewey opposes the "bare feeling" of passive
pleasure to true interest, which is active, but he does not eliminate feeling
from interest. Interest is a feeling that reaches outward. The activity to
which interest leads and in which it is manifest thus reconciles self and
world. If objects have to be made interesting, Dewey maintains, then a
"divorce between object and self" is being expressed. But our genuinely
interested actions place us in and with the world which we help form:
"genuine interest in education is the accompaniment of the identification,
through action, of the self with some object or idea, because of the necessity of that object or idea for the maintenance of self expression."[49] Interest therefore "marks the annihilation of the distance between subject and
object; it is the instrument which effects their organic union."[50]

In "Interest in Relation to the Training of the Will," Dewey stresses the connections to the world that interest encourages and produces, and in "My Pedagogic Creed," published a year later, in 1897, he explores the many different "objects" with which interest may connect us. These include not just material objects but the entire "funded capital of civilization."[51] Education is not to be separated from the life it learns about: It is "a process of living and not a preparation for future living . . . that education which does not occur through forms of life, forms that are worth living for their own sake, is always a poor substitute for the genuine reality, and tends to cramp and to deaden."[52] If the Romantics find the experience of the adult to be a dead and restricted one, then Dewey is saying that society should counter in its schools such forms of being-in-the-world.

The forms of life that Dewey stresses, such as gardening or sewing, are physical, because he believes that muscular development must precede sensory and intellectual development. Consciousness "is essentially motor or impulsive." However, Dewey recognizes that movement of the wrong sort can be just as routinized and deadening as is confinement to a fixed table and chair. The key to a child's (or an adult's) development lies in his or her interests. Find these, nurture them, and the development will follow: Interests "are the signs and symptoms of growing power. I believe that they represent dawning capacities. Accordingly the constant and careful observation of interests is of the utmost importance for the educator."[53] But – in contrast with the position of some of his followers, and with the position attributed to Dewey by some of his detractors – Dewey clearly warns against humoring interest. Interest encourages "intellectual curiosity and alertness" and "initiative," but if an educator is guided only by interest, he or she will substitute "the transient for the permanent. The interest is always the sign of some power below; the important thing is to discover this power. To humor the interest is to fail to penetrate below the surface, and its sure result is to substitute caprice and whim for genuine interest . . . next to deadness and dullness, formalism and routine, our education is threatened with no greater evil than sentimentalism."[54] Dewey's theory thus requires great attention on the part of the teacher, who must provide each child with those cultural influences that will accord with the child's budding interests. Then those interests will lead to the continuing reconstruction of experience that is education.

III. DEWEY'S MATURE PHILOSOPHY
In "The Copernican Revolution," the concluding chapter to his 1929 lectures published as *The Quest for Certainty*, Dewey distinguishes three forms of idealism. The first, plainly the Hegelian variety, idealizes the world "through purely intellectual and logical processes, in which

reasoning alone attempts to prove that the world has characters that satisfy our highest aspirations." The second is based on experience, on
"moments of intense emotional appreciation when, through a happy
conjunction of the state of the self and of the surrounding world, the
beauty and harmony of existence is disclosed in experiences which are
the immediate consummation of all for which we long." This is a remark
about the experiential territory James explores in *Varieties,* about Emerson's walk in the "blithe air," Whitman's bus ride, Wordsworth's universe "apparelled in celestial light." Dewey finds this way of idealizing
the world "while it lasts . . . the most engaging. It sets the measure of
our ideas of possibilities that are to be realized by intelligent endeavor."
But such consummate experiences are impermanent, so that we require
a third form of idealism, one that through intelligent effort seeks the
secure instantiation "of the values that are enjoyed by grace in our happy
moments."[55]

Dewey makes clear the important role the emotions play in the latter
two forms of idealism, and in doing so, he enunciates the thesis maintained by Wordsworth, Coleridge, Emerson, and James, that we understand the world as much by feeling as by thought. "Our affections, when
they are enlightened by understanding, are organs by which we enter
into the meaning of the natural world." But – and here he speaks of the
third form of idealism, the one that "gets results" – this "deeper and
richer intercourse with things can be effected only by thought and its
resultant knowledge."[56] This deeper and richer intercourse is what
Dewey both seeks and claims to find through his philosophical analyses
of experience and nature.

According to Dewey, "nature is capable of giving birth to objects that
stay with us as ideal. . . . Nature . . . lends itself to operations by which
it is perfected."[57] Into the naturalistic and instrumentalist philosophy he
developed during the first three decades of this century, Dewey incorporates this third form of idealism. He shows ideal objects to be a part of
nature, that is, how the secular and sacred (as well as many other oppositions) can be reconciled. And he attempts to identify in his wide-ranging
discussions of philosophy, science, art, and education those operations
that our active human intelligence can seize on in perfecting and reconstructing the world.

Emerson
Although Dewey's allegiance to Hegelian terminology (as well
as to orthodox Christianity) faded in the 1890s, his respect for another
Romantic idealist – Ralph Waldo Emerson – did not. This accords with
the threefold scheme just discussed, for Dewey correctly reads Emerson
as a representative of the second (experiential) and third (constructive)

idealism rather than – like Hegel – a representative of the first (artificial and abstract) form. Dewey was forty-four in 1903 when he delivered his talk on Emerson at the ceremonies honoring the centenary of Emerson's birth. Dewey's spirited defense of the claim that Emerson is America's greatest philosopher came during the beginning of his philosophical maturity, during the time he was composing the *Studies in Logical Theory* and other works about logic and inquiry that set the course for his "pragmatism." The essay on Emerson is a revelation of Dewey's expository talents and a guide to his overall project of achieving a vitalized ordinary experience of the world.

Dewey singles out two strands of what he calls Emerson's idealism. The first is the reconstructive power of thought, what Dewey later termed intelligence, to transform the world: "His idealism is the faith of the thinker in his thought raised to its nth power. 'History,' he says, 'and the state of the world at any one time is directly dependent on the intellectual classification then existing in the minds of men.' . . . There are times, indeed, when one is inclined to regard Emerson's whole work as a hymn to intelligence, a paean to the all-creating, all-disturbing power of thought."[58] Dewey's career equally expresses this faith. In *The Necessity of Pragmatism,* Sleeper shows that Dewey maintained that both our logic and our ontology are provisional, made to suit our purposes in interacting with the world, so that "ontology . . . becomes a provisional and transactional affair."[59] Dewey preserves the realistic sense that we have to deal with, and to some degree fit, a world independent of us, but he also stresses (as befits his Kantian and Emersonian inheritance) the many ways in which the world with which we grapple is our own construction. Dewey tries to persuade human beings to assume the responsibility appropriate to this condition.

The second strand of idealism that Dewey discerns in Emerson is his construing of ideal or spiritual matters as affairs of human experience. This acts as a corrective to what could be a misreading of Dewey's and Emerson's emphasis on the role that thought or intelligence plays in forming (our account of) the world, for it might seem as if Dewey is preserving the "thought – content" split that is traditional in Western philosophy, maintaining that thought overrides or determines content. Dewey rightly credits Emerson with making radiant intelligence not "apart thought" but concrete human experience: "He takes the distinctions and classifications which to most philosophers are true in and of and because of their systems, and makes them true of life, of the common experience of the everyday man." When Dewey calls Emerson an idealist, he means that Emerson holds "ideas" – philosophical, spiritual, poetic – to be essentially experiential, not deriving from, mirroring, or imposed by something "apart" from human life. According to Dewey, then, the "idealism which is a thing of the academic intellect to the professor . . . is to Emerson a narrowly accurate description of the facts of the most real world in which all earn their living."[60] Like the Hegel that he depicted in 1885, the Emerson that Dewey depicts in 1903 reconciles the empirical and the ideal.

In accordance with his notion of a concrete or realistic idealism, Dewey denies that Emerson is a transcendentalist. Rather, Emerson's ideas "are not fixed upon any Reality that is beyond or behind or in any way apart. . . . The reputed transcendental worth of an overweening Beyond and Away, Emerson, jealous for spiritual democracy, finds to be the possession of the unquestionable present."[61] Dewey's naturalism stands out even in the midst of his defense of ideals.

In contrast with James and anticipating Cavell, Dewey defends the claim that Emerson is a philosopher. "I am not acquainted with any writer, no matter how assured his position in treatises upon the history of philosophy, whose movement of thought is more compact and unified." If critics complain that Emerson has no logic, this simply reveals their "incapacity to follow a logic that is finely wrought."[62] Still, Emerson is above all for Dewey a philosopher of experience, for whom "perception was more potent than reasoning; the deliverances of intercourse more to be desired than the claims of discourse; the surprise of reception more demonstrative than the conclusions of intentional proof."

As in "Poetry and Philosophy" thirteen years earlier, Dewey defends the poet's claim to truth in his Emerson essay. Indeed, Dewey shies away even from the claim that philosophers and poets have "some distinction of accent in thought and of rhythm in speech."[63] Suggesting that the philosopher analyzes rather than uncovers, classifies rather than discerns, "reads, but does not compose," he immediately reconsiders: "One, however, has no sooner drawn such lines than one is ashamed and begins to retract. Euripides and Plato, Dante and Bruno, Bacon and Milton, Spinoza and Goethe, rise in rebuke. The spirit of Emerson rises to protest against exaggerating his ultimate value by trying to place him upon a plane of art higher than a philosophic platform." Emerson, like Plato, is a thinker and an artist, a writer who thinks but who also feels the world: "It is no more possible to eliminate love and generation from the definition of the thinker than it is thought and limits from the conception of the artist. It is interest, concern, caring, which makes the one as it makes the other. It is significant irony that the old quarrel of philosopher and poet was brought off by one who united in himself more than has another individual the qualities of both artist and metaphysician."[64] (In reading Dewey, it is helpful to take seriously the Heideggerian resonances of such expressions as "caring" and "thinking."[65] At his best, Dewey emerges as a cracker-barrel Heidegger: deep, but without the pretensions.)

Dewey insists that Emerson is a philosopher and a great one, the one American fit to be ranked with Plato. After William James's death in 1910, Dewey admitted him to the American philosophical pantheon, but his place of honor was alongside Emerson:

> America will justify herself as long as she breeds those like William James; men who are thinkers and thinkers who are men. I love, indeed, to think that there is something profoundly American in his union of philosophy with life; in his honest acceptance of the facts of science joined to a hopeful outlook upon the future; in his courageous faith in our ability to shape the unknown future. When our country comes to itself in consciousness, when it transmutes into articulate ideas what are still obscure and blind strivings, two men, Emerson and William James, will, I think, stand out as the prophetic forerunners of the attained creed of values.[66]

Dewey's picture of James as a man whose thinking is part of his life is profoundly Emersonian (cf. "The American Scholar"), and his description of the thinker as one who accepts the facts of science while confident in our ability to shape the unknown future fits Dewey himself at least as well as it does James.

Dewey was a theorist of inquiry, modifying and expanding the "doubt–belief" theory he inherited from Peirce.[67] He was a metaphysician who characterized the world as a mixture of tight completenesses and loose uncertainties. He was a reformer in education and politics. But his career also continues the Romantic project of naturalizing supernaturalism, a project for which the term "natural supernaturalism" was coined by Emerson's great friend Thomas Carlyle. Dewey remained an Emersonian idealist throughout his life, believing that the ideal, or spiritual, or "supernatural" is natural, part of the natural world that we help shape.

Survey of Empiricisms

All the Romantic writers we have examined were committed to experience as the basic source of knowledge, but they criticized traditional empiricism for its impoverished idea of experience. Dewey makes a major contribution to thinking about empiricism in his gradually evolving survey of kinds of empiricism and in his attempts to develop a new experimental and imaginatively reconstructive philosophy.

Democracy and Education contains an important early statement of Dewey's approach in which he reviews and criticizes previous empiricisms, beginning with Greek forms. For Plato, "experience meant habituation, or the conservation of the net produce of a lot of past chance trials." Plato and Aristotle had respect for the more or less dependable, trial-and-error knowledge of the craftsperson but compared it unfavorably with the insight into the nature of things provided by theoretical sciences like geometry, which consist of necessary and universal truths. There is a revolutionary cast to Greek rationalism as Dewey portrays it: "Devotion to the cause of reason meant breaking through the limitations of custom and getting at things as they really were."[68]

Dewey sees a second doctrine about experience emerging in seventeenth- and eighteenth-century Europe. Experience now plays the role played by reason in Greek philosophy; it cuts through the old customs and received doctrines to the very nature of things: "Appeal to experience marked the breach with authority. It meant openness to new impressions; eagerness in discovery and invention instead of absorption in tabulating and systematizing received ideas."[69]

These quotations show that Dewey has a good deal of sympathy even for the views of those philosophers, such as Plato and Locke, with whom he fundamentally disagrees. Indeed, Dewey uses Plato to criticize Lockean sensationalism when he contrasts the passivity of the Lockean mind, a blank tablet on which sensation is imprinted, with the "practical meaning" that experience "had borne from the time of Plato." Plato may have devalued experience, but he prefigured Dewey's own activist and reconstructive account (as Dewey tells the tale) in regarding experience as "ways of doing and being done to."[70]

Dewey attacks Lockean empiricism not only for its passive picture of experience but also for its separation of the mind from the rest of nature. In this way sensationalistic empiricism becomes for Dewey a "perversion" of the democratic and libertarian social movement that spawned it, for people wanted not "isolation from the world, but a more intimate connection with it."[71]

Dewey discusses these two basic conceptions of experience, the Greek and the sensationalistic, in greater detail in a 1935 paper entitled "An Empirical Survey of Empiricisms." Here he stresses the "dissolvent," skeptical side of eighteenth-century empiricism and the evident need "for a new type of philosophy," to which the "rationalistic and spiritualistic" Kantian and post-Kantian philosophies were a reaction. Dewey expresses respect for the impulse behind "the whole romantic and neo-romantic period of German philosophy," which begins with Kant, while rejecting the nonempirical method (among other things) of its major practitioners. Among empiricists he singles out Mill as someone who "through the direct influence especially of Coleridge and Wordsworth . . . felt the defects of historical empiricism and the need of something that would give a more stable, constructive ground for belief and conduct."[72] However, Mill did not provide this new form of empiricism.

The "third view of experience" that Dewey discerns "is still more or less inchoate, because it is still in process of development." But Dewey does characterize it by saying that it takes a "biological" approach, according to which "sensations are part of the mechanisms of behavior." And he contrasts it with the older empiricism that tested ideas by tracing them back to sensations; the new emerging empiricism looks forward to results. The older empiricism had an "introvert psychology" and a tendency to solipsism, isolation. The newer empiricism notes that science requires ideas with "a free imaginative quality" rather than mere "copies of sensations."[73]

These new approaches are, of course, Dewey's own. In *The Quest for Certainty*, for example, he calls for "a genuinely experimental empiricism" that will treat ideas as operations to be performed, their soundness to be proved by their consequences rather than by a correspondence with their antecedents.[74] And he condemns the tendency – observable in empiricism from Locke to Russell – to treat sensory qualities as "the antecedent models with which ideas must agree if they are to be sound or 'proved'."[75]

Dewey's new conception of experience is influenced by his poetic, moral, and spiritual leanings as well as by his scientific ones. In *Reconstruction in Philosophy*, he praises the progressive spirit of eighteenth- and nineteenth-century thought but complains of "the unimaginative conception of experience which professed philosophic empiricists have entertained and taught." Such narrow notions of experience give support, Dewey alleges, to those philosophers who appeal to "fixed principles transcending experience."[76] Dewey escapes the charge of narrowness which he makes against other empiricists while at the same time avoiding the appeal to transcendent principles of explanation in his account of naturally imaginative and spiritualized experience. According to Dewey, we experience the world through "seeing, hearing, loving, imagining," which all are "intrinsically connected with the subject-matter of the world. . . . Experience . . . is not a combination of mind and world, subject and object . . . but is a single continuous interaction of a great diversity (literally countless in number) of energies."[77] Dewey works at doing what Mill did not: incorporating such Romantic ideas as imagination, revitalization, and the ethereal into empiricism, into the heart of his theories of inquiry and experience.

In so doing, Dewey stresses the continuous, creative transitions that experience is capable of providing. In "The Need for a Recovery of Philosophy," he states that "the function of mind is to project new and more complex ends – to free experience from routine and from caprice."[78] In opposing caprice, he means to attack the idea of change merely for change's sake and to highlight the role of intelligent foresight in experience. But he also attacks the unthinking mechanism, rigidity, and routine to which Romanticism stands opposed. Emerson had written that "the one thing in the world of value, is, the active soul," that truth lies in the transitions between things, so that one must choose between "truth" and "repose," and that a "strong" and "quick" soul will burst its boundaries, achieving "immense and innumerable expansions."[79] Dewey expresses his own search for such fluid and creative expansions at the end of "The Need for a Recovery" when he writes that "action directed to ends to which the agent has not previously been attached inevitably carries with it a quickened and enlarged spirit. A pragmatic intelligence is a creative intelligence, not a routine mechanic."[80]

The project of achieving the blending of "science and emotion," of "practice and imagination" – what one might call Dewey's Romantic empiricism[81] – is the stated goal of *Reconstruction in Philosophy*, one of the most powerful and coherent of Dewey's middle works. *Reconstruction*'s title gives its flavor: Dewey emphasizes the overcoming, transcending, transformative elements of his philosophy. (There are clear Hegelian overtones here, though Dewey stresses humanity's, rather than reason's, transformative powers.) The word "reconstruction" is a marvelously effective one. It is not negative or dogmatic (as if everything had to be torn apart) like "deconstruction." It is less uncompromising and "apart" than "transcendence" and indicates more closeness to what already exists than the starting-from-scratch tone of "construction" (as in Nelson Goodman's "constructionalism").[82] But "reconstruction" is a critical term: If things are in order, they will not need to be reconstructed. It expresses Dewey's position, at once humble and forceful, that we can actively recover and renew our traditions – our moral and aesthetic values, our ways of thinking and experiencing – but that we must shape these cultural inheritances to fit our current situation and not treat them as inviolate.

At the end of *Reconstruction in Philosophy*, in a chapter on reconstruction and social philosophy, Dewey's peroration achieves an almost Emersonian force and confidence:

> As the new ideas find adequate expression in social life, they will be absorbed into a moral background, and the ideas and beliefs themselves will be deepened and be unconsciously transmitted and sustained. They will color the imagination and temper the desires and affections. They will not form a set of ideas to be expounded, reasoned out and argumentatively supported, but will be a spontaneous way of envisaging life. Then they will take on religious value. The religious spirit will be

revivified because it will be in harmony with men's unquestioned scientific beliefs and their ordinary day-by-day social activities. It will not be obliged to lead a timid, half-concealed and half-apologetic life because tied to scientific ideas and social creeds that are continuously eaten into and broken down. But especially will the ideas and beliefs themselves be deepened and intensified because spontaneously fed by emotion and translated into imaginative vision and fine art.[83]

Two key points emerge at the climax of Dewey's discussion: first, that the reconstitutions he envisages will not be merely doctrinal or formal but will characterize – in ways we can now only guess – the entire fabric of human life and, second, that the envisioned reconstruction of human thought, experience, and culture is secular, not meaning separate from the religious but, rather, long term. The changes he calls for in philosophical thinking, in social thought, and in education may take many generations to be made. But Dewey's use of the simple future tense expresses his confidence that these changes will come to pass.

Dewey considers his work in relation to the tradition of European philosophy, arguing that that tradition has been dominated by "the problem of adjusting the dry, thin and meagre scientific standpoint with the obstinately persisting body of warm and abounding imaginative beliefs." We cannot go back; we cannot restore an imaginative life (if we ever had one) by "lingering in the past." But we can "expedite the development of the vital sources of a religion and art that are yet to be." We must overcome the division between "intelligence" and "aspiration," which means accepting, not rejecting, science and "the daily detail" and also taking "faith in the active tendencies of the day." Philosophy's task is to guide this reconnection of intelligence and aspiration, of love and thought, of what we discover and what we value. Dewey calls for nothing less than the attention of philosophers to the Romantic project of reconciling the noumenal and the phenomenal, of sanctifying the ordinary. And so he ends *Reconstruction in Philosophy* on an ecstatic note (but also a cautionary one, as we are still "in days of transition"): "When philosophy shall have cooperated with the course of events and made clear and coherent the meaning of the daily detail, science and emotion will interpenetrate, practice and imagination will embrace. Poetry and religious feeling will be the unforced flowers of life. To further this articulation and revelation of the meanings of the current course of events is the task and problem of philosophy in days of transition."[84]

Metaphysics

Dewey is sometimes regarded as having no metaphysics, or as reducing the world to experience. He does emphasize experience, but he places it differently than do the traditional empiricists: not in the head but in the interaction between self and world. He does not reduce the world to experience;[85] rather, he maintains that experience reveals the world. Dewey thus does have a metaphysical picture, expressed most succinctly in the following passage from *Experience and Nature:* "We live in a world which is an impressive and irresistible mixture of sufficiencies, tight completenesses, order, recurrences which make possible prediction and control, and singularities, ambiguities, uncertain possibilities, processes going on to consequences as yet indeterminate."[86]

Dewey says a lot here. First, "we live in a world." The world does not live in us, but we in it. Dewey is not a subjective idealist. Second, the world is a mixture of order and disorder. Like James, whose radical empiricism countenanced both conjunctive and disjunctive relations, or Emerson, whose idealism incorporates both law and surprise, Dewey refuses to see the world as either a totality or a chaos. To those who see order, whether in the form of scientific law or spiritual insight, Dewey says, "Yes, that's there." But to the Emerson of "Fate" who wrote of the "wild, rough, incalculable road" of our experience, he says, "Yes, that is there, too." Emerson reminds us of our kinship to the "crickets, which, having filled the summer with noise, are silenced by a fall of the temperature of one night,"[87] and Dewey shares Emerson's sense of the world's contingency, of the fragility and impermanence that characterize even those "tight completenesses" – customs, family, physical environment – that form the bedrock of our lives.

If Dewey sees us living in a precarious and impermanent world, he does not therefore advocate our passive acceptance of it. In his phrase "prediction and control" he expresses his characteristic stress on the malleability of the world. Dewey portrays human experience itself as basically transformational, not a passive reception of something imprinted from without but an active engagement with the environment. As he explained in *Art as Experience:* "In an experience, things and events belonging to the world, physical and social, are transformed through the human context they enter."[88] Dewey lauds our transformative powers – he admired the ships and steam engines of his day – but he urges us to guide those powers by intelligence, by feeling, and by art.

Dewey emphasizes the power we have to transform both the world and our experience of it, but he always counters this idealistic and reconstructive side with an affirmation of realism. Thus, in *Reconstruction in Philosophy* he writes: "Although it is surprising how little check the environment actually puts upon the formation of ideas, since no notions are too absurd not to have been accepted by some people, yet the environment does enforce a certain minimum of correctness under penalty of extinction." (He mentions as examples that "water drowns" and "fire burns.")[89] Later in the book, he maintains that our system of classifications, our logic, does not fit a preexisting structure but evolves to serve our purposes: A classification is "a repertory of weapons for attack upon the future and the unknown." As such, it need not correspond to any preexisting form. But even though we design such classifications, they "must take effect in the world" and so are constrained by the world's conditions.[90] In general, one can say that Dewey sees a world "out there" but that he sees us out there too: He tries to counter "our old assumption of the self as outside of things."[91]

In "The Need for a Recovery of Philosophy" Dewey attacks the implicit idealism of traditional empiricism, expressed in the crucial assumption "that experience centres in, or gathers about, or proceeds from, a centre or subject which is outside the course of natural existence, and set over against it."[92] Dewey tries to overcome this point of view by claiming that experience itself reveals an objective world, not just a world of impressions and ideas: "According to tradition, experience is (at least primarily) a psychical thing, infected throughout by 'subjectivity.' What experience suggests about itself is a genuinely objective world which enters into the actions and sufferings of men and undergoes modifications through their responses."[93] Experience does not take place in a vacuum: "Experiencing means living; and that living goes on in and because of an environing medium."[94]

In his 1930 autobiography, Dewey speaks of his youthful need for "unification" and the liberation that the Hegelian philosophy provided. But no more in his later than in his earlier philosophy could Dewey tolerate the divisions and separations that he mentions there: "of self from the world, of soul from body, of nature from God."[95] He may have given up Hegelian categories for more scientific, pragmatically established, and open-ended ones, but he never abandoned the project of giving an account of self and world, values and facts, natural and spiritual, which while acknowledging their difference portrays their fundamental connection. Two central chapters of *Experience and Nature,* entitled "Nature, Mind and the Subject" and "Nature, Life and Body-Mind," illustrate this point by their treatment of the emergent novelty of mind within a fundamental unity of mind and nature. Mental qualities are not " 'in' the organism"; rather, they are somehow in the world's interaction with us, "qualities of interactions in which both extra-organic things and organisms partake."[96] Mind is an emerging property of natural processes, or interactions. Some interactions – for example, the ingestion and excretion carried out by an amoeba – do not have mental properties. Others, like the entrance of a cold cave man into his cave, do. Mind for Dewey is "a mode of natural existence in which objects undergo directed reconstitution."[97] It is "directed" because mental events are in some sense intelligent, responsive to the uncertainty of an objective situation (e.g., the situation that consists of a snowstorm, a cold human body, and a nearby cave). The distinction between the physical and the mental is thus "one of levels of increasing complexity and intimacy of interaction among natural events. The idea that matter, life and mind represent separate kinds of Being" is a fallacy springing from the conversion of "consequences of interaction of events into causes of the occurrence of these consequences."[98] Mind is not, as Dewey later observed in *The Quest for Certainty*, "an intruder from without."[99]

In his chapters on "body-mind" Dewey even manages to speak of "soul" and to distinguish it from the "mind" (the capacity for intelligent manipulation of the environment) while avoiding transcendental or unverifiable claims: A soulful person "has in marked degree qualities of sensitive, rich, and coordinated participation in all the situations of life." Similarly, "works of art, music, poetry, painting, architecture, have soul, while others are dead, mechanical."[100] These soulful interactions – whether thought of through the object as properties of an artwork or through the subject as a character of his or her experience – are Dewey's concern in *Art as Experience*.

Theory of Knowledge

The transactional unity of self and world that Dewey portrays in his metaphysics naturally has consequences for his theory of knowledge. One consequence is the sidestepping of skepticism. Dewey admits uncertainty into his picture of our cognitive situation, as we have seen. But uncertainty is not just subjective; it is a feature of the world, "a real property of some natural existences." Our human intelligence operates not just to give us a convincing account of knowledge but also to transform an objective situation from a more doubtful to a more secure or coherent state: "[a] *situation* undergoes, through operations directed by thought, transition from problematic to settled, from internal discontinuity to coherency and organization."[101] Dewey's picture of inquiry, including the uncertainty to which it responds, places it "in" the world, leaving no room for the skeptic to drive a radical wedge, no "gap" between self and world. Dewey in fact has little to say about overcoming skepticism because his basic picture of the world does not allow it to get a foothold. "The world is subject-matter for knowledge," he writes in *Experience and Nature*, "because mind has developed *in* that world."[102] Again, in *The Quest for Certainty*, he maintains that the "organs, instrumentalities and operations of knowing are inside nature, not outside. Hence they are changes of what previously existed: the object of knowledge is a constructed, existentially produced, object."[103] Rather than questioning our ability to know the world, Dewey tends to praise the "liberation and expansion" that a naturally rooted intelligence may bring about: "It is nature realizing its own potentialities in behalf of a fuller and richer issue of events. Intelligence within nature means liberation and expansion, as reason outside of nature means fixation and restriction."[104] For Dewey, the function of intelligence is not to grasp already given structures but to project and create new ones. We are part of nature and free, within bounds, to shape it. To use Nietzsche's metaphor, "The sea, *our* sea, lies open again; perhaps there has never yet been such an 'open sea'."[105]

Dewey attempts to frame alternatives to what he calls "spectator" theories, which place us outside the world we are said to know.[106] We are not passive with respect to the world but are active manipulators of it; not just minds containing ideas, but body-minds feeling and reconstructing the world. The explorations of an infant give some idea of Dewey's outlook. The child reaches out in the world – first on its back as an infant, swatting at the rattles strung above it, later grasping and manipulating stuffed animals, rocks, clay, water, and other children. These exploratory interactions become knowledge when they become predictable and intelligent: "directed."[107] Knowing is then only a special form of interaction and transformation, not a process starting in a private subjective mind, on which all contact with the world is based. It is not – like watching a faraway bird through fixed binoculars – viewing something from a distance but, rather, actually encountering the world.

Education

Dewey's thoughts about children were obviously shaped by the writings of Rousseau, which he uses extensively in his comprehensive writings on education published in the second decade of this century. *Schools of Tomorrow*, published jointly with his daughter Evelyn Dewey in 1915, is a case in point.[108] For the most part the book is a description and evaluation of successful experimental schools, such as the Fairhope School in Alabama, the Howland School in Chicago, and the Teachers' College kindergarten in New York City. But its opening chapter is almost pure Rousseau, with Dewey using Rousseau's *Emile* to develop such themes as the importance of experience, play, and the body. Central to Rousseau's outlook, as it is to Wordsworth's, is a sense of the inherent powers of the child. "Rousseau said, as well as did, many foolish things," Dewey begins *Schools of Tomorrow*. "But his insistence that education be based upon the native capacities of those to be taught and upon the need of studying children in order to disclose what these native powers are, sounded the key-note of all modern efforts for educational progress."[109] Dewey praises the Fairhope school for putting into practice "Rousseau's central idea; namely: The child is best prepared for life as an adult by experiencing in childhood what has meaning to him as a child; and further, the child has a right to enjoy his childhood."[110] Dewey praises Rousseau's conjunction of joy and activity and quotes this passage from *Emile*: "You are afraid to see him spending his early years doing nothing. What! Is it nothing to be happy, nothing to jump and run all day? He will never be so busy again all his life long."[111] A properly expansive and educating "busyness" – our true business in life, one might say – can only be accomplished with enthusiasm. Dewey finds the children at Fairhope "uniformly happy in school," proclaiming "their 'love' for it."[112] They learn "the meaning of the words pistils, stamens, and petals with flowers they have gathered" or about "the ordinary tools of life," such as scissors, knives, needles, and saws, by using them rather than sitting at some "cramping desk" passively receiving "knowledge."[113]

Dewey credits Rousseau with discovering that an active education develops a lively and interested experience of the world. The idea in Rousseau's time and still prevailing to a great extent was, Dewey maintains, "that the senses were a sort of gateway and avenue through which impressions traveled and then built up knowledge pictures of the world. Rousseau saw that they are a part of the apparatus of action by which we adjust ourselves to our environment, and that instead of being passive receptacles they are directly connected with motor activities – with the use of hands and legs."[114] (The senses, then, are natural reconstructing devices.)

Dewey takes up Rousseau again in his educational magnum opus of 1916, *Democracy and Education,* in which he offers the most extensive discussion of his educational views and which he credits (in his autobiography) with having been for many years the book in which his philosophy was most fully expounded.[115] He again praises Rousseau for encouraging respect for the natural aims and interests of the child and for stressing the body's role in developing them. But he criticizes Rousseau for equating the natural with the physical and devaluing our intellectual side. In contrast, Dewey regards what he calls the "body-mind," with its intellectual interests and anticipations, as no less natural than a blade of grass.[116] Moreover – and here again is the point that both Dewey's followers and his critics sometimes miss – children need guidance, and Dewey takes issue with Rousseau for thinking that everything can just be left to nature: "To leave everything to nature was, after all, but to negate the very idea of education; it was to trust to the accidents of circumstance."[117]

Rather than looking to Rousseau for a fully adequate position, Dewey turns to Emerson. Warning against "idealizing" childhood by accepting everything the child does as an end in itself but at the same time committed to respecting the child's "natural instincts," Dewey finds that "the true principle of respect for immaturity, cannot be better put, than in the words of Emerson," who wrote that one should "respect the child" and not be "too much his parent" and also that one should respect oneself: "The two points in a boy's training are, to keep his *naturel* and train off all but that; to keep his *naturel,* but stop off his uproar, fooling, and horseplay; keep his nature *and arm it with knowledge in the very direction in which it points.*"[118] This arming with knowledge is the teacher's function; here the subject matter in a teacher's repertoire comes into play.

Dewey wants children interested so that they will learn, but he sees such learning ideally as the track left by a life absorbed in the values of the present. For Dewey, learning is not an end product. In *Reconstruction in Philosophy,* published in 1920, Dewey defines education as "getting from the present the degree and kind of growth there is in it." This statement reflects the present-tense orientation of a section of *Democracy and Education* entitled "Education as Reconstruction," in which Dewey argues that the reorganizing (i.e., what he often calls "growth" in *Reconstruction*) effected by education is constant, that its goal, the "chief business of life," is to "make living . . . contribute to an enrichment of its own perceptible meaning."[119] This "enrichment" of our experience is the function Dewey terms imaginative in *Art as Experience.* In 1916, when *Democracy and Education* was written – no less than in 1920 in *Reconstruction in Philosophy,* 1934 in *Art as Experience,* or 1890 in "Poetry and Philosophy" – Dewey is talking about the imaginative reconstruction of experience: "There is no limit to the meaning which an action may come to possess. . . . The reach of imagination in realizing connections is inexhaustible."[120]

In his educational theory and practice Dewey looks to imagination and interest, to a "caring" attention to the world, to bring about a more "intimate connection" with it.[121] Philosophy guides us in life; it is not just a set of theories to be put in "cold storage." The test of a philosophy lies in its philosophy of education,[122] in the kind of life it means to inculcate.

The kind of life Dewey sought was a Romantic's, in which the "glad animal movements" of Wordsworth become the form of life and in which intelligence and imagination are set free to realize the vast human potential. "Man is the dwarf of himself," Emerson complained. Dewey tried to show that dwarf how to grow.

IV. "ART AS EXPERIENCE"

Art as Experience is the capstone to the Romantic project that inspired John Dewey as a young man. In this work he places the artist in the role of Emerson's scholar or poet, as one who inspires. But what he most basically calls for is the generalization of such artistic inspiration to common experience; indeed, his book could justly have been

called "experience as art." The goal of "reawakening . . . a truly spiritual religion" of experience, which Dewey found in Marsh and Coleridge, is renewed in Dewey's late aesthetic work, in which the religious –
at least in its nontheistic, Romantic form – coincides with the poetic.
There also is a voluntaristic streak in *Art as Experience,* an expression of
Dewey's sense that human beings can play a significant role in reconstructing their own experience. And there is a strong reconciling tendency. *Art as Experience* demonstrates that Dewey never ceased believing
what he believed in the 1880s: that there is no conflict between science
and "ideals."

Dewey's professional interest in poetry reaches back at least to his 1890
essay "Poetry and Philosophy."[123] During his time at Columbia University (1905–39) his interest in the visual arts, particularly in painting, was
stimulated by Albert C. Barnes, a wealthy chemist, inventor, and art
collector. Barnes's discussions with Dewey; his extensive collection of
paintings by Picasso, Cézanne, Renoir, Manet, and others; and the
Barnes Foundation's sponsorship of Dewey's 1926 summer tour of European museums were important stimulants in Dewey's thinking about
art.[124] (Dewey, by the way, had little interest in, or appreciation of, music.) Although there are numerous remarks about art scattered throughout his mature writings, and a whole chapter of *Experience and Nature*
entitled "Experience, Nature, and Art," Dewey evidently wanted to
produce a more complete discussion of aesthetic issues and took the op-
portunity of an invitation to deliver the first William James lecture at
Harvard in 1931 to develop it. But *Art as Experience* is more than just
Dewey's thoughts about one side of human experience: It is a full philosophical vision. It is a work whose stature and comprehensiveness make
plausible Sleeper's suggestion that in it Dewey had already offered the
revision of *Experience and Nature* (for which he planned the title "Experience and Culture") that, near the end of his life, he wrote to his friend
Arthur Bentley of wanting to produce.[125]

In the context of my interest in an American Romantic philosophical
tradition, *Art as Experience* is striking because of Dewey's extensive use
of Romantic writings.[126] It is not simply that he uses the poems or essays
of Wordsworth or Keats as examples for analysis – something any book
on aesthetics might do – but that he also embraces some of their most
important philosophical ideas. Dewey places these ideas among the main
elements of his mature philosophy, where they lie as naturally as a plant
grows in the soil. The passion with which Dewey writes of and utilizes
Romantic ideas is also striking, especially when one considers that
Dewey was seventy-five years old in 1934, when *Art as Experience* was
published. The springs of feeling and thought flowed exuberantly from
him in the 1930s (his *Logic: The Theory of Inquiry* was still to be published

in 1938). More than Wordsworth or Emerson, Dewey maintained a
youthful and hopeful outlook on life.

Art as Experience begins in a reconciling mode, with an attack on the
separation of art from life. There is "a chasm between ordinary and es-
thetic experience,"[127] Dewey complains, and this is reflected in theories
of art that place the aesthetic in a transcendental domain, a place apart
from human experience. In contrast, Dewey sees aesthetic experience as
rooted in ordinary human life:

> The sources of art in human experience will be learned by him who
> sees how the tense grace of the ball-player infects the onlooking crowd;
> who notes the delight of the housewife in tending her plants . . . the
> zest of the spectator in poking the wood burning on the hearth and in
> watching the darting flames and crumbling coals. . . . He does not re-
> main a cold spectator. What Coleridge said of the reader of poetry is
> true in its way of all who are happily absorbed in their activities of mind
> and body: "The reader should be carried forward, not merely or chiefly
> by the mechanical impulse of curiosity, not by a restless desire to arrive
> at the final solution, but by the pleasurable activity of the journey it-
> self."[128]

This "happy absorption" in one's activities is just the form Dewey had
identified as necessary for a successful education; in *Art as Experience* it
is identified as the form of a properly aesthetic or imaginative human
life.

Dewey sees the aesthetic as the domain in which his second and third
types of idealism – in which the ideal and the experienced come together – are most clearly manifested: "Art itself is the best proof of the
existence of a realized and therefore realizable, union of material and
ideal."[129] He notes the similarities between artistic, and religious and
mystical experience, citing W. H. Hudson, who "found the world so
agreeable and interesting as to be in love with it," and Emerson, whose
"perfect exhilaration" occurred during an ordinary winter's walk across
a "bare common, at twilight, under a clouded sky."[130] These experiences – and Dewey keeps stressing that they are that – demonstrate the
possibility of reconciling the ordinary and the spiritual or ideal. "There
is no limit to the capacity of immediate sensuous experience to absorb
into itself meanings and values that in and of themselves – that is in the
abstract – would be designated 'ideal' and 'spiritual'."[131] In *Art as Experience* Dewey reconceives his reconstructive task as one of expanding these
human experiential capacities.

The book's second chapter, entitled "The Live Creature and 'Etherial
Things'," considers this reconciliation of the ideal and the experiential.
The title derives from Keats, who wrote: "The Sun, the Moon, the Earth
and its contents, are material to form greater things, that is etherial

things – greater things than the Creator himself made."[132] This quotation perfectly expresses the natural supernaturalism typical of Romanticism. Dewey follows Keats and other Romantics in his sense of the richness that experience might have – and for some people sometimes does have – and of the contrast with its ordinary, flat, impoverished content. "Only occasionally in the lives of many are the senses fraught with the sentiment that comes from deep realization of intrinsic meanings. We undergo sensations as mechanical stimuli or as irritated stimulations, without having a sense of the reality that is in them and behind them."[133]

In his well-known sonnet "The World Is Too Much with Us," Wordsworth writes:

> The world is too much with us; late and soon,
> Getting and spending, we lay waste our powers:
> Little we see in Nature that is ours;
> We have given our hearts away, a sordid boon!
> This sea that bares her bosom to the moon;
> The winds that will be howling at all hours,
> And are up-gather'd now like sleeping flowers;
> For this, for everything, we are out of tune;
> It moves us not.

Even this much of the poem raises such Romantic themes as a lost intimacy with nature, the importance of feeling, and humanity's great but wasted powers. Wordsworth examines and characterizes our ordinary lives, so much in contrast with the "ethereal" possibilities stressed by Keats and by Wordsworth himself. With Wordsworth's sonnet in our ears, let us now listen to Dewey in *Art as Experience:* "Ordinary experience is often infected with apathy, lassitude and stereotype. We get neither the impact of quality through sense nor the meaning of things through thought. The 'world' is too much with us as burden or distraction. We are not sufficiently alive to feel the tang of sense nor yet to be moved by thought."[134] Dewey is alluding to Wordsworth's sonnet in the third sentence quoted and may plausibly be supposed to be drawing the word "moved" in his last sentence from Wordsworth's "It moves us not." Dewey calls for us to respond not only to sensation but also to thought, which for Dewey is a feature of experience.

Much of our life is so lax or distracted, Dewey maintains, that it does not achieve the ideal he calls "*an* experience." But this ideal is not unattainable; it is achieved by everyone at some times. *An* experience occurs when a dramatic unity, a "particular rhythmic movement," occurs, with an inception, development, and "consummation"; for example, "That meal in a Paris restaurant . . . that storm one went through in crossing the Atlantic – the storm that seemed in its fury, as it was experienced, to sum up in itself all that a storm can be, complete in itself, standing out because marked out from what went before and what came after."[135] There is not enough drama or interest to our experience, Dewey believes. We suffer, on the one hand, from "submission to convention in practice and intellectual procedure" and, on the other hand, from "dissipation, incoherence, and aimless indulgence."[136]

If he criticizes our ordinary experience for being narrow and unimaginative, that is not because Dewey urges us to fly to some superexperiential realm beyond the world. The feelings of "exquisite intelligibility and clarity" that he seeks might seem to be of another world, "a world beyond this world," but they are really introductions to "the deeper reality of the world in which we live in our ordinary experiences."[137] Hudson, whom Dewey names "a person of extraordinary sensitiveness to the sensuous surface of the world," wrote: "I rejoiced in colors, scents, in taste and touch: the blue of the sky, the verdure of the earth, the sparkle of light on water, the taste of milk, of honey, the smell of dry or moist soil, of wind and rain." Dewey emphasizes the realism and objectivity of Hudson's account. Hudson's joy in the world is not just a response to his private sensations: "The enjoyment is of the color, feel, and scent of *objects:* blades of grass, sky, sunlight and water, birds."[138] Near the end of *Art as Experience,* Dewey employs an extract from Browning's (the hero of "Poetry and Philosophy") essay on Shelley to make this realistic point again: "It is with this world, as starting point and basis alike, that we shall always have to concern ourselves; the world is not to be learned and thrown aside, but reverted to and relearned."[139] Dewey remains a realist in *Art as Experience,* committed to the existence of the physical world. But he refuses to see any version of that world as final, and he advocates its continual creative reconstruction.

Following basic Romantic doctrine, Dewey credits both art and nature with the power to carry us "to a refreshed attitude toward the circumstances and exigencies of ordinary experience."[140] Thus, new movements in painting are "the discovery and exploitation of some possibility of vision not previously developed – as Dutch painters grasped the intimate quality of interiors . . . as Cézanne re-saw the volume of natural forces in their dynamic relations."[141] Like Wordsworth and Emerson, Dewey finds poetry in the homespun or ordinary. He quotes a weather report in its entirety, with its drama of storms and extreme temperatures. Dewey finds the beauty of it to come in part from "the euphony of the geographical terms" ("along the Mississippi Valley and into the Gulf of Mexico"), in part from the sense of "the wide spaciousness of the earth" that such reports create.[142] A sense of mystery and romance may thus inhabit our ordinary experience. We can learn to "*celebrate* the familiar," so that "the old takes on a new guise in which the sense of the familiar is rescued from the oblivion that custom usually effects."[143]

Romantic writers and philosophers such as Coleridge, Schelling, Schiller, and Wordsworth give the name "imagination" to the power within us that accomplishes this transformation of the ordinary. Dewey does not have a faculty psychology like Schelling's and he is more theoretical than Wordsworth, but he too gives a crucial role to our imaginative capacities. Imagination, he writes, "is a *way* of seeing and feeling things as they compose an integral whole. It is the large and generous blending of interests at the point where the mind comes in contact with the world."[144] Dewey characteristically stresses experience here: He is not speaking of a transcendental faculty but of what James would have called a piece of pure experience, "a way of seeing and feeling," that is available to any human being. The conjunction and equality of seeing and feeling show that Dewey, no less than James or Wordsworth, works at developing the human "feeling intellect."

In discussing imagination, Dewey considers Coleridge's description of the imagination in the *Biographia Literaria* as "esemplastic." Dewey points out his calling attention "to the welding together of all elements . . . into a new and completely unified experience." Discarding his terminology but explicitly accepting Coleridge's basic idea, Dewey maintains that "an imaginative experience is what happens when varied materials of sense quality, emotion, and meaning come together in a union that marks a new birth in the world."[145] Every word in this definition is important. Dewey does not talk of imagination but of "imaginative experience," thereby indicating his experiential and processual basis. His portrayal of the union or synthesis of diverse materials show his links with Hegel and Kant. The word "new" indicates Dewey's sense of what Emerson called the surprise of existence, the eruption of novelty. The word "emotion" indicates the important role Dewey gives to feeling in his account not just of imaginative experience but of all experience, for "imaginative experience exemplifies more fully than any other kind of experience what experience itself is in its very movement and structure."[146] Imagination "is the only gateway through which . . . meanings can find their way into a present interaction."[147] It is that blending of meanings and memories that makes even the most ordinary experience possible. Even such a humble experience as that of burning the toast requires connecting this smell in my kitchen with what I remember of past burnings of toast and other things. Such connecting is part of the function Coleridge calls esemplastic.

The ordinariness of imaginative experience allows Dewey to build a sense of its vast reconstructive powers. Imagination "designates a quality that animates and pervades all processes of making and observation." Indeed, imagination is portrayed as the unifying element – the cement – that binds self and world or, to mirror more faithfully Dewey's reconstructive purposes, the function that allows their opposition to each other to be eliminated: "It is the large and generous blending of interests at the point where the mind comes in contact with the world. When old and familiar things are made new in experience, there is imagination. When the new is created, the far and strange become the most natural inevitable things in the world. There is always some measure of adventure in the meeting of mind and universe, and this adventure is, in its measure, imagination."[148] (A brilliant sidestep by Dewey, and completely consistent with his notion of body-mind, to place imagination not in the mind but in the "adventure" of the mind–universe meeting.)

Even while Dewey attempts, through his treatment of imagination, to dissolve the old antagonism, or opposition, between self and world, he highlights the human contribution to that dissolution. "The medium of expression in art is neither objective nor subjective. It is the matter of a new experience in which subjective and objective have so cooperated that neither has any longer an existence by itself." But what he calls "the individual person" has an essential role to play in this cooperation: "Objective material becomes the matter of art only as it is transformed by entering into relations of doing and being undergone by an individual person with all his characteristics of temperament, special manner of vision, and unique experience."[149] Dewey uses lines from Coleridge's "Dejection" (discussed in connection with "voluntaristic structures" of knowledge and being in Chapter 1) to make his point:

> The work [of art] takes place when a human being cooperates with the product so that the outcome is an experience that is enjoyed because of its liberating and ordered properties. Esthetically at least
> "we receive but what we give,
> And in our life alone does nature live;
> Ours is her wedding garment; ours her shroud."[150]

Dewey echoes these lines from Coleridge's poem earlier in the book, when he contrasts "perception," which is productive and creative, with mere "recognition" or "bare identification." "Perception is an act of the going-out of energy in order to receive."[151] Dewey does not believe in a faculty of "will," but he does identify the human facet of the world as being responsible for imaginatively reconstructing it. "Only imaginative vision elicits the possibilities that are interwoven within the texture of the actual."[152]

Dewey calls for a "revolution" of "the imagination and emotions of man."[153] Indeed, this is something of a redundant demand, as he understands "imaginative experience" to include emotion, along with meaning and sense quality. In common with his Romantic progenitors, then, Dewey finds emotion to be a key feature of all experience, a point he makes in *Art as Experience* and elsewhere: "Experience is emotional but there are no separate things called emotions in it";[154] "Where there is life, there are already eager and impassioned activities";[155] and " 'Feeling' is in general a name for the newly actualized quality acquired by events previously occurring upon a physical level, when these events come into more extensive and delicate relationships of interaction."[156]

In *Art as Experience,* Dewey stresses the caring and feeling nature of human consciousness: "Mind denotes every mode and variety of interest in, and concern for, things: practical, intellectual, and emotional. . . . Nor is mind . . . purely intellectual. The mother minds her baby; she cares for it with affection. Mind is care in the sense of solicitude, anxiety, as well as of active looking after things that need to be tended; we mind our step, our course of action, emotionally as well as thoughtfully."[157] (Again, Dewey's language – mind as "care" – is reminiscent of Heidegger.) Aesthetic experience involves an intensification of the emotional factors present in any human experience.

Dewey illustrates this "care" in action with his example of a mechanic, "artistically engaged" in his job and "caring for his materials and tools with genuine affection."[158] Through such affection the mechanic transforms his ordinary experience, just as Coleridge's Mariner transforms the world through his affection for the water snakes. The mechanic loves his tools and work, just as the Mariner learns to love "all things both great and small."

If the "reconstructive doing" that makes consciousness "fresh and alive"[159] takes place, we need not rush through life "getting and spending." Dewey urges us to slow down and explore the connections within our experience, instead of shutting them out. He calls for a new order, a new ruler of our experience: not the forces of the marketplace or of technological development but imagination, our underdeveloped power to move from a tread-worn to a richly novel path through this world. An imaginatively developed world will have public brilliancy, as in the Renoir paintings that Dewey so much admired, but it will be as comfortable as morning tea: "I do not see why in drinking tea from a cup [one] is necessarily estopped from enjoying its shape and the delicacy of its material. Not every one gulps his food and drink in the shortest possible time in obedience to some necessary psychological law."[160]

Dewey ends *Art as Experience* by considering Shelley's view that "imagination is the great instrument of moral good." He distinguishes between institutional moralities and the imaginative "moral prophets" who "have always been poets even though they spoke in the verse or the parable." Like Emerson, Dewey contrasts the poet's "vision of possibilities" with the "hardened" facts, rules, and institutions into which they are converted. Poets present "ideals which should command thought and desire" and imagination – ours and the records of theirs –

is necessary to a morality that will free us from the "constrictions that hem us in."[161] Poetry is expansive, what Shelley called "a going out of our nature" that yet does not result in the overcoming of that nature. It is an "identification of ourselves in the beautiful which exists in thought, action, or person, not our own" and so reproduces the combination of intimacy and alterity of the marriage of self and world.[162] But Dewey, again like Emerson, emphasizes the energy of the expansion that Shelley describes, drawing the moral that poetry is objective and transformative at once; in short, that the imagination is reconstructive.

Dewey's message in *Art as Experience* is that imagination can be brought to earth, that the natural world can be imaginatively reconstructed. As he insisted in "Poetry and Philosophy" over forty years earlier, poetry is therefore concerned with truth, with the facts of this world. Dewey's work on aesthetics is a major contribution to the "fuller and freer philosophy" that he called for in "Poetry and Philosophy," to the religion considered as a "state of the will and the affections" that he found in Coleridge, to the transformative idealism that he identified in *The Quest for Certainty,* and to the blending of "science and religion," "poetry and religious feeling," and "the daily detail" that he foresaw in *Reconstruction in Philosophy.*

EPILOGUE

A wise writer will feel that the ends of study and composition are best
answered by announcing undiscovered regions of thought, and so com-
municating, through hope, new activity to the torpid spirit.

Ralph Waldo Emerson, *Nature*

"The heart of pragmatism," writes Hilary Putnam in *The Many Faces of
Realism* – "of James's and Dewey's pragmatism, if not of Peirce's – was
the insistence on the supremacy of the agent point of view. If we find
that we must take a certain point of view, use a certain 'conceptual system', when we are engaged in practical activity, in the widest sense of
'practical activity', then we must not simultaneously advance the claim
that it is not really 'the way things are in themselves.' "[1] To those who
see Putnam's recent work as an important break with the Anglo-American tradition of which he has been so distinguished an exponent, such
claims have something of a revolutionary air, by representing not simply
a new sort of epistemological perspective but a renunciation as well, an
admission that we are at last coming to the end of an older way of thinking about the mind and the world. Yet the identical claim has, as Putnam
is perfectly aware, a venerable status in American philosophy, being in
its way simply what William James said long ago in *The Will to Believe*,
that as human beings we will accept no "philosophy whose principle is
so incommensurate with our most intimate powers as to deny them all
relevancy in universal affairs."[2]

In the same way, we find Putnam a few pages later invoking Dewey
in the name of a realm of human needs to which an adequate epistemology must grant objective relevance: "It is because there are real human
needs, and not merely desires, that it makes sense to distinguish between
better and worse values. . . . Dewey tells us that human needs . . . do

not pre-exist, that humanity is constantly redesigning itself, and that we *create* needs."[3] Nor, in the context of an established analytic tradition, is it hard to see why such claims are being felt as somehow revolutionary, for it is the burden of his argument that values – earlier placed in a separate noumenal realm of "things as they are in themselves" and more recently denied any authority or existence at all – are just as much a part of the world as either the objects or laws of science. And both are intimately related to the way in which human beings think and feel and act. "The trail of the human serpent," in Putnam's favorite paraphrase of James, "is over all."[4]

The mode of Putnam's recent work is a neo-Wittgensteinian and neo-pragmatic analysis of the primordial role of human needs, interests, and activities in determining reality, but his project has, for all that, a certain recognizable shape: Putnam is, in Kantian or Romantic terms, working to recover the noumenal world by humanizing it. The emblematic or symbolic value of a work like *The Many Faces of Realism* thus is precisely that it represents at once a new departure and a return: a departure from the Anglo-American tradition in whose immediate background loom the figures of Russell and Carnap and the early Wittgenstein, a return to the American tradition of "Romantic" epistemology whose outlines I have attempted to trace in these pages. The ultimate value of *The Many Faces of Realism* is perhaps that it represents the passing of an eclipse, a long period during which the lingering spirit of an earlier positivism had meant that such thinkers as James and Dewey could not be regarded seriously as philosophers, or Emerson regarded as a philosopher at all.

Perhaps no less emblematic is Putnam's role as a member of the Harvard philosophy department, not simply because his occupancy of the Pearson Professorship of Mathematical Logic so unmistakably symbolizes his earlier commitment to formal or analytical methods, or because his return to William James has been carried out in the very department of which James was once the most famous member, but also because it is the department of Stanley Cavell. Putnam's recent criticisms of "scientism" and "method fetishism" in contemporary philosophy, as well as his new emphasis on "moral images of the world" – pictures "of how our virtues and ideals hang together . . . and of what they have to do with the position we are in"[5] – may be regarded as an enlistment in Cavell's ongoing project of creating alternatives to what we "call *arguments*" in philosophy, alternative modes of "rigor" and "conceptual accuracy."[6] Putnam focuses on the moral image that "inspires" Kant's arguments, without which they "don't make sense,"[7] while Cavell posits what he calls "reading," the more purely meditative or interpretive style of an Emerson or Thoreau or Wittgenstein, as an alternative method of "argumentation in philosophy" and an ultimate means of "accepting full responsibility for one's own discourse."[8]

This, too, is a return. In his essay on literary ethics, Emerson can be heard to lament the "mediocre and sordid" forms in which he saw scholarship in the America of his day: "The intellect still wants the voice that shall say to it, 'sleep no more'."[9] As a general indictment of a characteristically American sort of shallowness or philistinism, no doubt, the claim is not without merit, but the truth is also that American philosophy has never been without such voices, the distinctly human voices of what Emerson himself called men "raised above themselves by the power of principles."[10] Such principles were evidently at work in Emerson's own delineations of the lords of life and the American scholar, in James's intricate explorations of the varieties of human experience, and in Dewey's attempts to reconstruct philosophy and education from within. They are no less at work today in the myths of skepticism and recovery given voice in Cavell's work.

If we have been unaware of this tradition as a tradition, it is perhaps because we have mistaken the nature of its own claims to be distinctively or authentically American, as though this must mean, if it is to mean anything, some style of thinking carried out in isolation from Europe. Nor, as Cavell has shown in the case of Emerson and Thoreau, is this a notion entirely without warrant. The quest for a philosophy calling itself American, Emerson asserted, must begin with a search for an American scholar who, not lost in words and schools, "converses with things"; only such a thinker could lead a nation that would "for the first time exist."[11] The mistake, however, lies in thinking that such a project must begin in a renunciation of Europe and its intellectual traditions, an inference that would have dismayed Emerson himself. For the project of bringing to birth a "new America" was always, as we have seen in the preceding pages, associated in Emerson's mind with Romanticism as his own immediate source of inspiration; the alteration of consciousness that he so fervently hoped to see taking place in Pennsylvania, New Jersey, and Massachusetts would have as its source the "blood-warm" writings of "Goethe, Wordsworth, and Carlyle."[12]

The Romantic tradition in American philosophy, then, amounts to a renunciation not of Europe but of certain separations between mind and world that can be seen as the terminal illness of European philosophy in its institutionalized modality, the spiritual dilemma of which Romanticism itself, in its European context, was meant to resolve or cure. To lead thought back into the realm of actual human existence, to give voice to the moral urgency of Goethe and Wordsworth and Carlyle as a mode of philosophical investigation, would thus constitute the American revolution in philosophy, a redirection or reinflection of European Romanticism that would offer it a permanent home in the New World in the altered guise of philosophical discourse. This, or at any rate something very like it, is what Dewey had in mind when he confessed that he loved "to think that there is something profoundly American in James's union of philosophy with life" or when he predicted that Emerson and James would be the two key figures if and when America "comes to itself in consciousness."[13]

Philosophy may thus be seen as becoming "American" in Dewey's sense at just the point when it enters a perpetual struggle against the divorce of thought from experience, mind from world. This is the struggle James has in mind in reviewing "the present situation in philosophy" in 1908, for instance, when he issues a warning about "the overtechnicality and consequent dreariness of the younger disciples at our American universities," about their "fear of popularity," about "the professorial game" played when "they think and write from each other and for each other and at each other exclusively." The same warning is being issued today, implicitly or explicitly, by philosophers like Cavell and Putnam, and what gives it a peculiarly American tonality – what allows it to be heard as American philosophy calling itself back to itself – is precisely the determination that philosophy should not lose contact, in James's phrase, with "the open air of human nature," enter and lose itself in that hermetic realm where "true perspective gets lost" and "extremes and oddities count as much as sanities."[14]

Dewey's place in this same tradition derives, as we have seen, from his own steady determination to emancipate philosophy from any concern with narrow technical problems, to recover and maintain its engagement with contemporary life. This is the sense in which Dewey comes to embody in his own career the Emersonian thinker, the "realist . . . convers[ing] with things." Philosophy returns to itself, Dewey says in his great essay on the recovery of philosophy, only "when it ceases to be a device for dealing with the problems of philosophers and becomes a method, cultivated by philosophers, for dealing with the problems of men." Only in this lies the promise of "a deeper and more adventurous wisdom" and a philosophy that might even yet "somehow bring to consciousness America's own needs and its own implicit principle of successful action."[15]

There is in Dewey's words, as there is today in the writings of Cavell, an intimation of American philosophy conceived less as a tradition of thought than as an unending tradition of struggle within thought, against the bewitchments of an intellect bent on floating free of mere cluttered actuality and toward the acknowledgement of our inevitable situatedness as conscious or thinking beings. It is this notion of a ceaseless and yet necessary struggle that has made Romanticism, in Harold Bloom's phrase, a "perpetually self-renewing" tradition and that allows us to grasp the thought of Emerson and James and Dewey as a perpetuation in philosophy of the original Romantic enterprise.[16] To call American philosophy by its name is perhaps in the end to do no more than to think of "America" as that inward landscape glimpsed nearly two centuries ago by Goethe and Wordsworth and Carlyle, the scene of thought remembering its own birth in the domain of an unexalted actuality and, remembering, determined to return there.

NOTES

PREFACE

1 Stanley Cavell, *The Senses of Walden: An Expanded Edition* (San Francisco: North Point Press, 1981), pp. 32–3.

2 See John Stuhr, *Classical American Philosophy* (New York: Oxford University Press, 1987); Elizabeth Flower and Murray Murphey, *A History of Philosophy in America* (New York: Putnam, 1977); Joseph Blau, *Men and Movements in American Philosophy* (Englewood Cliffs, N.J.: Prentice-Hall, 1952); and John Smith, *The Spirit of American Philosophy* (New York: Oxford University Press, 1963). One writer who does give Emerson a prominent place is Paul K. Conkin, in his *Puritans and Pragmatists: Eight Eminent American Thinkers* (Bloomington: Indiana University Press, 1968).

3 Richard Poirier, *The Renewal of Literature: Emersonian Reflections* (New York: Random House, 1986); Cornel West, *The American Evasion of Philosophy: A Geneology of Pragmatism* (Madison: University of Wisconsin Press, 1989). See also my "Reconstructing American Philosophy: Emerson and Dewey," given in June 1988 at a Texas A&M University conference, "Frontiers in American Philosophy," and forthcoming in *Texas A&M Studies in American Philosophy.*

4 A primary goal of many Greek and Roman philosophers. See, for example, Martha Nussbaum, "Undemocratic Vistas," *New York Review of Books,* November 5, 1987, p. 20. Romanticism is in many ways an attempt to recover Greek and Roman ways of thinking and being, and this is nowhere clearer than in the American transcendentalists, for example, in the connections between Thoreau and the Stoics, or Emerson and the Platonic tradition.

5 Stanley Cavell, "Genteel Responses to Kant? In Emerson's 'Fate' and in Coleridge's *Biographia Literaria,*" *Raritan* 3, no. 2 (1983): 35.

6 In Morris Eaves and Michael Fischer, eds., *Romanticism and Contemporary Criticism* (Ithaca, N.Y.: Cornell University Press, 1986), pp. 183–239. This paper furnishes the title of, and appears in, Cavell's subsequent book, *In Quest of the Ordinary: Lines of Skepticism and Romanticism* (Chicago: University of Chicago Press, 1988).

7 Cavell, "Genteel Responses," p. 34.
8 *The Middle Works of John Dewey*, ed. Jo Ann Boydston (Carbondale: Southern Illinois University Press, 1976–83), 6:97.
9 Ralph Waldo Emerson, *English Traits* (Boston: Houghton Mifflin, 1903), p. 14.
10 Henry James, *A Small Boy and Others* (New York: Scribner, 1913), p. 8.
11 Stanley Cavell, *The Claim of Reason* (New York: Oxford University Press, 1979), p. 455.
12 William James, *Pragmatism* (Cambridge, Mass.: Harvard University Press, 1975), p. 24.
13 *The Collected Works of Ralph Waldo Emerson*, ed. Robert Spiller et al. (Cambridge, Mass.: Harvard University Press, 1971–), 3:41.

CHAPTER 1

1 Stanley Cavell, "Being Odd, Getting Even: Threats to Individuality," *Salmagundi* no. 67 (Summer 1985): 97–8.
2 In Stanley Cavell, *Must We Mean What We Say?* (1962; reprint, Cambridge, England: Cambridge University Press, 1969), pp. 44–72; hereafter cited as *MWM*.
3 Ludwig Wittgenstein, *Philosophical Investigations*, trans. G. E. M. Anscombe (New York: Macmillan, 1958), para. 129; hereafter cited as *PI*.
4 Ibid., para. 133.
5 Cavell, *MWM*, pp. 70–2.
6 This is true of philosophies other than Cavell's, as he himself suggests in his treatments of Wittgenstein's therapeutic voices or in his use of the terms "recital" and "moment" to characterize the argument of Descartes's *Meditations* (Cavell, *The Claim of Reason* [New York: Oxford University Press, 1979], pp. 420–1; hereafter cited as *CR*). The musicality of Cavell's writing shows also in the form of Part IV of *CR*: not chapters, propositions, or essays, but a series of "entries" with breaks between, which Cavell characterizes as "convenient resting places, to let the mind clear, or a thought complete itself – matters which may or may not coincide with the introducing or the dropping of a theme." Indeed, although Cavell associates the themes in his table of contents – such as "slaves," "seeing human beings as human beings," or "The Outsider" – with specific sections of his text, he also warns that "shifting numbers of them may simultaneously extend over one or more segments of the whole" (Cavell, *CR*, p. viii). Especially in this key part of *The Claim of Reason*, Cavell resembles a jazz musician, stating, developing, provoking, and undermining his themes. Those tracing biographical sources for this propensity should note that Cavell's undergraduate degree (at Berkeley) was in musicology, that he studied piano and composition at Juilliard, and that he played jazz saxophone in Oakland before he entered college. Cf. James Conant, "An Interview with Stanley Cavell," in Richard Fleming and Michael Payne, eds., *The Senses of Stanley Cavell* (Lewisburg, Pa.: Bucknell University Press, 1989), pp. 21–72.
7 Wittgenstein, *PI*, para. 133, 123, 129.
8 Cavell, *CR*, p. 453.
9 Cavell, *MWM*, p. 286.
10 Cavell, *MWM*, pp. 279, 278.

11 Ibid., p. 324. All italics in original unless otherwise noted.

12 Cavell, *CR*, p. 352.

13 See, for example, Cavell, *CR*, pp. 384–6.

14 Social contract: Cavell, *CR*, p. 438; insanity: Cavell, *CR*, p. 460.

15 "The dawning of an aspect, and its presentation of a physiognomy, sketch the logic, I mean the myth, of knowing another mind" (Cavell, *CR*, p. 370). Cf. Northrop Frye, *A Study of English Romanticism* (Chicago: University of Chicago Press, 1968), p. 5.

16 Cavell, *CR*, pp. 364, 368.

17 Wittgenstein, *PI*, para. 371.

18 See Ludwig Wittgenstein, *Culture and Value*, ed. G. H. von Wright and trans. Peter Winch (Chicago: University of Chicago Press, 1980), p. 16.

19 This quotation and much of the text that follows align Cavell with "transformational" writers. See John Taber, *Transformational Philosophy* (Honolulu: University of Hawaii Press, 1983).

20 Wittgenstein, *Culture and Value*, p. 68.

21 Stanley Cavell, "The Division of Talent," *Critical Inquiry* 11 (June 1985):520.

22 Cavell, *CR*, p. 377.

23 Ibid., p. 424. I have added the circumflex to *l'âme*.

24 Wittgenstein, *PI*, p. 178; cf. Cavell, *CR* pp. 340–1, 399.

25 Cavell, *CR*, p. 421; cf. p. 423. It is helpful in evaluating the force of this "with" to remember that such an attitude, is, like Kant's "respect," demanded or claimed from us and that for Kant such claims ultimately require a community, a "kingdom of ends."

26 Cavell, *MWM*, pp. 263–4.

27 Søren Kierkegaard, *Either/Or*, trans. Walter Lowrie (Princeton, N.J.: Princeton University Press, 1949), 2:143.

28 Cavell, *CR*, p. 361.

29 Ludwig Wittgenstein, *Notebooks 1914–16* (Oxford, England: Blackwell Publisher, 1969), p. 81.

30 Cf. Thomas Nagel, "What Is It Like to Be a Bat?" *Philosophical Review* 83 (October 1974): 435–50.

31 Cavell, *CR*, p. 425.

32 Ibid., p. 432.

33 Cavell, *MWM*, p. 290.

34 Cavell, *CR*, p. 439.

35 On the "oscillation between sensing an asymmetry under each symmetry, and a symmetry under each asymmetry," see ibid., p. 451.

36 Ibid., p. 437. However, Cavell's subsequent work on Coleridge and Wordsworth, suggesting connections between "dejection" and external world skepticism, shows that this asymmetry is unstable.

37 Ibid., p. 449.

38 Ludwig Wittgenstein, *On Certainty* (Oxford, England: Blackwell Publisher, 1969), para. 117.

39 Ibid., para. 7.

40 Quoted in Stanley Cavell, *Pursuits of Happiness: The Hollywood Comedy of Remar-*

riage (Cambridge, Mass.: Harvard University Press, 1981), p. 21; hereafter cited as *PH*.
41 Cavell, *CR*, p. 432. Cavell thus records the "diasparactive" moments in our knowledge of other minds. See Thomas McFarland, *Romanticism and the Forms of Ruin* (Princeton, N.J.: Princeton University Press, 1983); hereafter cited as *RFR*.
42 Cavell, *CR*, p. 451.
43 Cavell, "The Division of Talent," p. 521. Philippe Lacoue-Labarthe and Jean-Luc Nancy provide an important discussion of Schlegel's doctrine that "poetry and philosophy should be made one" and other positions of Jena Romanticism in *The Literary Absolute: The Theory of Literature in German Romanticism* (Albany: State University of New York Press, 1988); hereafter cited as *LA*. Cavell acknowledges his "American belatedness" in learning about the Jena Romantics, and his "education in public" by Lacoue-Labarthe's and Nancy's book. In *Quest of the Ordinary: Lines of Skepticism and Romanticism* (Chicago: University of Chicago Press, 1988), p. xii; and *This New Yet Unapproachable America* (Albuquerque, N.M.: Living Batch Press, 1989), p. 8.
44 Stanley Cavell, "Genteel Responses to Kant? in Emerson's 'Fate' and Coleridge's *Biographia Literaria*," *Raritan* 3 (1983): 55; hereafter cited as *GR*. Lacoue-Labarthe and Nancy also give Kant a central place in opening up "the possibility of Romanticism," though they focus on Kant's views about the subject rather than about noumena (*LA*, p. 29).
45 Samuel Taylor Coleridge, *Biographia Literaria*, ed. James Engell and Walter Jackson Bate (Princeton, N.J.: Princeton University Press, 1983), 2: 25–6; hereafter cited as *BL*.
46 "In Quest of the Ordinary," in Morris Eaves and Michael Fischer, eds., *Romanticism and Contemporary Criticism* (Ithaca, N.Y.: Cornell University Press, 1986), p. 185; hereafter cited as *IQO*.
47 Cavell states: "Like many other people, I've learned a lot, I hope, from having read M. H. Abrams, Geoffrey Hartman, Paul de Man, and Harold Bloom on these topics. I'm not talking about some of their recent work so much as the work in the sixties and the early seventies when they lived and died with Romanticism, before the theoretical controversies that, you may say, either grew out of their work or allowed them not to think anymore about that work" (Cavell, *IQO*, pp. 230–1). Some important works on Romanticism not already cited are by Jacques Barzun, *Romanticism and the Modern Ego* (Boston: Little, Brown, 1947) and *Berlioz and the Romantic Century*, 2 vols. (New York: Columbia University Press, 1969); Harold Bloom, *The Ringers in the Tower* (Chicago: University of Chicago Press, 1971), *A Map of Misreading* (New York: Oxford University Press, 1975), and *Agon: Towards a Theory of Revisionism* (New York: Oxford University Press, 1982); M. H. Abrams, *The Mirror and the Lamp: Romantic Theory and the Critical Tradition* (New York: Oxford University Press, 1953) (hereafter cited as *ML*), and *Natural Supernaturalism: Tradition and Revolution in Romantic Literature* (New York: Norton, 1971) (hereafter cited as *NS*); Geoffrey Hartman, *Wordsworth's Poetry 1787–1814* (New Haven, Conn.: Yale University Press, 1964); and Thomas McFarland, *Coleridge and the Pantheist Tradition* (New York: Oxford University Press, 1969) (hereafter cited as *CPT*).

48 Cf. Cavell, *CR*, p. 455.
49 *Immanuel Kant's Critique of Pure Reason*, trans. Norman Kemp Smith (London: Macmillan, 1963), B xvi; hereafter cited as *CPR*. Also see the discussion in Abrams, *ML*, pp. 58 ff.
50 Frye, *A Study of English Romanticism*, p. 5. Cf. Lacoue-Labarthe and Nancy, *LA*, p. 36.
51 Kant himself responds to such deficiencies in the *Critique of Judgment*, in which he speaks of the soul (geist) of a work of genius and of the necessity of our pleasure in experiencing the beautiful (this necessity is asserted in what he calls "the judgment of taste"). See Immanuel Kant, *Critique of Judgment*, trans. J. H. Bernard (New York: Hafner, 1968), pp. 132, 156; hereafter cited as *CJ*. The judgment, the transcendental faculty that Kant studies in this third *Critique*, is "a middle term between the understanding and the reason" (p. 13). It discovers the unified purposiveness of nature and its source in the harmony of our faculties of understanding and imagination.

In discussing genius, Kant assigns the imagination the role of "creating another nature, as it were, out of the material that actual nature gives it." For this purpose it utilizes "aesthetical ideas," which occasion "much thought, without however any definite thought, i.e., any *concept*, being capable of being adequate to [them]." The poet employing these aesthetical ideas "tries, by means of imagination, which emulates the play of reason in its quest after a maximum, to go beyond the limits of experience and to present them to sense with a completeness of which there is no example in nature" (pp. 157, 158). On the role of the *Critique of Judgment* in sketching a resolution to problems posed by Kant's earlier writings, see Lacoue-Labarthe and Nancy, *LA*, pp. 31–2.
52 Cavell, *GR*, p. 55. This is bound to be a controversial interpretation of Coleridge, on historical as well as textual grounds. As to the first, Coleridge had not yet traveled to Germany and probably had not even read Kant when he wrote "The Rime of the Ancient Mariner." Cavell responds to this as follows: "I am not saying that when he wrote his poem he meant it to exemplify Kant's *Critique of Pure Reason*, merely that it does so, and that there are passages in the *Biographia* where Coleridge virtually states as much" (Cavell, *GR*, p. 59). Second, Coleridge's avowed enemies throughout the *Biographia* are writers such as Locke, and Kant is taken not as his enemy but as the giant who "disciplined my understanding" (Coleridge *BL*, I, 153). Yet, Coleridge has to do quite a bit of interpretation to make Kant express his ideas ("In spite . . . of his own declarations, I could never believe it was possible for him to have meant no more by his *Noumenon*, or THING IN ITSELF, than his mere words express" (Coleridge, *BL*, I, 155). He points out that Kant offers an analysis "not of human nature in toto, but of the speculative intellect alone" (which he also calls "the point of *reflection*," using a variant of the word that he had associated with death) (Coleridge, *BL*, I, 154). Such passages support Cavell's view that Coleridge is criticizing, if only as part of revising, Kant's idea of the phenomenal world, the world of Understanding.
53 Cavell, *IQO*, p. 193.
54 Ibid., p. 190.

55 Ibid., p. 203.
56 Sharon Cameron, *Writing Nature* (New York: Oxford University Press, 1985), p. 11.
57 *The Collected Works of Ralph Waldo Emerson*, ed. Robert Spiller et al. (Cambridge, Mass.: Harvard University Press, 1971–), 1:43; hereafter cited as *CW*. Of course, who "we" are ultimately is also questioned by Romanticism. The self is no more fixed than is the self–world relationship.
58 To Plotinus may be traced the Romantic concern with alienation and the recovery of a primal unity, the picturing of this unity as the relation of lover and beloved, and the common Romantic figure of creation as emanation (Abrams, *NS*, pp. 146–9; Abrams, *ML*, p. 58).
59 See P. F. Strawson, *The Bounds of Sense* (London: Methuen, 1966), esp. pp. 122–32. See also Strawson's *Individuals* (London: Methuen, 1959) for other statements of this kind of argument.
60 Kant, *CPR*, B xxvi.
61 Cavell, *IQO*, pp. 190, 191.
62 William Wordsworth, *The Poetical Works of Wordsworth* (Boston: Houghton Mifflin, 1982), p. 231 (*The Recluse*, lines 800–8); hereafter cited as *W*.
63 Abrams, *NS*, p. 68. Cf. Lacoue-Labarthe and Nancy, *LA*, p. ix, in which the translators, Philip Barnard and Cheryl Lester, speak of a condition in which "the absolute might be experienced."
64 Wordsworth, *W*, p. 231 (*The Recluse*, Lines 822–4).
65 Abrams, *NS*, p. 281. This remark applies most clearly to Fichte and Schelling. Hartman similarly maintains that "Wordsworth cannot be said to discover nature as such, but rather the reality of the relation between nature and mind" (Hartman, *Wordsworth's Poetry*, p. 170). See also McFarland, *RFR*.
66 Harold Bloom, ed. *William Wordsworth* (New York: Chelsea House, 1985), p. 113.
67 Ibid., p. 188.
68 Wordsworth, *W*, pp. 222 (*The Recluse*, 50–1) and 215 (*The Prelude*, XIII, 290–3).
69 Paul de Man writes, for example, that "critics who speak of a 'happy relationship' between matter and consciousness fail to realize that the very fact that the relationship has to be established within the medium of language indicates that it does not exist in actuality." "Intentional Structure of the Romantic Image," in Bloom, *William Wordsworth*, p. 28. See also M. H. Abrams, "Two Roads to Wordsworth," in Bloom, *William Wordsworth*, and McFarland, *RFR*.
70 Wordsworth, *W*, p. 165 (*The Prelude*, VI, 526–8).
71 For example, ibid., pp. 218–19 (*The Prelude*, XIV, 188ff).
72 Ibid., p. 166 (*The Prelude*, VI, 592–7).
73 Hartman, *Wordsworth's Poetry*, p. 350.
74 Wordsworth, *W*, p. 217 (*The Prelude*, XIV, 74–5, 105).
75 Cavell, *GR*, p. 56. In "Revelations," chap. 21, Coleridge's biblical source for the idea of a "new heaven and a new earth," the power of producing them is divine, not human.
76 Kant, *CPR*, B 44, A 27–8, B 52, A 35–6.

77 Coleridge, *BL*, I, 261–2.
78 Samuel Taylor Coleridge, *The Friend*, ed. Barbara E. Rooke (Princeton, N.J.: Princeton University Press, 1969), 1:497. See the discussion of this and the preceding quotations in Owen Barfield, *What Coleridge Thought* (Middletown, Conn.: Wesleyan University Press, 1971), p. 65.
79 Quoted in McFarland, *CPT*, p. 185.
80 Coleridge, *BL*, II, 158–9.
81 McFarland, *CPT*, p. 228.
82 Ibid., pp. 221–2.
83 See Oscar Cullman, "Immortality of the Soul or Resurrection of the Dead? The Witness of the New Testament," in Terence Penelhum, ed., *Immortality* (Belmont, Calif: Wadsworth, 1973), pp. 53–85.
84 Barfield, *What Coleridge Thought*, p. 37; see also chap. 11, "Coleridge and the Cosmology of Science." There is, of course, a long-standing alliance of science and mysticism, for example, in medieval alchemy.
85 Raimonda Modiano, *Coleridge and the Concept of Nature* (London: Macmillan, 1985), p. 144.
86 Ibid., p. 6.
87 Coleridge, *BL*, II, p. 5.
88 Emerson, *CW* 3:48.
89 Stanley Cavell, *The Senses of Walden* (San Francisco: North Point Press, 1981), p. 126; hereafter cited as *SW*.
90 Robert Langbaum, *The Poetry of Experience* (New York: Random House, 1957), pp. 35, 22. Ernest Lee Tuveson finds relations between Romanticism and the thought of John Locke, a philosopher usually regarded as the champion of the passive mind and hence an opponent of the active, overflowing mind that the Romantics depict. Tuveson maintains that because of his discovery of unconscious associations of ideas, Locke had discovered the living, nonmechanical Romantic mind: "Experience for Locke is not a mere automatic connection of impressions, as if an adding machine were being set up. He always has the sense of a living being . . . but its area is not sharply defined, and its boundaries expand and contract with the exigencies of the creature's total response to its ever-changing environment." See Ernest Lee Tuveson, *The Imagination as a Means of Grace* (Berkeley and Los Angeles: University of California Press, 1960), p. 39. For seventeenth- and early eighteenth-century precursors of Romanticism, see Walter Jackson Bate, *From Classic to Romantic* (New York: Harper Torchbooks, 1946). For Wordsworth's relation to the empiricist tradition deriving from Newton, see Fred Wilson, "Wordsworth and the Culture of Science," *Centennial Review* 33 (Fall 1989): 322–92.
91 Although they owe much to empiricist writers such as Locke; see Bate, *From Classic to Romantic*.
92 Wordsworth, *W*, p. 92.
93 Ibid., p. 791.
94 Coleridge, *BL*, II, 7.
95 See Barzun, *Berlioz and the Romantic Century*; and Bloom, "Romanticism and the Rational," in Bloom, *The Ringers in the Tower*, pp. 323–37.
96 Wordsworth, *W*, p. 213 (*The Prelude*, XIII, 141–6).

97 Ibid., pp. 791, 796.

98 Cavell, *GR*, p. 56.

99 Hartman, *Wordsworth's Poetry*, p. 80.

100 As quoted in Abrams, *NS*, pp. 435–6 (*The Prelude*, II, 401 ff.).

101 Cavell, *GR*, pp. 40–1.

102 Wordsworth, *W*, p. 791.

103 Bate, *From Classic to Romantic*, p. 174. Cf. Coleridge, *BL*, I, 80.

104 On the pre-Romantic association between feeling and subtlety of discrimination, see Bate, *From Classic to Romantic*, pp. 129–31.

105 Cavell, *MWM*, p. 325, n. 15.

106 Cavell, *SW*, p. 104.

107 Coleridge, *BL*, I, 304. Cf. the account of the relation among aesthetic Ideas, action, and will in Lacoue-Labarthe and Nancy, *LA*, p. 35. For application of this passage to Emerson, see Julie Ellison, *Emerson's Romantic Style* (Princeton, N.J.: Princeton University Press, 1984), p. 182.

108 For the last phrase, see "Expostulation and Reply," in Wordsworth, *W*, p. 83.

109 William James, *The Will to Believe and Other Essays* (Cambridge, Mass.: Harvard University Press, 1979), p. 18.

110 Cavell, *CR*, p. 397.

111 Immanuel Kant, *Groundwork of the Metaphysic of Morals*, trans. H. J. Paton (New York: Harper Torchbooks, 1964), pp. 100–3.

112 Wordsworth, *W*, p. 211 (*The Prelude*, XII, 276–7).

113 Augustine, *Later Works*, trans. John Burnaby (Philadelphia: Westminster Press, 1955), 8:71, 54–5.

114 Ibid., pp. 70–1. For Augustine, a certain kind of love – not eros, which involves a lack, but a constantly fulfilled love – is the perfection of the will that unites self and world. See Hannah Arendt, *Willing* (New York: Harcourt Brace Jovanovich, 1978), p. 102.

115 Coleridge, *BL*, I, 153.

116 Kant, *Groundwork*, p. 125.

117 Coleridge, *The Friend*, I: 519–20.

118 Ibid, p. 521.

119 Kant, *CPR*, A 816–17, B 844–5. I am indebted to Brom Anderson for pointing out the relevance of this paragraph to my account. Kant takes up the theme of the fit between our faculties and the phenomenal world in Kant, *CJ*; see especially the "Introduction."

120 Barfield, *What Coleridge Thought*, p. 14.

121 Arendt, *Willing*, p. 29.

122 Cavell, *IQO*, p. 197.

123 Stanley Cavell, *Pursuits of Happiness: The Hollywood Comedy of Remarriage* (Cambridge, Mass.: Harvard University Press, 1981), p. 142; hereafter cited as *PH*.

124 Ibid., pp. 126–7.

125 Cf. Wittgenstein's remark that "love is not a feeling; love is put to the test" in *Zettel* (Berkeley and Los Angeles: University of California Press, 1967), para. 504.

126 Cavell, *PH*, pp. 166–7.

127 Arendt, *Willing*, p. 102.
128 Cavell, *PH*, p. 87. The dominant meaning of "conversation" in Milton's time, however, was not "talk" but something more like "intercourse."
129 Ibid., p. 172.
130 Ibid., p. 236.
131 Ibid., p. 88.
132 Ibid., p. 260.
133 Ibid., p. 103.
134 Cavell, *In Quest of the Ordinary*, p. 178.
135 Cavell, *CR*, p. 399.
136 Kant, *Groundwork*, pp. 68–9n. Some writers, for example, Beck, translate the German *Achtung* as "respect," whereas others, for example, Paton, use "reverence." In order to match Cavell's discussion, I shall follow him and Beck in using "respect," even when I am otherwise employing Paton's translation. See Lewis White Beck, *Foundations of the Metaphysics of Morals* (Chicago: University of Chicago Press, 1950).
137 Cavell, *CR*, p. 389.
138 Kant, *Groundwork*, p. 69n. Cf. Immanuel Kant, *Critique of Practical Reason*, trans. Lewis White Beck (Indianapolis: Bobbs-Merrill, 1956), p. 83.
139 Cavell, *CR*, p. 377.
140 Cavell's inspiration is the Wittgenstein of the *Philosophical Investigations*, but it is noteworthy that Wittgenstein wrote in the *Notebooks* that "the will is an attitude of the subject to the world." Wittgenstein, *Notebooks*, p. 87.
141 See, for example, Cavell, *CR*, p. 370.
142 Although as my colleague Brom Anderson reminds me, it is not always a mistake to avoid others.
143 Cavell, *SW*, p. 4.
144 Ibid., pp. 11–12.
145 Ibid., p. 88.
146 Ibid., pp. 33–4.
147 Ibid., p. 80.
148 Henry David Thoreau, *Walden and Other Writings* (New York: Modern Library, 1965), p. 7. Cavell again records a voluntarist structure of reading, in which our "knowing" depends on what "we will," by focusing on Thoreau's statement that "there are probably words addressed to our condition exactly, which, if we could really hear and understand, would be more salutary than the morning." Cavell comments that these "are words with our names on them" but that we need to be reborn to hear them (*SW*, p. 16). Some such words, he continues, contain "a rebuke of our lives by what we may know of them, if we will" (*SW*, p. 92).
149 Cavell, *SW*, p. 65.
150 Wittgenstein, *Zettel*, para. 155.
151 Cavell, *SW*, pp. 103, 104.
152 Ibid., p. 106n.
153 Ibid., p. 105.
154 Cavell, *IQO*, p. 185. On Wittgenstein and Heidegger, see Friedrich Wais-

mann, "Notes on Talks with Wittgenstein," *Philosophical Review* 74 (1965):12–16. The original title of these notes was "On Heidegger." See Michael Murray, "A Note on Wittgenstein and Heidegger," *Philosophical Review* 83 (1974):501–3.
155 William James, *Varieties of Religious Experience* (Cambridge, Mass.: Harvard University Press, 1985), p. 395, n. 8.

CHAPTER 2

1 Gay Wilson Allen, *Waldo Emerson* (New York: Penguin, 1982), p. 187.
2 Harold Bloom, *The Ringers in the Tower* (Chicago: University of Chicago Press, 1971), p. 297. See also Bloom's discussion of "Romanticism and the Rational," pp. 323–38 of *The Ringers;* his discussion of "Emerson and His Influence," in his *A Map of Misreading* (New York: Oxford University Press, 1975), pp. 160–76; and B. L. Packer, *Emerson's Fall* (New York: Continuum, 1982), *passim.* On Emerson's use of the marriage metaphor for expressing the mind–world relationship, see Eric Cheyfitz, *The Trans-Parent: Sexual Politics in the Language of Emerson* (Baltimore: Johns Hopkins University Press, 1981), pp. 69 ff.
3 See notes 2 and 3 in the Preface.
4 John Dewey, *The Middle Works* (Carbondale: Southern Illinois University Press, 1976–83), 3:191 (hereafter cited as *MW*).
5 William James, *Essays in Religion and Morality* (Cambridge, Mass.: Harvard University Press, 1982), p. 114.
6 Stanley Cavell, "Thinking of Emerson" and "An Emerson Mood," in *The Senses of Walden* (San Francisco: North Point Press, 1981), hereafter cited as *SW;* "Genteel Responses to Kant? In Emerson's 'Fate' and Coleridge's *Biographia Literaria*," *Raritan* 3 (1985):34–61; hereafter cited as *GR;* and "Being Odd, Getting Even: Threats to Individuality," *Salmagundi* no. 67 (Summer 1985):97–128, hereafter cited as *BO* (the two previous papers are reprinted in Cavell's *In Quest of the Ordinary: Lines of Skepticism and Romanticism* (Chicago: University of Chicago Press, 1988); David Van Leer, *Emerson's Epistemology* (Cambridge, England: Cambridge University Press, 1986), Cornel West, *The American Evasion of Philosophy: A Geneology of Pragmatism* (Madison: University of Wisconsin Press, 1989); and Packer, *Emerson's Fall*. See also Julie Ellison, *Emerson's Romantic Style* (Princeton, N.J.: Princeton University Press, 1984); and Evan Carton, *The Rhetoric of American Romance: Dialectic and Identity in Emerson, Dickenson, Poe, and Hawthorne* (Baltimore: Johns Hopkins University Press, 1985) for application of the deconstructive philosophy of Barthes and Derrida to Emerson's works.
7 Emerson is often treated as a moral philosopher. See, for example, Ellen Kappy Sukiel, "Emerson on the Virtues," in Marcus G. Singer, ed., *American Philosophy* (Cambridge, England: Cambridge University Press, 1985), pp. 135–52. West understands him to be a political philosopher who "evades" traditional epistemological issues.
8 For a comparison of Dewey's and James's evaluations of Emerson, see John McDermott, "Spires of Influence: The Importance of Emerson for Classical American Philosophy," in his *Streams of Experience* (Amherst: University of Massachusetts Press, 1986), pp. 29–43. Poirier argues in *The Renewal of Litera-*

ture: Emersonian Reflections (New York: Random House, 1986) – convincingly in my view – that whether or not he acknowledged it, James was profoundly influenced by Emerson, for example, in his focus on action and transition (pp. 9–17).

9 *The Collected Works of Ralph Waldo Emerson,* ed. Robert E. Spiller et al. (Cambridge, Mass.: Harvard University Press, 1971–), 3:48; hereafter cited as *CW.*

10 See the interpretation of "Experience," provided by Sharon Cameron in "Representing Grief: Emerson's Experience," *Representations* 15 (Summer 1986):15–41.

11 Emerson, *CW,* 1:7–70.

12 Ibid., 1:7.

13 Ibid., 1:56.

14 A point stressed by Ellison, *Emerson's Romantic Style, passim.*

15 Emerson, *CW,* 1:56.

16 Emerson, *CW,* 2:28. For the idea that the scholar's freedom is essentially interpretive, see Ellison, *Emerson's Romantic Style,* pp. 97–104.

17 Emerson, *CW,* 1:63–4.

18 Such forward looking is a link between Emerson and the pragmatists. "Genius looks forward," Emerson stated, "The eyes of man are set in his forehead, not in his hindhead. Man hopes. Genius creates" (Ibid., 1:57).

19 Ibid., 1:64.

20 Ibid., 1:65.

21 Ibid., 1:52, 70.

22 Ibid., 1:89.

23 Ibid., 1:82.

24 For the contemporary reaction to the address, see Allen, *Waldo Emerson,* pp. 316 ff. Emerson was attacked for his "infidelity, pantheism, and atheism" (p. 322).

25 Emerson, *CW,* 1:90.

26 Ibid.

27 See his essay on Emerson.

28 Emerson, *CW,* 2:179.

29 Ibid., 2:180–1.

30 Ibid., 2:190. I broach the subject of Emerson's transitional metaphysics in my paper "Freedom in the Philosophy of Ralph Waldo Emerson, *Tulane Studies in Philosophy* 35 (1987):7.

31 Emerson, *CW,* 2:189. On the notion of transition or flux in Emerson, see Poirier, *The Renewal of Literature, passim;* West, *The American Evasion,* pp. 15 ff.; and my paper "Reconstructing American Philosophy: Emerson and Dewey," given at a conference, "Frontiers in American Philosophy," in June 1988 and forthcoming in *Texas A & M Studies in American Philosophy.* Cf. Friedrich Schlegel's idea that becoming is the essence of Romantic poetry, in *Friedrich Schlegel's Lucinde and the Fragments,* trans. Peter Firchow (Minneapolis: University of Minnesota Press, 1971), p. 173 (Athenaeum Fragment 116); and the discussion in Philippe Lacoue-Labarthe and Jean-Luc Nancy, *The Literary Absolute: The Theory of Literature in German Romanticism* (Albany: State University of New York Press, 1988), p. 43.

32 For some treatments of Emerson and Nietzsche, see Van Leer, *Emerson's Epistemology,* p. 217, n. 52.

33 Emerson, *CW,* 2:186.

34 Ibid., 2:187.

35 See note 6.

36 Emerson, *CW*, 2:38. Van Leer's discussion of this passage suggests his unfamiliarity with the Cartesian source, for he maintains that Emerson's statement of it lacks a "therefore" (Van Leer, *Emerson's Epistemology*, p. 136). "I think, therefore I am" occurs in the *Discourse on the Method* but not in the *Meditations*, in which Descartes writes " 'I am, I exist' is necessarily true whenever I utter it or conceive it in my mind," using exactly the words that Emerson reproduces.

37 See Søren Kierkegaard, *Concluding Unscientific Postscript* (Princeton, N.J.: Princeton University Press, 1941). For a brief account of Kierkegaard's picture of human existence, see Section III of my paper "How a Thing Is Said and Heard: Wittgenstein and Kierkegaard," *History of Philosophy Quarterly* 3 (July 1986): 335–53.

38 Cavell, *BO*, p. 102.

39 Emerson, *CW*, 2:27.

40 Emerson, *CW*, 3:31.

41 Ibid.

42 Emerson, *CW*, 2:29.

43 Ralph Waldo Emerson, *The Conduct of Life* (Boston: Houghton Mifflin, 1904), p. 20; hereafter cited as *CL*. A classic discussion of Emerson's dialectic of freedom and fate occurs in Stephen Whicher's *Freedom and Fate: An Inner Life of Ralph Waldo Emerson* (Philadelphia: University of Pennsylvania Press, 1953).

44 Emerson, *CL*, pp. 8–9.

45 Ibid., p. 15; for the view that Emerson is not talking about his earlier thought in this passage, see Cavell, *GR*, p. 43.

46 Emerson, *CL*, pp. 41–2.

47 Ibid., p. 48.

48 But, one might ask, why shouldn't the way we handle it be part of fate, as our temperament is?

49 Emerson, *CL*, p. 47.

50 Ibid., pp. 47–8.

51 David Hume, *An Inquiry Concerning Human Understanding* (Indianapolis: Bobbs-Merrill, 1955), p. 104.

52 Emerson, *CW*, 3:32.

53 Ibid., 3:42.

54 The Heraclitean side of Plato emerges, however, in such dialogues as the *Phaedrus* and *Symposium*.

55 Emerson, *CW*, 4:91.

56 Ibid., 2:202.

57 Ibid., 4:101.

58 Ibid., 3:48.

59 Cavell's discussion is in Cavell, *SW*, pp. 142–3.

60 Emerson, *CW*, 1:37–8.

61 Ibid., 1:10.

62 Ellison argues that these are essential to Emerson's "aggressive" project of mastering the universe by interpreting it.

63 Allen, *Waldo Emerson*, p. 278.

64 Emerson, *CW*, 3:35.

65 See note 6.

66 Van Leer comes at Emerson's Kantianism independently of Cavell's work, producing an original argument about the Kantian claims of *Nature* and also enlightening discussions of many other Emersonian texts.

   Although he is familiar with many philosophical sources, Van Leer's understanding of philosophical literature is somewhat shaky. For example, in discussing criticisms of Emerson for missing the distinction between "transcendental" (a priori and in some sense human) and "transcendent" (apart from all determination by what is human, beyond "the bounds of sense") in Kant, he misstates that very distinction by understanding transcendent principles as "organizing mental principles that are inaccessible to experience." For Kant they are illusions, not existing but inaccessible principles. The point of them (in the illusory tale, as it were) is that they are not mental and not subjective but, rather, that they reflect things as they are in themselves. Again, Van Leer takes transcendental idealism to mean that space and time are illusions; for example, he speaks of the rapidity with which "time and space vanish . . . in Kant's Aesthetic" (*Emerson's Epistemology*, p. 40) and maintains that "transcendental idealism ensures that experience will always be illusion, a tempest of fancies" (p. 163). Kant's project was to justify the objectivity of space and time.

   More technically, Van Leer confuses entailment with identity (p. 91), gives an account of transcendental argument in which that notoriously difficult notion amounts merely to showing entailments ("that certain concepts are logically built into other concepts," p. 112); misses Austin's notion of a performative, for example, by saying that "performatives are oughts" (p. 243, n. 91); (If I insult you, I do not necessarily command you; only some performatives are "oughts"); and is unreliable on Wittgenstein – remarking (p. 175) that "a pain is not a possessing or even a content of any kind, but a behavioral act" or (p. 176) that in Wittgenstein's parable of the beetle in the box, pain drops out like the beetle (which misses Wittgenstein's point that this is so only if we "construe" pain "on the model of object and designation").

67 Emerson, *CW*, 3:48. Cf. Cavell, *SW*, p. 126.

68 Cavell, *SW*, p. 126.

69 Ibid., p. 125. This is a point that Van Leer fails to consider, for example, when he interprets Emerson's discussions as having moved beyond epistemology when they reach a sentiment such as Romantic joy (*Emerson's Epistemology*, p. 92). Van Leer, in fact, has an extremely puzzling notion of epistemology, maintaining for example, that Emerson's essay "Montaigne; or the Skeptic" is not about an epistemological topic (pp. 194–5). He appears to believe that if one regards faith or mystical experience (or, as one might say, a certain mood) as superseding doubt and as leading to truth, as Emerson does in "Montaigne" (and elsewhere), then one has somehow passed beyond the domain of epistemology. But this is to restrict epistemology, the theory of knowledge, to certain kinds of knowledge.

70 Emerson, *CW*, 3:30.

71 Ibid., 3:30, 45–6.

72 Ludwig Wittgenstein, *Tractatus Logico-Philosophicus* (London: Routledge & Kegan Paul, 1961), para. 6.43.
73 Cavell, *SW*, p. 125.
74 William James, *The Principles of Psychology* (Cambridge, Mass.: Harvard University Press, 1981), p. 1182.
75 Emerson, *CW*, 2:182.
76 Ibid., 4:99.
77 Ibid.; here the "common" is not to be embraced but avoided.
78 Cavell, *SW*, p. 128.
79 Emerson, *CW*, 3:48.
80 Cavell, *SW*, p. 126.
81 Cavell does not actually suggest this use of the "lords" in *SW*, though his interpretation of Emerson led me to it. Cf. Stanley Cavell, *This New Yet Unapproachable America: Lectures After Emerson After Wittgenstein* (Albuquerque, N.M.: Living Batch Press, 1989), p. 88. Van Leer also treats the lords as Kantian categories or forms in his discussion of "Experience" (*Emerson's Epistemology*, pp. 150–87).
82 Emerson, *CW*, 3:39; Van Leer, *Emerson's Epistemology*, p. 158.
83 Emerson, *CW*, 3:33.
84 Cameron, "Representing Grief," p. 21.
85 Emerson, *CW*, 3:31.
86 Ibid., 3:32.
87 Ibid., 3:57.
88 Ibid., 3:61, 57.
89 As Milly Theale does to Lord Mark in Henry James's *The Wings of the Dove*.
90 Emerson, *CW*, 3:64.
91 Ibid., 2:34.
92 Ibid., 3:54.
93 Ibid., 3:40.
94 Ibid., 3:29–30.
95 Ibid.
96 "There is no mark by which we can tell dreaming from waking." René Descartes, *Meditations on First Philosophy*, trans. Donald A. Cress (Indianapolis: Hackett, 1979). Cf. J. L. Austin, *Sense and Sensibilia* (New York: Oxford University Press, 1962), pp. 48–9.
97 Emerson, CW, 3:30.
98 Ibid., 3:43.
99 Ibid., 1:10.
100 James in *Varieties of Religious Experience*, and Dewey in *Democracy and Education*. See Chapters 3 and 4 in this text.
101 Emerson, *CW*, 1:10.
102 Ibid., 3:40.
103 Ibid., 2:189–90.
104 The contrast between the Platonic idea of knowledge as recollection and Emerson's idea of losing our memory is also striking.
105 Emerson, *CW*, 3:189 ("Circles"); *CW*, 3:39 ("Experience").
106 Ibid., 2:195.

107 Ibid., 1:41.

108 Ibid., 3:33.

109 Van Leer makes this point (*Emerson's Epistemology*, p. 165), though he does not seem to see the problem it raises for his claim that surprise is a category.

110 Emerson, *CW*, 3:47.

111 Allen, *Waldo Emerson*, p. 209.

112 Gay Wilson Allen, "A New Look at Emerson and Science," in Robert E. Burkholder and Joel Myerson, eds., *Critical Essays on Ralph Waldo Emerson* (Boston: G. K. Hall, 1983), pp. 339–40.

113 Emerson, *CW*, 1:35.

114 Ibid., 4:89. The last sentence is Montaigne's famous slogan in *Essays*, bk. 1, chap. 47.

115 Ibid., 3:43.

116 Montaigne, "On Experience," in *Selected Essays* (New York: Penguin, 1958), p. 348.

117 Emerson, *CW*, 1:58.

118 Ibid., 1:59, 150.

119 *The Later Works of John Dewey*, ed. Jo Ann Boydston (Carbondale: Southern Illinois University Press 1981–), 4:164–5.

120 Emerson, *CW*, 1:39.

121 Ibid., 1:31.

122 Ibid., 2:198.

123 Dewey, *MW*, p. 3

124 Emerson, *CW*, 3:20; William James, *Pragmatism* (Cambridge, Mass.: Harvard University Press, 1979), p. 34; *The Later Works of John Dewey*, 4:92; and R. W. Sleeper, *The Necessity of Pragmatism* (New Haven, Conn.: Yale University Press, 1986), p. 69. Cf. Poirier, *The Renewal of Literature*, pp. 33, 58; and West, *The American Evasion*, p. 36.

125 Emerson, *CW*, 2:188.

126 Ibid., 1:69.

127 Oscar W. Firkins, *Ralph Waldo Emerson* (Boston: Houghton Mifflin, 1915), p. 68.

128 Ibid., p. 33.

129 Emerson, *CW*, 1:83.

130 Ibid., 1:85. There is a voluntarist structure of evidence here, in that "my heart" provides the criterion of "origin in heaven."

131 Ibid., 1:12.

132 Samuel Taylor Coleridge, *Biographia Literaria*, ed. James Engell and Walter Jackson Bate (Princeton, N.J.: Princeton University Press, 1983), chap. 13. On the links with Coleridge, see Packer, *Emerson's Fall*.

133 Emerson, *CW*, 1:44.

134 Ibid., 1:31.

135 James, *Pragmatism*, p. 37. Cf. Hilary Putnam, *The Many Faces of Realism* (La Salle, Ill.: Open Court, 1987).

136 Emerson, *CW*, 2:43.

137 Ibid., 3:80–1.

138 Bloom, *The Ringers*, p. 337.

CHAPTER 3

1 Ralph Barton Perry, *The Thought and Character of William James* (Boston: Little, Brown, 1935), 1:387; hereafter cited as Perry. Cf. his statement to G. H. Howison that he "wanted to make something entirely popular, and as it were emotional, for technicality seems to me to spell 'failure' in philosophy," in *The Letters of William James*, ed. Henry James (Boston: Atlantic Monthly Press, 1920); hereafter cited as *Letters*.

2 Perry, 2:207.

3 *The Poetical Works of Wordsworth* (Boston: Houghton Mifflin, 1982), pp. 793–4.

4 Perry, 1:339–40.

5 William James, *Talks to Teachers on Psychology: And to Students on Some of Life's Ideals* (New York: Henry Holt, 1904), p. 244; hereafter cited as *TT*.

6 Ibid., p. 245.

7 Quoted in ibid., p. 249.

8 Ibid., pp. 252–3.

9 Ibid., p. 245.

10 William James, *A Pluralistic Universe* (Cambridge, Mass.: Harvard University Press, 1977), pp. 14–15; hereafter cited as *PU*. Cf. Friedrich Schlegel's view that *"philosophy is properly only what it is only in and through the individuality of a philosopher,"* discussed in Philippe Lacoue-Labarthe and Jean-Luc Nancy, *The Literary Absolute: The Theory of Literature in German Romanticism* (Albany: State University of New York Press, 1988), p. 116.

11 Cf. Perry, 1:449ff.

12 Perry, 2:443 (1905–6); compare his remarks about the alliance of "the thicker and more radical empiricism" with the religious life in James, *PU* p. 142.

13 James, *TT*, p. 244.

14 In "Self-Reliance," in *The Collected Works of Ralph Waldo Emerson*, ed. Robert Spiller et al. (Cambridge, Mass.: Harvard University Press, 1971–), 2:44; hereafter cited as *CW*.

15 William James, *Pragmatism* (Cambridge, Mass.: Harvard University Press, 1979), p. 125; hereafter cited as *P*. For the relation to Emerson's view in "Circles," see Richard Poirier, *The Renewal of Literature: Emersonian Reflections* (New York: Random House, 1986), p. 197.

16 James, *TT*, p. 264.

17 Ibid., p. 252.

18 William James, *Memories and Studies* (New York: Longmans, Green, 1912), pp. 148, 149. Cf. Jacques Barzun, *A Stroll with William James* (New York: Harper & Row, 1983), p. 199.

19 William James, *The Principles of Psychology* (Cambridge, Mass.: Harvard University Press, 1981), p. 323; hereafter cited as *PP*. He contrasts his experiential account with the "hypotheses" of "the Kantian philosophy" on p. 339. For some problems with this sort of account, see the discussion in Sidney Shoemaker, *Self Knowledge and Self Identity* (Ithaca, N.Y.: Cornell University Press, 1963).

20 James, *PP*, p. 237.

21 Ibid., p. 238.

22 Ibid., pp. 238–9.

23 Ibid., p. 243.

24 Ibid., p. 462.
25 Ibid., p. 381.
26 Ibid., p. 788.
27 Ibid., p. 246.
28 Ibid., p. 915.
29 Ibid., p. 1182. Note the pronounced Emersonian tone (e.g., in the phrase "lords of life") of James's remarks on this and the preceding page.
30 Ibid., p. 226; see also p. 227.
31 See James M. Edie, "Notes on the Philosophical Anthropology of William James," in James M. Edie, *An Invitation to Phenomenology* (Chicago: Quadrangle Books, 1965), pp. 110–32; and Bruce Wilshire, *William James and Phenomenology* (Bloomington: Indiana University Press, 1968).
32 Poirier, *The Renewal of Literature*, p. 47.
33 James, *PP*, pp. 227, 228.
34 Emerson, *CW*, 3:33.
35 Though Gerald Myers maintains that "odd as it may seem, he was a Hegelian at heart, excited by the vision of an impending theoretical insight in which apparent opposites are reconciled in an overarching unity"; see his *William James, His Life and Thought* (New Haven, Conn.: Yale University Press, 1986), p. 396. Professor Myers's fine book has been of help to me in thinking about some of the knottier problems connected with James's views on science, religion, materialism, and radical empiricism.
36 James, *PP*, p. 271.
37 Ibid., p. 692. This is not to say that he found all empiricists sterile. See the discussion of his interest in Stumpf and Mach, and that of his rejection of "blind expertise" in "narrow" sciences in Daniel W. Bjork, *William James: The Center of His Vision* (New York: Columbia University Press, 1988), pp. 138–41.
38 James, *PP*, p. 480.
39 This is why, for example, James sees no problem in explaining why the hand-as-seen and the hand-as-felt are taken to lie in one space (*PP*, p. 462). (Actually, James does take the confusion to have a feature – unity.)
40 Stanley Cavell, "The Division of Talent," *Critical Inquiry* 11 (June 1985):532.
41 "Tintern Abbey."
42 James, *PP*, p. 247.
43 Quoted in M. H. Abrams, *Natural Supernaturalism* (New York: Norton, 1971), p. 379.
44 Henry James, *A Small Boy and Others* (New York: Scribner, 1913), p. 234. There was no "keeping Sunday" in the James household. See Henry James, *Notes of a Son and Brother* (New York: Scribner, 1914), p. 168.
45 William James, *The Varieties of Religious Experience* (Cambridge, Mass.: Harvard University Press, 1985), p. 270; hereafter cited as *V*.
46 Ibid., p. 34.
47 James, *PP*, pp. 303–4.
48 Perry, 1:458–9.
49 James, *V*, p. 188.
50 Ibid., p. 41.
51 Ibid., pp. 36–7.

52 Ibid., pp. 41–2.
53 See Søren Kierkegaard, *Either/Or*, vol. 1, trans. D. F. Swenson and L. M. Swenson, vol. 2, trans. W. Lowrie (Princeton, N.J.: Princeton University Press, 1971); and Søren Kierkegaard, *Concluding Unscientific Postscript*, trans. D. F. Swenson and W. Lowrie (Princeton, N.J.: Princeton University Press, 1941).
54 James, *V*, pp. 136–8.
55 James employs Emerson to represent the healthy-minded tendency in *Varieties* but, in his talk at the Emerson centennial celebrations, places him correctly in the twice-born class, contrasting him with Whitman. See William James, *Essays in Religion and Morality* (Cambridge, Mass.: Harvard University Press, 1982), p. 62.
56 James, *V*, p. 155.
57 James, *P*, p. 124.
58 James, *V*, p. 189.
59 Ibid., p. 281.
60 Ibid., p. 202.
61 Ibid., p. 201; cf. James, *PU*, p. 143, in which James writes that our "acts redetermine the previous nature of the world."
62 Myers, *William James*, p. 452.
63 See James, *PU*; and cf. Nelson Goodman, "The Way the World Is," in Nelson Goodman, *Problems and Projects* (Indianapolis: Bobbs-Merrill, 1972), pp. 24–32.
64 James, *V*, p. 29.
65 Ibid., p. 216.
66 Ibid., pp. 115–6. Again, this resembles Kierkegaard's view.
67 Ibid., p. 197, also pp. 305, 307.
68 Ibid., pp. 307–8. James describes his experiments with nitrous oxide in *The Will to Believe* (Cambridge, Mass.: Harvard University Press, 1979), pp. 217–21; hereafter cited as *WB*.
69 See H. S. Thayer's account of the term's origin in Paul Edwards, ed., *Encyclopedia of Philosophy* (New York: Macmillan, 1967), 6:431.
70 James, *P*, p. 5.
71 Ibid., p. 12.
72 Ibid., p. 13.
73 Ibid., p. 32.
74 Ibid., p. 40.
75 Ibid., p. 41 (italics removed).
76 Ibid., p. 44.
77 On this topic, see Gardner Murphy and Robert O. Ballou, *William James on Psychical Research* (London: Chatto & Windus, 1961).
78 Gay Wilson Allen, *William James: A Biography* (New York: Viking, 1967), pp. 465–6.
79 Myers, *William James*, p. 613.
80 Myers notes "the tension in James's mind between religion as a matter of faith different from science and religion as a respectable discipline related to science" (ibid., p. 611).
81 James, *WB*, p. 48.

82 William James, *Essays in Religion and Morality* (Cambridge, Mass.: Harvard University Press, 1982), p. 88.

83 James, *P*, p. 140.

84 In James, *V*, *P*, and in *PU*, end of penultimate chapter.

85 William James, *Some Problems of Philosophy* (Cambridge, Mass.: Harvard University Press, 1979), p. 54.

86 Wordsworth, pp. 231 (*The Recluse*, 793), 203 (*The Prelude*, XI, 143–5); See M. H. Abrams's discussion in *Natural Supernaturalism*, p. 65.

87 Wordsworth, *W*, p. 794.

88 James, *Letters*, 2:12–13. When pressed, however, James could be devastating at criticism. See, for example, his "Remarks on Spencer's Definition of Mind as Correspondence," *Journal of Speculative Philosophy*, January 1878, pp. 1–18.

89 James, *P*, p. 10.

90 James, *WB*, p. 77.

91 Wordsworth, *The Prelude*, XIV, 226; James is not so much interested (as some contemporary theorists are) in the cognitive side of feelings as he is in the feeling side of our cognitions. See, for example, Jerome Neu, "Jealous Thoughts," in Amelie Rorty, ed. *Explaining Emotions* (Berkeley and Los Angeles: University of California Press, 1982). James held that mental states may be correctly called either feelings or thoughts. See James, *PP*, p. 186.

92 Ibid., p. 380.

93 James, *P*, p. 122.

94 Here one may think of Kierkegaard's definition of the self as "a relation that relates itself to its own self," in *The Sickness unto Death*, trans. W. Lowrie (Princeton, N.J.: Princeton University Press, 1968), p. 146.

95 James, *PP*, p. 304. Notice that consciousness is defined by things here – James is thinking, for example, of our bodies and of the interest we take in them – which is consistent with his project of overcoming mind–body dualism.

96 Ibid., p. 277.

97 James, *P*, p. 13.

98 Ibid., p. 14.

99 Ibid., p. 23.

100 James, *PP*, p. 448.

101 James, *P*, pp. 124, 125. William James, *Essays in Radical Empiricism* (Cambridge, Mass.: Harvard University Press, 1976); hereafter cited as *ERE*.

102 James, *ERE*, p. 141.

103 Ibid., pp. 140–1.

104 Ibid., pp. 141–3

105 James, *P*, p. 24.

106 James, *PU*, pp. 14–15.

107 James, *P*, p. 140.

108 Ibid., pp. 141, 140; cf. Cavell's diagnosis of a "fear of experience" in philosophy.

109 James, *P*, p. 142.

110 James, *WB*, p. 57.

111 Ibid., p. 58. Again, an objector will want to say that relief is one thing and

harmonic order another, and James, that this is a secondary, "intellectualist" distinction.

112 Ibid., p. 70.

113 The preceding three quotations from ibid., p. 71.

114 Ibid., pp. 70–1. If one were to push James and argue that what seemed rational to us might not really be rational, he could reply that there is no meaning to the term outside the human sentiments that are its basis. This is the sort of standpoint he developed in *Pragmatism*, in which he writes that "the trail of the human serpent is . . . over everything" (p. 37).

115 James, *WB*, pp. 15–16.

116 Ibid., p. 17.

117 Ibid., p. 19; or as he puts it in *P*, p. 100, truth comes on the credit system.

118 James, *WB*, p. 21.

119 Ibid., p. 22.

120 James, *Letters*, 2:49.

121 James, *WB*, p. 26.

122 Ibid., p. 22.

123 James, *Letters*, 1:131.

124 James, *P*, p. 122.

125 James, *WB*, pp. 28, 29.

126 Myers criticizes James for confusing the consequences following from God's existence with the consequences following from the belief in God's existence and for suggesting "that faith in a god will somehow help to create that god" (Myers, *William James*, p. 452). However, if God emerges in the form of a deified humanity, as Emerson and other naturalizers of the supernatural suggest, then perhaps such faith – as in the "secular" cases James also discusses – can create its object.

127 James, *P*, p. 124.

128 James, *PU*, p. 14.

129 "Immortality Ode." Cf. the end of Emerson's "Experience": "up again old heart!" (Emerson, *CW*, 3:49).

130 James, *WB*, p. 54.

131 Stanley Cavell, *The Claim of Reason* (New York: Oxford University Press, 1979), p. 361.

132 James, *WB*, p. 18.

133 Ibid., p. 55; cf. James, *PU*, p. 143: "Philosophies are intimate parts of the universe, they express something of its own thought of itself. A philosophy may indeed be a most momentous reaction of the universe upon itself."

134 James, *WB*, p. 71.

135 Wordsworth, *W*, p. 215 (*The Prelude*, XIII, 290–3).

136 James, *V*, p. 395n. (cont'd).

137 Some writers claim to pin down precise variations in James's basic metaphysical beliefs. Marcus Peter Ford writes, for example: "From 1900 to 1904 James was a panpsychist, from 1904 to 1905 he oscillated between being a phenomenist and a panpsychist, and from 1905 until his death in 1910 he was, again, a panpsychist"; see *William James's Philosophy* (Amherst: University of Massachusetts Press, 1982), p. 75. Though there is evidence for such

assertions, I shall instead follow James's own metaphilosophical suggestion that each major philosopher has one simple, personal view of things by looking for James's peculiar lifelong vision. Cf. the discussion of Ford's book in Myers, *William James*, pp. 612–13.

138 James, *PU*, chap. 1.

139 Henry James, *A Small Boy and Others*, p. 259.

140 Allen, *William James*, p. 47.

141 Henry James, *Notes of a Son and Brother*, p. 138.

142 James, *Letters*, 1:54, 55.

143 James, *PP*, p. 609.

144 Ibid., p. 534.

145 Ibid., p. 531. For the trouble James had in reconciling this dualistic stance with his radical empiricism, see Perry, 2:393 ff.

146 Wilshire, *William James and Phenomenology*, p. 35.

147 Emerson, *CW*, 1:35.

148 The tone of this remark is remarkably like that of many in Wittgenstein's *Philosophical Investigations*.

149 James, *PP*, pp. 681–2. Cf. *PP*, p. 653, in which James writes, "The first time we see *light*, in Condillac's phrase, we *are* it rather than see it. But all our later optical knowledge is about what this experience gives."

150 His position here anticipates Dewey's.

151 James, *PP*, p. 461; cf. p. 219.

152 Ibid., p. 679.

153 Wilshire puts this by saying that it is as if James had "blasted open" the self and "distributed [it] across the face of the lived-world" (*William James and Phenomenology*, p. 125). He also finds in James the argument that the specification of conscious states requires reference to the world.

154 James, *ERE*, pp. 36–7.

155 Ibid., p. 73.

156 Compare this statement from "The Thing and Its Relations," also published in 1905: "Pure experience is the name which I gave to the immediate flux of life which furnishes the material to our later reflection with its conceptual categories. Only newborn babes, or men in semi-coma from sleep, drugs, illnesses, or blows, may be assumed to have an experience pure in the literal sense of a *that* which is not yet any definite *what*, tho' ready to be all sorts of whats . . . the flux of it no sooner comes than it tends to fill itself with emphases." (ibid., p. 46).

157 James, *P*, p. 122.

158 James, *ERE*, p. 4.

159 Ibid., pp. 42–3.

160 James develops this thought in the direction of panpsychism, according to which "our only intelligible notion of an object *in itself* is that it should be an object *for* itself." See Perry, 2:446.

161 James is not without a skeptical side, however. Recall that he holds it possible, even likely, that our relation to the universe is about as full and accurate as those our dogs and cats have to our human practices.

162 James, *ERE*, p. 120.

163 Perry, 2:763. One of James's anti-idealistic and antiskeptical tactics in the *Essays in Radical Empiricism* is to focus on the publicity of the body. One's body is not an isolated, disconnected atom but a "place" like those in the *Psychology*, in which different experiences mingle. Some of these experiences – yours, for instance – include "warm" or "intimate" feelings of the body, whereas others – mine, say – are cooler and more distant. But James insists that when I see your body I "share" it with you, even though our relations to it are not the same.

Our relations even to our own bodies may vary. Catching an unexpected glimpse of ourselves in a mirror we treat our body as a foreign object; working on math or philosophy we forget it entirely (a fact on which Plato based his theory of the soul); making love or sitting in the sun, we merge with it. "Our body itself," James writes, "is the palmary instance of the ambiguous. Sometimes I treat my body purely as a part of outer nature. Sometimes, again, I think of it as 'mine,' I sort it with the 'me'" (James, *ERE*, p. 76). Our relations to our own bodies are somewhat "loose" in James's picture.

164 William James, *The Meaning of Truth* (Cambridge, Mass.: Harvard University Press, 1975), p. 7. This is a passage rightly emphasized by John McDermott. See James, *ERE*, p. xxvii.

165 Ibid., p. 24.

166 Emerson, *CW*, 1:25.

167 James, *P*, p. 123.

168 Emerson, *CW*, 1:31.

169 James, *P*, p. 123; italics removed.

170 Ibid., p. 37. See Thomas Kuhn, *The Structure of Scientific Revolutions* (Chicago: University of Chicago Press, 1970).

171 Emerson, *CW*, 2:181.

172 James, *P*, p. 122. Cf. Hilary Putnam's idea of the "interest-relativity" of explanation in *Meaning and the Moral Sciences* (London: Routledge & Kegan Paul, 1978), pp. 45–8.

173 James, *P*, p. 117.

174 Ibid., p. 119. Poirier stresses the limitations this picture places on the "possibilities for newness or for originality or for freedom" (Poirier, *The Renewal of Literature*, p. 47). But must newness come only from the "nonhumanized core" rather than from new interpretations of and in the already "humanized mass?"

175 James, *P*, p. 122.

176 Ibid., *P*, p. 120. Cf. James, *ERE*, p. 120.

177 James, *P*, p. 120.

178 James, *PU*, p. 13. I have capitalized "American," "German," and "English."

179 Ibid., p. 145.

180 Perry, 2:748–9.

181 James, *PU*, p. 19. Cf. Cavell's remarks on the relation between skepticism and jealousy, discussed in Chapter 1 of this text.

182 James, *PU*, p. 16. Note that James rejects materialism but embraces empiricism.

183 Ibid., p. 16.
184 Ibid., p. 18.
185 Ibid., p. 16.
186 Ibid., p. 23.
187 James, *ERE*, p. 30.
188 James, *PU*, p. 145.
189 Ibid., p. 144.
190 Ibid., p. 135.
191 Ibid., p. 21; Cf. James's project of uniting spiritualism with empiricism.
192 Ibid., p. 142, *The Meaning of Truth*, p. 7.
193 James, *PU*, p. 146.
194 Ibid., p. 144. On marriage as conversation, see Stanley Cavell, *Pursuits of Happiness: The Hollywood Comedy of Remarriage* (Cambridge, Mass.: Harvard University Press, 1981).

CHAPTER 4

1 *The Philosophy of John Dewey*, ed. John J. McDermott (Chicago: University of Chicago Press, 1973), p. xi.
2 *The Later Works of John Dewey*, ed. Jo Ann Boydston (Carbondale and Edwardsville: Southern Illinois University Press, 1981), 5:155. Hereafter, references to the Southern Illinois University edition of the complete works of John Dewey will be as follows: *EW* for volumes of *The Early Works of John Dewey* (1969–72), *MW* for volumes of *The Middle Works of John Dewey* (1976–83), and *LW* for volumes of *The Later Works of John Dewey*.
3 Dewey, *MW*, 9:82.
4 Harold Bloom, *The Ringers in the Tower* (Chicago: University of Chicago Press, 1971), pp. 336, 337.
5 Dewey, *MW* 3:191. This position is reaffirmed in ibid., 4:241.
6 Dewey, *LW* 5:156.
7 *Dialogue on John Dewey*, ed. Corliss Lamont (New York: Horizon Press, 1959), *passim*.
8 Ibid., p. 40.
9 *The Collected Works of Ralph Waldo Emerson*, ed. Robert Spiller et al. (Cambridge, Mass.: Harvard University Press, 1971–), 1:58; hereafter cited as *CW*.
10 Ralph Sleeper, *The Necessity of Pragmatism* (New Haven, Conn.: Yale University Press, 1986); Neil Coughlan, *Young John Dewey* (Chicago: University of Chicago Press, 1975); and Bruce Kuklick, *Churchmen and Philosophers* (New Haven, Conn.: Yale University Press, 1985).
11 Kuklick, *Churchmen and Philosophers*, p. 252.
12 See Perry Miller, *The Transcendentalists* (Cambridge, Mass.: Harvard University Press, 1950), pp. 34–9.
13 Lamont, *Dialogue*, pp. 15, 16.
14 Dewey, *LW* 5:182.
15 Ibid., 5:181.
16 Cf. Jacques Barzun, *Romanticism and the Modern Ego* (Boston: Little, Brown, 1947), preface and chap. 1.
17 See Sleeper, *The Necessity of Pragmatism*, esp. chap. 4.

18 Dewey, *LW* 5:186.
19 For example, in his view our logic is a human construction. See Sleeper, *The Necessity of Pragmatism, passim;* Michael Buxton, "The Influence of William James on John Dewey's Early Work," *Journal of the History of Ideas* 45 (July 1984):452–3; and Dewey's discussion of the Copernican revolution in Dewey, *LW*, 4, chap. 11.
20 Dewey, *LW*, 5:189.
21 Ibid., 5:153.
22 Coughlan, *Young John Dewey*, pp. 58–9.
23 Ibid., p. 54.
24 Dewey, *EW*, 3:16.
25 Ibid., 3:20.
26 Ibid., 3:23.
27 Hannah Arendt, *Willing* (New York: Harcourt Brace Jovanovich, 1978), pp. 40–50.
28 Thomas McFarland, *Romanticism and the Forms of Ruin* (Princeton, N.J.: Princeton University Press, 1981), p. 346. *Friedrich Schlegel's Lucinde and the Fragments,* trans. Peter Firchow (Minneapolis: University of Minnesota Press, 1971), p. 157 (Critical Fragment 115).
29 Stanley Cavell, "The Division of Talent," *Critical Inquiry* 11 (June 1985):521.
30 John Dewey was only thirty-one in 1890, but he already had a successful academic career. Hired for a junior position at the University of Michigan in 1884, Dewey established himself as an able defender of Hegelian ideas, an opponent of reductionistic forms of materialism, and an advocate of psychological methods. He was lured in 1888 to the University of Minnesota by the offer of the professorship of mental and moral philosophy but remained there only a year, returning to Michigan as a professor of philosophy after the sudden death of his mentor and sponsor George Sylvester Morris. A year later, in the early summer of 1890, the eminent young Michigan professor gave "Poetry and Philosophy" as the commencement address at Smith College, and it was first published in the *Andover Review.* See George Dykhuizen, *The Life and Mind of John Dewey* (Carbondale: Southern Illinois University Press, 1973), pp. 47–8.
31 Dewey, *EW*, 3:110.
32 Ibid., 3:111, 112.
33 Ibid., 3:113.
34 Ibid., 3:114, 115.
35 Ibid., 3:118–9.
36 Ibid., 3:119.
37 Ibid., 3:119, 120, 121.
38 Ibid., 3:117, 122, 123.
39 "Immortality Ode."
40 Emerson, *CW*, 2:28–9.
41 Wordsworth, "Immortality Ode."
42 Stanley Cavell, "In Quest of the Ordinary: Texts of Recovery," in Morris Eaves and Michael Fischer, eds., *Romanticism and Contemporary Criticism* (Ithaca, N.Y.: Cornell University Press, 1986), p. 186.
43 Dewey, *EW*, 5:120, 121.

44 Ibid., 5:119.

45 Ibid., 5:cxlvi.

46 Ibid., 5:117, 118.

47 Ibid., 5:120.

48 Ibid., 5:122.

49 Ibid., 5:121.

50 Ibid., 5:122. I follow the 1896 edition here.

51 Ibid., 5:84.

52 Ibid., 5:87.

53 Ibid., 5:91, 92.

54 Ibid., 5:93.

55 Dewey, *LW*, 4:240, 241.

56 Ibid., 4:237.

57 Ibid., 4:241.

58 Dewey, *MW*, 3:187.

59 Sleeper, *The Necessity of Pragmatism*, p. 122; cf. his characterization of the *Studies in Logical Theory:* Dewey there "treats essences as provisional" (p. 69). Note also Dewey's early (and more Emersonian sounding) statement that "the 'facts' are not rigid, but are elastic to the touch of theory" (Dewey, *EW*, 3:87, cited in Sleeper, *The Necessity of Pragmatism*, p. 23).

60 Dewey, *MW* 3:188.

61 Ibid., 3:189–90.

62 Ibid., 3:184.

63 This and the preceding quotation are from ibid., 3:185.

64 Ibid., 3:186.

65 See Martin Heidegger, *Being and Time*, trans. J. Macquarrie and E. Robinson (Oxford, England: Blackwell Publisher, 1967). In the "Letter on Humanism" Heidegger writes that "man is the shepherd of Being. It is in this direction alone that *Being and Time* is thinking when ecstatic existence is expressed as 'care.'" *Martin Heidegger, Basic Writings*, ed. David Farrell Krell (New York: Harper & Row, 1977), p. 210. Richard Rorty discusses some of the links between Heidegger and Dewey in *Philosophy and the Mirror of Nature* (Princeton, N.J.: Princeton University Press, 1979).

66 Dewey, *MW*, 6:96–7.

67 Sleeper, *The Necessity of Pragmatism*, p. 49.

68 Dewey, *MW*, 9:275.

69 Ibid., 9:276.

70 Ibid., 9:276.

71 Ibid., 9:302, 303.

72 John Dewey, "An Empirical Survey of Empiricisms," in Department of Philosophy of Columbia University, ed., *Studies in the History of Ideas* (New York: Columbia University Press, 1935), p. 18.

73 Ibid, p. 20.

74 Dewey, *LW*, 4:90, 92.

75 Ibid., 4:90.

76 Dewey, *MW*, 12:137.

77 Ibid., 9:174.

78 Ibid., 10:45.
79 Emerson, *CW*, 1:56; *CW*, 2:202, 181.
80 Dewey, *MW*, 10:45.
81 For the claim that Romanticism is itself a form of empiricism, see Robert Langbaum, *The Poetry of Experience* (New York: Random House, 1957).
82 Nelson Goodman, "The Significance of *Der Logische Aufbau*," in Paul Schilpp, ed., *The Philosophy of Rudolf Carnap* (New York: Library of Living Philosophers, 1963), pp. 552–8.
83 Dewey, *MW*, 12:200.
84 Ibid., 12:200, 201.
85 See Sleeper's criticism of Bernstein and Rorty on this issue, in *The Necessity of Pragmatism*, p. 132.
86 Emerson, *LW*, 1:47.
87 Emerson, "Fate," in *Complete Works* (Boston: Houghton Mifflin, 1904), 6:7–8.
88 Dewey, *LW*, 10:251.
89 Dewey, *MW*, 12:85.
90 Ibid., 12:168.
91 Ibid., 10:32.
92 Ibid., 10:22.
93 Ibid., 10:6.
94 Ibid., 10:7.
95 Dewey, *LW*, 5:153.
96 Ibid., 1:198–9.
97 Ibid., 1:171.
98 Ibid., 1:200.
99 Ibid., 4:184.
100 Ibid., 1:223.
101 Ibid., 4:184, 185.
102 Ibid., 1:211.
103 Ibid., 4:168.
104 Ibid., 4:171.
105 Friedrich Nietzsche, *The Gay Science*, trans. Walter Kauffman (New York: Vintage, 1974), p. 280 (section 343).
106 Dewey, *MW*, 10:41. Dewey traces the "spectator theory" back to Plato, diagnosing it as the ideology of a leisured class attempting to justify its idleness. See also Dewey, *LW* 4, chap. 1.
107 Dewey, *LW*, 4:168, 170.
108 Dewey, *MW*, 8:205–404. The influence of both Evelyn and his wife, Alice, on John Dewey deserve much more attention than I can give them here.
109 Ibid., 8:211.
110 Ibid., 8:222.
111 Ibid., 8:214.
112 Ibid., 8:226.
113 Ibid., 8:231, 232, 230.
114 Ibid., 8:217.
115 Dewey, *LW*, 5:156.

116 Dewey, *MW*, 9:118 ff.
117 Ibid., 9:99. To what degree Rousseau actually holds the position that Dewey attributes to him is a question that I cannot address here.
118 Ibid., 9:57.
119 Ibid., 9:82.
120 Ibid., 9:215.
121 Ibid., 9:347 ("intimate participant"), 303 ("intimate connection").
122 Ibid., 9:338–41.
123 Dewey also wrote poetry, much of it inspired by his relationship with the writer Anzia Yezierska, one of his students at Columbia. See *The Poems of John Dewey*, ed. Jo Ann Boydston (Carbondale: Southern Illinois University Press, 1977).
124 Dykhuizen, *The Life and Mind of John Dewey*, pp. 221–3.
125 Sleeper, *The Necessity of Pragmatism*, p. 186.
126 Dewey's pronounced interest in Romantic poets and Romanticism generally is noted by Thomas Alexander in "John Dewey's Theory of Aesthetic Meaning (Ph.D. diss., Emory University, 1984), chap. 2, n. 3. See also Thomas Alexander, *John Dewey's Theory of Art, Imagination and Experience: The Horizons of Feeling* (Albany, N.Y.: State University of New York Press, 1987). I am grateful to Professor Alexander for his valuable comments on an early version of this chapter.
127 Dewey, *LW* 10:15.
128 Ibid., 10:11.
129 Ibid., 10:34.
130 Ibid., 10:35.
131 Ibid., 10:35–6.
132 Ibid., 10:26.
133 Ibid., 10:27.
134 Ibid., 10:264.
135 Ibid., 10:42, 43.
136 Ibid., 10:47.
137 Ibid., 10:199.
138 Ibid., 10:131.
139 Ibid., 10:326.
140 Ibid., 10:144.
141 Ibid., 10:239. Cf. Nelson Goodman, *Ways of Worldmaking* (Indianapolis: Hackett, 1978), p. 105.
142 Dewey, *LW*, 10:228.
143 Ibid., 10:145.
144 Ibid., 10:271.
145 Ibid., 10:272.
146 Ibid., 10:286.
147 Ibid., 10:276.
148 Ibid., 10:271–2.
149 Ibid., 10:292.
150 Ibid., 10:218.
151 Ibid., 10:59, 60.

152 Ibid., 10:348.
153 Ibid., 10:346.
154 Ibid., 10:48.
155 Dewey, *MW* 9:47.
156 Dewey, *LW*, 1:204.
157 Ibid., 10:268.
158 Ibid., 10:11.
159 Ibid., 10:59.
160 Ibid., 10:266.
161 Ibid., 10:349, 351.
162 Ibid., 10:352.

EPILOGUE

1 Hilary Putnam, *The Many Faces of Realism* (La Salle, Ill.: Open Court, 1987), p. 70; hereafter cited as *MF*.
2 William James, *The Will to Believe* (Cambridge, Mass.: Harvard University Press, 1979), pp. 70–1.
3 Putnam, *MF*, p. 79.
4 Ibid., pp. 16 ff.
5 Hilary Putnam, *Reason, Truth and History* (Cambridge, England: Cambridge University Press, 1981), pp. 188–200; Putnam, *MF*, p. 46.
6 Stanley Cavell, *In Quest of the Ordinary* (Chicago: University of Chicago Press, 1988), p. 14.
7 Putnam, *MF*, p. 51.
8 Cavell, *In Quest of the Ordinary*, p. 14.
9 *The Collected Works of Ralph Waldo Emerson*, ed. Robert Spiller et al. (Cambridge, Mass.: Harvard University Press, 1971), 1:100.
10 Ibid., 1:157.
11 Ibid., 1:100, 70.
12 Ibid., 1:68.
13 *The Middle Works of John Dewey* (Carbondale: Southern Illinois University Press), 6:96–7; hereafter cited as *MW*.
14 William James, *A Pluralistic Universe* (Cambridge, Mass.: Harvard University Press, 1977), p. 13
15 *The Early Works of John Dewey* (Carbondale: Southern Illinois University Press), 3:123; and *MW* 10:47.
16 Harold Bloom, *The Ringers in the Tower* (Chicago: University of Chicago Press, 1971), p. 324.

INDEX

Cambridge Studies in American Literature and Culture

Editor

Albert Gelpi, Stanford University

Lynn Keller, *Re-Making It New: Contemporary American and the Modernist Tradition*

Anne Kibbey, *The Interpretation of Material Shapes in Puritanism: A Study of Rhetoric, Prejudice, and Violence*

Robert Lawson-Peebles, *Landscape and Written Expression in Revolutionary America: The World Turned Upside Down*

Robert S. Levine, *Conspiracy and Romance: Studies in Brockden Brown, Cooper, Hawthorne, and Melville*

John Limon, *The Place of Fiction in the Time Of Science: A Disciplinary History of American Writing*

Jerome Loving, *Emily Dickinson: The Poet on the Second Story*

Susan Manning, *The Puritan–Provincial Vision: Scottish and American Literature in the Nineteenth Century*

Elizabeth McKinsey, *Niagara Falls: Icon of the American Sublime*

John McWilliams, *The American Epic: Transformation of a Genre, 1770–1860*

David Miller, *Dark Eden: The Swamp in Nineteenth-Century American Culture*

Warren Motley, *The American Abraham: James Fenimore Cooper and The Frontier Patriarch*

Brenda Murphy, *American Realism and American Drama, 1800–1940*

Michael Oriard, *Sporting with the Gods: The Rhetoric of Play and Game in American Literature*

Majorie Perloff, *The Dance of the Intellect: Studies in Poetry in the Pound Tradition*★

Tim Redman, *Ezra Pound and Italian Fascism*

Karen Rowe, *Saint and Singer: Edward Taylor's Typology and the Poetics of Mediation*

Barton St. Armand, *Emily Dickinson and Her Culture: The Soul's Society*★

Eric Sigg, *The American T. S. Eliot: A Study of the Early Writings*

Tony Tanner, *Scenes of Nature, Signs of Man: Essays in 19th and 20th Century American Literature*★

Brook Thomas, *Cross Examinations of Law and Literature: Cooper, Hawthorne, Stowe, and Melville*★

Albert von Frank, *The Sacred Game: Provincialism and Frontier Consciousness in American Literature, 1630–1860*

David Wyatt, *The Fall into Eden: Landscape and Imagination in California*★

Lois Zamora, *Writing the Apocalypse: Ends and Endings in Contemporary U.S. and Latin American Fiction*

★Now available in hardcover and paperback